Y0-BCV-472

Oct, 197L

AN ANVIL ORIGINAL
under the general editorship of Louis L. Snyder

THE RISE AND DECLINE OF JACKSONIAN DEMOCRACY

GLYNDON G. VAN DEUSEN
Research Professor of History Emeritus
The University of Rochester

VAN NOSTRAND REINHOLD COMPANY

New York Cincinnati Toronto London Melbourne

For Philip, Rachael, and David

Van Nostrand Reinhold Company Regional Offices:
Cincinnati, New York, Chicago, Millbrae, Dallas

Van Nostrand Reinhold Company Foreign Offices:
London, Toronto, Melbourne

Published by Van Nostrand Reinhold Company
450 West 33rd Street, New York, N.Y. 10001

Published simultaneously in Canada by
Van Nostrand Reinhold (Canada), Ltd.

10 9 8 7 6 5 4 3 2 1

Preface

Ever since Andrew Jackson strode upon the historical stage, historians have attempted to analyze the character and significance of the man, and of the movement generally known as Jacksonian Democracy. Both have been subject to a bewildering variety of interpretations.

Some critics have portrayed Jackson as a frontier bully and opportunist, a demagogue, an ignorant and tyrannical incompetent who vulgarized and corrupted politics. Others have regarded him as a symbol of the frontier and of American individualism, a man of high ideals who ennobled politics and invoked the power of the executive branch of the national government to curb the selfish greed of the business community.

Historians have differed just as widely about the character of Jacksonian Democracy. It was a popular movement to ensure justice and opportunity for the common man. It was the triumph of the frontier. It represented the aims and aspirations of the urban workers as well as the spirit of the frontier. It operated in ignorance of sound financial principles. It foreshadowed the era of Franklin D. Roosevelt in its effort to limit the power of the business class. Its primary purpose was to help the rising entrepreneurial class. It probably derived from ethnic and religious differences and local conditions. It reeked of demagoguery, ruthlessness, and corruption.

It is self-explanatory why both the movement and the man have produced much scholarly debate. This clash of interpretations persists to the present day.

This account of the rise and decline of Jacksonian Democracy is based upon years of writing and teaching about the pre-Civil War period of American history and upon an intensive examination of pertinent articles and monographs that have appeared during the past two decades. It seeks to portray what actually happened in and to the Jacksonian movement and why it took the course it did take over a period of some forty years.

I wish to express my heartfelt thanks to my wife, Ruth Litteer Van Deusen, who found time to type the manuscript and offered valuable stylistic suggestions.

GLYNDON G. VAN DEUSEN

Table of Contents

PART II—READINGS

Part I

THE RISE AND DECLINE OF JACKSONIAN DEMOCRACY

CHAPTER 1

The Background

Jacksonian Democracy—a political movement with social and economic connotations—did not, like Athena, spring into existence fully armed with all the panoplies of power. It grew out of conditions and ideas that characterized American life during the first decades of the nineteenth century.

Political Antecedents. The political background of Jacksonian Democracy properly begins with the establishment of the national government under the federal constitution, for in the preceding period political parties, as the term is understood today, were non-existent. The Founding Fathers, when they met at Philadelphia, had no prevision of any such development, and provided no blueprint for political organization along party lines. Unwittingly, however, they furnished a basis for future party organization. The Constitution provided for the choice of members of the House of Representatives "by the people of the several states." Also, it made the selection of the President a national affair, with the ballots of the presidential electors of the several states opened and counted in the presence of the Senate and the House of Representatives at the national capital. (*See Reading No. 1.*)

Utilization of these constitutional provisions, so far as party formation was concerned, did not immediately take place. When Congress met for the first time, in 1789, its members had been chosen, not by regularly organized parties, but by shifting groups or cliques of prominent citizens rallying to a particular candidate. State and national political parties, formed around a set of principles and held together by partisan loyalty, had not appeared. There was little evidence that they would ever come into existence.

During President Washington's two terms of office, serious political divisions appeared. These manifested themselves in Congress, and were the result of men taking sides with Alexander Hamilton and John Adams, or with Thomas Jefferson

and James Madison. The conflict between these leaders lay
mainly in the realm of social and economic ideals, but it also
involved differing conceptions about the structure and functions
of the national government. The contest for the presidency in
1796 between Jefferson and Adams dramatized this cleavage. It
also helped to spread the Congressional political division into
the states, where social and economic problems helped further
to define these differences of opinion. It was at this point that
national political parties with fairly specific creeds emerged
as the Federalists and the Jeffersonian Republicans. (*See Reading No. 2.*)

The Federalist party of Hamilton and Adams put its faith in
a strong central government. This should be based on a broad
construction of the Constitution, and should be administered
by the rich, the well-born, and the able. It would promote national prosperity by establishing a national bank and a protective tariff. In foreign affairs the Federalists, confronted by the
French Revolution of 1789 and war between revolutionary
France and England, viewed French radicalism with distaste.
Federalist sympathies were all with England. (*See Reading
No. 3.*)

The Jeffersonian Republicans believed in a limited national
government. Their motto was "that government governs best
that governs least." In their view the central government should
seek to promote justice for all, especially for the common man,
but it should be economical, should always be tender of the
rights of the states, and strict construction of the Constitution
should keep its activities within narrow limits. These Republicans looked to agricultural America for their chief support; in
their view the farms and plantations were the true basis of
American prosperity. They had no enthusiasm for a national
bank, and they regarded a protective tariff as a harmful measure catering to the interests of an urban manufacturing class.
In foreign affairs their disposition was to pursue an isolationist
policy, but their sympathies lay with France, where the Revolution was seeking to establish a new regime of liberty, equality,
and fraternity. (*See Reading No. 4.*)

Breakup of the First Party System.   These two parties had a brief and curious history. The Federalists elected John Adams President in 1796. Some of their measures were unpopular, the followers of Hamilton and Adams quarreled, and in 1800 Jefferson defeated Adams for the presidency. The Federalists never elected another President. They opposed the War of 1812, some of their New England brethren threatened secession during that struggle, and thereafter their political organization disintegrated. Individual Federalists joined the Republican party or abandoned politics altogether.

Jeffersonian Republicanism triumphed over its rival, but in the process the party suffered a strange transformation. Under the pressure of circumstances its leaders, even Thomas Jefferson himself, felt constrained to expand the activities of the central government, and to that end began interpreting the Constitution in a broad manner. Jefferson purchased Louisiana without strict constitutional warrant. During his administrations his Secretary of the Treasury, Albert Gallatin, drew up a magnificent plan for constructing roads and canals at national expense and Congress authorized the building of a great national highway, the Cumberland Road. In a flareup of Republican zeal the party narrowly refused to recharter the First National Bank in 1811, but five years later Republicans established the Second Bank of the United States. They enacted the protective tariff of 1824, and only the constitutional scruples of Presidents Madison and Monroe kept them from inaugurating a great national system of internal improvements. By 1824 Republicanism had come to resemble its defeated rival in many ways. It had, indeed, put on Federalism, and Old Federalists and Old Republicans cooperated more or less happily in its ranks.

While one party disappeared and the other suffered a sea change, political activity on the national level became more and more disorganized. As Federalist opposition faded out, Republicanism became full of factional struggles, and its machinery as a national party rusted from lack of need to confront a powerful adversary. One political practice that owed much to Jefferson's sanction, the legislative caucus for nominations, did remain in vogue, but even this orderly procedure was beginning to stale with custom. Political activity at the state or local level, of which there was plenty, manifested itself in a confused manner. It was often difficult for a candidate to tell to what "party" he belonged, or for what his "party" stood.

Changing Social and Economic Factors.   During this period of transformation in the party structures, American social and economic conditions also were changing in significant fashion. The working men in the growing urban centers became restless. They, and the common folk in general, began demanding social reforms such as better schools, freedom from imprisonment for debt, and abolition of the onerous militia system which took a good many working days out of the ordinary man's life. Such discontents grew apace, and as they did so men became aware that the improvements they wanted could best be achieved by means of the ballot box.

Another cause of social unrest was the panic of 1819–1823. Boom times following the War of 1812 had fostered a speculative mania, lax and over-easy bank credit policies, and extravagant purchases of European goods. Then came a reaction as cotton glutted foreign markets, prices sank, and the contraction of bank loans brought foreclosures and ruin in its train. For some four years the country was in the grip of a depression which was most severe in agricultural communities and especially so in the South. As a result there arose cries for relief legislation, demands that came from the haves as well as from the have nots. The depression helped to create a popular feeling that American political leadership left something to be desired; that Americans should be in a position to elect statesmen who would make the United States in fact as well as in name a land of equal opportunity.

The crisis over slavery expansion in 1819–1820 also helped to promote a demand for improved political conditions. For the first time North and South clashed over the slavery issue. A political compromise quieted the controversy over admission of Missouri as a slave state but, as Jefferson remarked, this "firebell in the night" was a harbinger of stormy times ahead. It brought to many the conviction that sectional conflict would require the utilization of the best political talent that the nation could bring forth.

This realization of the need for political brains took on added

strength as the old generation of leaders, the Founding Fathers
and their associates, left the political stage. During the early
1820s, Jefferson, John Adams, and James Madison were in retirement. James Monroe's second term in the presidency was
moving toward its close. Henry Clay, John C. Calhoun, Daniel
Webster, and other young men were crowding toward the front
of the political stage, but they had yet to prove their worth as
statesmen of the first order. The country needed government
by all the talents, and many of those who held themselves tal-
ented saw in the championship of franchise reform a means of
achieving preferment and power.

The Development of Political Democracy. The political,
social, and economic conditions of the times fostered a general
belief that the great principles of the Declaration of Independence were profoundly true; that all white Americans had been
created equal, and that government should exist only with the
consent of the governed. It was, therefore, only natural that
there should be a movement toward broadening the suffrage.
The new western states, Ohio, Indiana, Illinois, and Missouri
provided practically complete voting rights for white males. In
the East, too, the limitations on the franchise were eased. Between 1800 and 1824 suffrage qualifications were at least partially removed in Connecticut, New York, New Jersey, Maryland, and North and South Carolina. By 1824, save for Rhode
Island, Virginia, and Louisiana, nearly all white males could
vote in presidential elections. Accompanying this increased use
of the ballot came a widening of voter responsibility. More and
more states provided for the election of judges and other public
officials, and for the choice of presidential electors by ballot
instead of by the state legislatures. The resultant increase in political activity received a further stimulus from a series of
dramatic political developments.

Presidential Candidates in 1824. James Monroe's second
administration marked the end of that "dynasty" of Virginia
statesmen that had occupied the President's Mansion for over
twenty years. Now five young leaders, four of them professional
politicians and one a military man, appeared on the presidential
scene. Two of them were southerners, two hailed from the
New West, one represented New England, and they engaged

in a political movement that was full of vitality, but that was
also formless and chaotic. There were no opposing parties.
All of the aspirants belonged to that political agglomeration
called Republican, and the candidates came before the public
eye through the medium of numberless committees of correspondence, nominating caucuses, and state and local conventions.

Both of the southern candidates were experienced politicians.
John Caldwell Calhoun of South Carolina, Secretary of War
in the Monroe administrations, was now in his early forties. He
was an angular individual, six feet two inches in height, his
rugged face marked by high cheek bones and a jutting chin.
Serious and humorless (it was common report that he had
written a poem beginning with the word "whereas"), he was
a stern logician and a remorseless fighter in the political arena.
His morality was unimpeachable, for he was as chaste in private as he was incorruptible in public life. Since the War of
1812 he had been a leader in the Federalization of the Republican party—a champion of the Second Bank of the United
States, of a protective tariff, and of internal improvements at
national expense. But ambition for the presidency, coupled with
his love for the South and his devotion to slavery, were already
casting him for a very different role.

The other southern candidate, William Harris Crawford of
Georgia, now Secretary of the Treasury, was some ten years
older than his South Carolina rival. Over six feet in height,
he was blessed with a more engaging presence than was Calhoun. Handsome, with fair complexion and brilliant blue eyes,
the Georgian seemed to radiate health and energy. Being a
famous storyteller and charming and affable when he chose
to exhibit that side of his nature, and possessing a keen mind
and powerful intellect, he was a formidable opponent on the
public platform.

Crawford also possessed less admirable qualities. A hard and
ruthless fighter—he had killed one man in a duel—he was in-
satiably ambitious. As a patronage dispenser, he had a reputation for using ignoble means in building up his corps of
supporters. His faction of so-called Radicals emphasized states'
rights, economy in government, and maintenance of the Re-

publican Congressional caucus in choosing a presidential candidate, but its leader's devotion to Old Republican principles was at least questionable. In 1811 he had introduced a bill to continue the First National Bank charter for twenty years, and supported it by a speech pleading the doctrine of implied powers in the Constitution. (*See Reading No. 5.*) As Secretary of the Treasury he was at least complaisant about internal improvements at federal expense, and about financial measures based on the same doctrine. Crawford also had a temper. On one occasion he called Monroe to his face a "damned, infernal old scoundrel." The President seized a pair of fire tongs and threatened his visitor with summary ejection from the White House. Subsequently he left statements impugning Crawford's good faith. It is likely that historians would have found the Georgian's personal papers interesting reading, but he burned them before his death.

New England's candidate was John Quincy Adams. In 1824, at fifty-one years of age, Adams had a long and distinguished record of public service. Read out of the Federalist party in 1808 on account of his heterodox opinions, he served with credit as Minister to Russia, as a member of the American peace commission at Ghent in 1814, and subsequently as minister to Great Britain. Since 1817 he had been Secretary of State in Monroe's Cabinet. There he had forcefully defended a nationalist policy. In so doing he had upheld Andrew Jackson's invasion of Florida in 1818, and by diplomatic pressure had forced Spain's cession of that country to the United States.

Adams believed that the national government was an instrument to be used with a minimum of constitutional scruple in advancing the national welfare. High principled, courageous, and pugnacious in defending what he held to be right, he was an opponent of slavery and a believer in freedom for all mankind. In private he had charm and social ease but, save in New England, he lacked popular appeal, for he had an astounding lack of talent in using the arts of the politician. Before the public, as he confessed in his diary, he was a man of "cold, austere and forbidding manners." He now sought the presidency as an advocate of internal improvements at national expense, and as a cautious supporter of a protective tariff.

Henry Clay of Kentucky, ten years the junior of Adams, was also a nationalist, and the outstanding exponent of the "American System"—a combination of national bank, protective tariff, and internal improvements as means of promoting national prosperity. Arrogant and often dictatorial, warm-hearted and charming, never profound but often persuasive, Harry of the West had been one of the War Hawks in 1811, had served with Adams on the peace commission that concluded the War of 1812, and subsequently had been an outstanding leader in the House. He was now Speaker of that body, and was ready to move heaven and earth in his effort to become Monroe's successor.

The other western candidate was Andrew Jackson of Tennessee, famous as an Indian fighter and victor over the British at New Orleans. Old Hickory, his soldiers had called him, and so he was known throughout the West. Violence marked his early career as a land speculator and planter in Tennessee. Strongly opinionated, hot-tempered, and utterly fearless, he had gunned down his opponent in a duel, engaged in a pistol fight with the Benton brothers, Thomas Hart, and Jesse, and during his army career had been quick to utilize the noose and the wall. Six militiamen had left his army without permission, although the evidence indicated that they believed their term of enlistment had expired. The court martial ordered death by shooting. The verdict came before Old Hickory for review just after the battle of New Orleans, but he saw no reason for leniency. He executed two British subjects during his 1818 Florida campaign. He told Monroe that, had he been in command of the military department in which the Hartford Convention met in 1814, he would have hung three of its leaders as being "really monarchist." (*See Reading No. 6.*)

But, prone though he was to violent emotions and acts, there was another side to Jackson's character. Advancing age—he was fifty-seven in 1824—and the life of a prosperous cotton planter had smoothed the rougher edges. Hot-tempered he was still, but he had acquired the deportment of a gentleman, one whose loyalty to his friends and whose integrity were beyond question. By nature simple and unreflective, he was also ambitious. He had sought wealth and glory, had achieved both, and now thought of himself as a western aristocrat, still full of vitality and ambition. He knew that he was a popular hero, famous in song and story, and when Tennessee politicians beckoned he was ready to respond.

How Jackson Became a Candidate. During the 1820s in Tennessee, two factions contended for control of the state. The Willie Blount-Judge John Overton group sought to wrest control from their rivals who were led by Colonel Andrew Erwin and Governor William Carroll. Several members of the Carroll entourage were personal enemies of Andrew Jackson, and he was loosely identified with the Overton coterie. Everyone recognized Old Hickory's popularity as a political asset and Overton, who had been for Clay in 1822, now turned to the Hero of New Orleans.

Then the plans for Jackson's advancement seemed to boomerang. Some time previously he had been badly hurt in land speculation, and had learned to distrust all banks. He now said so publicly. The Overton group, which had large banking interests, had already made him its candidate for the United States Senate. It now became cool, and he barely gained election.

Here was not an auspicious beginning for a political career, but elevation to the Senate stimulated popular interest in the Hero. Support for him as a presidential candidate began to appear in the southern states, and in Pennsylvania and New Jersey as well. Astute politicians climbed on the bandwagon. James Buchanan, a Pennsylvania Old Federalist, a standpatter at heart who prided himself on being a liberal, came out for Jackson in 1823. A Maryland Old Federalist named Roger Brooke Taney confided to a friend that he preferred the Hero because he was honest and was not brought forward by any particular class of politicians. Jackson-for-President enthusiasts were a mixed lot, so far as political antecedents were concerned, but the tide of public opinion was unmistakable. The Overton group in Tennessee had second thoughts and decided to join the procession.

When Jackson's friends had spoken to him of the White House in 1821, he had declared that he was unfit for the presidency. This modest self-appraisal may be taken with a grain of salt. It was, however, an opinion that Jefferson shared, and that con-

temporary evidence in part substantiated. Championship of the
mass of underprivileged voters has always been a prime asset for
a politician, but it was one that Jackson could not claim, for
he had none of the arts of the demagogue. During the panic of
1819–1823 he opposed relief for debtors, his remedy for their
hardships being simply industry and economy. So far as political
parties were concerned he was an amalgamationist, and had
counseled Monroe after his election in 1816 to ignore party in
making appointments to his Cabinet. In the Senate his record,
which lacked anything approaching distinction, was that of a
moderate nationalist. He did not oppose the Bank of the United
States and voted for the protective tariff of 1824. (*See Reading No. 7.*) He favored not only protection but also internal
improvements at federal expense where such measures would
enhance preparedness for war—a politician's rather than a statesman's attitude, but one that was sincere. If there was virtue in
this record, it lay in the fact that it could not offend any great
body of voters.

The Election of 1824. As 1824 approached, one aspirant
for the presidency dropped out and another was disqualified by
illness. Calhoun, his hopes blasted when the Pennsylvania state
convention refused to endorse him, resigned himself to being
a candidate for Vice President, an office for which he had no
serious competitor. Crawford lost ground, mainly because his
huge frame had been blasted by a paralytic stroke from which
he only slowly recovered, but also because of his nomination
by a Congressional caucus.

In that day of burgeoning democracy the caucus method
of choosing a presidential candidate had become distinctly unpopular, for it could not have been further from an expression
of the popular will. All the members of the House of Representatives had been chosen two years before the presidential
election. One-third of the Senate had been chosen six, one-third
four, and one-third two years before the election, and all the
Senators had been elected, not by the people, but by the state
legislatures. There was in addition the not unimportant fact that
Crawford had the support of some eighty Congressmen and was
bound to be nominated by the caucus.

Crawford did receive the Congressional caucus nomination on

February 14, 1824, but it was a mockery. Only 66 members of the 261 attended. Eight states, including Pennsylvania, were not represented, and a majority of those present came from four states. This was a blow to the Georgian's chances. It also marked the end of Congressional caucus nominations for the presidency, and was therefore a considerable step toward the democratization of the electoral process. Despite these setbacks to his presidential chances, Crawford stubbornly remained in the field. There were still four candidates for the presidency, the others having been nominated by state legislatures and popular mass meetings, and the contest bade fair to be close.

As election time came on, the supporters of each man filled the air with bitter recriminations against his opponents. The people heard that Crawford was incompetent; that Clay was a reckless gamester, and immoral to boot; that Jackson was a tyrant and full of uncontrollable impulses; that Adams was a conscienceless aristocrat. Ingenious politicians in various parts of the country tried to set up combinations of candidates. Crawfordites offered Clay a place on their ticket as Vice President. Adams offered Jackson the same office. These efforts illustrate the state of general confusion in which the election of 1824 took place.

Balloting in the twenty-four states took place from October 27 to December 1, a situation that, despite slowness of communication, gave some time for early returns to influence late voters. If such was the case, the advantage was on Jackson's side, for he jumped into an early lead in Pennsylvania. When the final results were in, however, a curious circumstance appeared. Despite all the name-calling, the voters had shown little interest. Voter participation in all the states averaged only 26.5 per cent.

Voter apathy was due to several factors. It was not a contest between regularly organized parties equipped to get out the vote, but a formless and chaotic race between the candidates. In a number of states (the New England states and Pennsylvania, for example) there was no real competition. In several states, voters were not accustomed to participation in presidential contests, their electors in the past having been chosen by the legislatures.

The election of 1824 could not, by any stretch of the imagination, be called a great triumph for anyone. Adams swept New England, but there only one voter out of five went to the polls. Jackson overwhelmed his opponents in Pennsylvania, but New York was about even between Adams and Crawford, and in Ohio, Indiana, and Illinois, no candidate received a majority of the popular vote. In no section of the country save New England was strong preference manifested for any one candidate.

So far as Jackson was concerned, the balloting indicated that he had an edge over his rivals. Though in some states the contest was very close, he did manage to carry eleven of the twenty-four. He had 99 votes in the electoral college to 83 for Adams, 41 for Crawford, and 37 for Clay.

Jackson's military reputation and his renown as an Indian fighter had been his stock in trade. As Mississippians said, he was a man who "fout." It is also possible that many voters believed that the election of a national hero would be a boon to national unity which was being strained by sectional disputes. Nevertheless he lacked a majority of votes in the electoral college, and the election was thrown into the House of Representatives.

The Election of 1825. The Constitution provides that, where there is no electoral college majority, only the three highest shall be candidates in the House of Representatives and each state shall cast one vote. (*See Reading No. 8.*) Clay was therefore out of the running but, as the influential Speaker of the House, he was in a position of great influence and power. As soon as Congress met in December the friends of all three candidates began to court him, (*See Reading No. 9.*) but he had come to Washington determined to support Adams.

There were a number of reasons why Clay should favor the New Englander rather than Old Hickory. Both Clay and Adams believed that there should be a protective tariff and internal improvements at federal expense. Their views on foreign policy ran along harmonious lines. Clay could reasonably hope to succeed Adams, whereas Jackson might well have other ideas. Then, too, Adams had had a long career of distinguished public service. Jackson's short term in 1821 as governor of Florida

Territory had demonstrated his penchant for high-handed justice rather than any real capacity for public administration. Military talent he possessed but, to Clay's mind, killing 2,500 Englishmen at New Orleans was scarcely a presidential qualification. And the General's ideas on the tariff and internal improvements were certainly nebulous. When it had been reported that Jackson was for a "judicious" tariff, Clay had tossed his head and declared with an oath he was for an "injudicious" tariff.

Shortly after the New Year celebrations, Clay had a three-hour conference with Adams, one that reinforced the Kentuckian's belief as to the similarity of their views on public policy. They skirted the question of reward for Clay's support, but he left convinced that he could have any place in the government that he wanted. (*See Reading No. 10.*)

When election day, February 9, arrived, the issue was still in doubt. The Kentucky and Ohio delegations had announced for Adams, but at most the New Englander could count on only twelve states out of the twenty-four. New York was crucial and its delegation was divided, seventeen for Adams, sixteen opposed, and one, old General Stephen Van Rensselaer, doubtful. Pressured by Crawfordites and by Adams supporters, Van Rensselaer went to his seat in an agony of doubt. He bowed his head in an appeal for divine guidance. As he finished, his gaze fastened on an Adams ticket lying on the floor at his feet. It seemed like the answer to his prayer, and he picked it up and dropped it in the ballot box. The presidential election was over. A few days later Adams offered and Clay accepted the State Department.

One of Adams's first moves after he took the oath of office was to send Clay's name to the Senate for confirmation. The vote, taken on March 7, showed 14 out of 41 Senators opposed. Prominent in the minority were Andrew Jackson and John H. Eaton of Tennessee, John Macpherson Berrien of Georgia, and Littleton W. Tazewell of Virginia. Rightly enough, Adams recognized it as "the first act of the opposition."

Jackson was furious, all the more so because what he regarded as the finagling of politicians had taken away from him in the House vote, four of the eleven states he had won in the electoral college. Forgotten was the way in which Adams had defended his actions in Florida, for the General was now convinced that he was the victim of an infamous bargain and sale. "No midnight taper burnt by me," he wrote Samuel Swartwout. "No secret conclaves were held, or cabals entered into, to persuade any to a violation of pledges given, or of instructions received." And he wrote to his old friend William B. Lewis that "the *Judas* of the West had closed the contract" for his thirty pieces of silver. (*See Reading No. 11.*) Adams wanted Jackson in the Cabinet as Secretary of War, but Old Hickory made it clear that he would not accept the post if it were offered.

CHAPTER 2

The Jacksonian Democratic Party Begins to Take Form

The Vulnerability of President Adams. Jackson and his disappointed supporters swore revenge. They looked to the followers of Crawford and Calhoun for support, nor were they to look in vain. Slowly the first outlines of the political movement that would become known as Jacksonian Democracy began to come into view.

President Adams had no sooner taken the oath of office than he began furnishing his enemies with ammunition for his overthrow. In his inaugural address he urged the necessity of internal improvements, and expressed his hope that doubts as to their constitutionality would vanish in an atmosphere of friendly discussion. This alarmed all proponents of states' rights, particularly those in the South who were fearful of the growing power of the northern protectionists at Washington; and Adams's obvious preference for loose construction of the Constitution laid him open to the charge of being an Old Federalist in disguise. His remarks also showed his dislike of what he called "the baneful weed of party strife," and his satisfaction at the disappearance of the two-party system. This was anathema to politicians who saw in political amalgamation only chaos and confusion, and who were avid for a reconstruction of parties as the safest and therefore the best means of acquiring power. (*See Reading No. 12.*)

When the President's first message to Congress in December, 1825 (in language that Franklin D. Roosevelt might well have used a century later), again emphasized the importance of a broad, national program of internal improvements, Old Republicans and contemporary states' rights southerners regarded it as virtually a declaration of war. (*See Reading No. 13.*)

Adams's opposition to a renewal of party politics alarmed Clay and others of the President's supporters. They urged the organization of a party that would back the President, and they took a hand in establishing committees of correspondence that would marshal support for Adams and his administration. Popular conventions and several legislatures passed resolutions commending Adams's course. But he himself would take no practical steps toward building up a party following. Furthermore, the appointments that emanated from the White House did nothing to conciliate any of the followers of Jackson, Crawford, or Calhoun; and Adams's belief that "government is founded on personal property" was scarcely in harmony with the democratic spirit of the age.

Elements of the Opposition. The President's lack of political sense, together with the hopes and frustrations of his defeated rivals and their followers, naturally led to a combination against him. The uneasy coalition that resulted first became known as the Opposition. A little later it took the name of Republican Democrats.

Jackson and his followers constituted the nucleus of this movement, as was natural since Old Hickory had been Adams's leading rival. Vice President Calhoun foresaw no hope for his presidential aspirations if Adams were in due time succeeded by Clay. The South Carolinian was also aware of his state's dislike for the protective tariff of 1824 and, for that matter, of any broad internal improvements program at the expense of the federal government. He felt that there was no real reason for loyalty to the administration of which he was a part, and he and his followers decided to rally around the Hero, who was trumpeting his grievances and seeking popular support. The Crawfordites, bereft of their ailing champion and thoroughly disliking Adams's nationalism, also moved into the Jackson camp. In so doing they provided the Opposition with a most astute and effective leader.

Martin Van Buren. Martin Van Buren was the acknowledged leader of the superbly organized Bucktail faction of the New York State Republican party. Son of a farmer and tavernkeeper of Dutch descent, he was forty-three years of age in 1825, and a wealthy lawyer. He was ambitious for preferment and he loved politics, which he saw as a means to place and power. Since 1821 he had represented New York State in the United States Senate, a post with which he professed great satisfaction. In 1823, however, he was willing to give up his Senate seat and a politician's career for a seat on the Supreme Court, but President Monroe passed him over, much to his disgust.

Van Buren was a little man who became stout as he grew older and his red hair and whiskers turned to a sandy grey. He had sharp eyes, a keen wit, and an ease of manner that gave him a sophisticated air. He was almost foppish in his dress, with a taste for decided but harmonious colors. Henry Stanton saw him in attendance at a Rochester church in 1828, arrayed in a snuff colored broadcloth coat with a velvet collar, an orange cravat with lace tips, pearl colored vest with silk hose to match, white duck trousers, yellow kid gloves, morocco shoes, and a long-furred beaver hat.

Suave, courteous, and conciliatory by nature, Van Buren sought to keep on friendly terms with all, including his political opponents, and he had great ability in the art of managing men. Fully aware that there are many pitfalls in politics, he early developed a penchant for hiding his own perplexities, and sometimes his convictions as to the proper course of action, in a haze of verbiage that enraged his enemies and perplexed even his friends. (*See Reading No. 14.*) As John Randolph said of him, he "rowed to his object with muffled oars." He usually had a destination in view, and at this time one of his objectives was the preservation, or rather the reestablishment, of party distinctions. He was known to friend and foe as "The Red Fox of Kinderhook," "The Magician," and "The American Talleyrand."

Van Buren Maneuvers for Position. The Red Fox had no patience with the amalgamation of parties that was so attractive to Adams and for that matter to Jackson. It was a development that he found abhorrent, for it obstructed his ideas of orderly and effective political procedure. He wanted a return to a two-party system such as had characterized the early days of the century. It seemed to him highly expedient to promote a movement that, in opposition to the nationalistic notions of Adams and Clay, would stand for states' rights and strict construction of the Constitution, giving it sanctity by calling it a return to old-time Jeffersonian principles.

There was some slight difficulty in this idea of returning to
Jeffersonian principles, for the Sage of Monticello was a man
many of whose views were either inconsistent or changed with
changing circumstances. He could denounce slavery as a vicious
and degrading evil, but could also have a runaway slave flogged,
and in his will leave over 260 slaves in bondage. He was an intense partisan in the 1790s, but in his 1801 inaugural address, he
had thrown down a challenge to partisan dissension with his
famous "We are all Republicans. We are all Federalists," and
in his later years he had lamented the prospect of a reappearance
of parties. In 1798 he had exalted the legislative branch against
the executive, or "monarchical" branch of the government, but
as President he had used the caucus system to exert his will over
Congress. Before becoming President he had been tender of
states' rights, and had favored a simple and limited national government, but during his presidency the true Old Republicans, John
Randolph's *Tertium Quids,* became disgruntled with his leadership and accused him of being recreant to the doctrine of states'
rights and the strict construction of the Constitution. The presidency broadened his perspective, and by 1816 he could declare
that constitutions must be subject to change, and institutions must
keep pace with the times. (*See Reading No. 15.*) This Delphic
utterance was not wholly in accord with the idea of a return to
the principles of Old Republicanism.

In 1824 Van Buren visited Jefferson at Monticello. Years
later, when writing his autobiography and unaided by any notes
or memoranda, the New Yorker's recollection was that his
own views on internal improvements, states' rights, and strict
construction were those of Jefferson. This may have been true.
Nevertheless, there can be no doubt that the New Yorker's
return to Jeffersonian principles was highly selective in character, based to a very considerable extent on his own ideas
as to what would be an attractive party platform.

States' rights and strict construction did hark back to Old
Republicanism, and in the latter 1820s such a program was
bound to enlist much southern support. It also accorded with
the interests of New York State, which was just completing
its Erie Canal without the aid of federal funds and had small
desire to see national revenues used for the internal improve-

ments of other states. Finally, calling the program Jeffersonian gave it the luster of a great name—a sort of involuntary accolade from one now generally revered as a Founding Father.

The Search for a Candidate.   Having provided himself with a platform, Van Buren looked about for a candidate whom he could support. This was 1824, and Adams, Clay, and Calhoun were all nationalist in outlook. Jackson shared this taint and, in addition, was an amalgamationist. This left only Crawford, although his devotion to Van Buren's set of principles was dubious. The New Yorker backed Crawford and turned his blandishments upon Clay, hoping that the latter would take second place on the Crawford ticket. When Clay refused, Van Buren turned to Albert Gallatin (scarcely a strict constructionist), and eventually accepted Calhoun for second place. The Red Fox also clung stubbornly to the Congressional caucus method of nomination for it was certain that there the Georgian would be selected. Then Crawford's illness and defeat blasted his chances, Adams became President, and Van Buren had to find another candidate.

The Adams inaugural and first message to Congress with their disclosures as to the President's program, hardened Van Buren's resolution to proceed with his plans, but he still had no candidate. With considerable reluctance he began taking a more favorable view of Andrew Jackson. The latter's public record certainly did not accord with the Old Republican principles that Van Buren wished to inscribe on his new party's standard, but the Tennesseean had prominent backers and he was indubitably a popular figure. Good fortune and good associations might be trusted to correct such errors as tarnished his Republican principles, and to control his tendency to rash and precipitate action. (*See Reading No. 16.*)

Organization of the Opposition.   Carefully Van Buren began bringing the elements opposed to Adams into focus. He cultivated New York's governor, DeWitt Clinton, his chief rival in New York politics but a strong backer of Andrew Jackson. He made overtures to southern politicians, for he was seeking an alliance between southern planters and the "plain Republicans" of the North. This was possible, he felt, if they could smooth over the ruffled southern feelings that were already apparent over slavery. In 1824 he had strenuously opposed a treaty with Great Britain that, had the Senate confirmed it, would largely have destroyed the slave trade on the high seas. Now he told Thomas Ritchie of Virginia that this proposed North-South alliance would quiet any northern clamors over slavery. He undoubtedly used this and similar arguments with Calhoun, and readily secured the South Carolinian's promise of cooperation. Then, in April, 1827, Ritchie, though fearful of Jackson's propensity for violent action, brought his powerful Richmond *Enquirer* to the aid of the coalition. That spring the Washington *National Intelligencer,* spokesman for the Adams administration, attacked Van Buren as the organizer of a new party.

Under the Little Magician's careful leadership and with the aid of a group of co-laborers, the Opposition gained substance. Some of the prominent figures in it operated out of Washington, some in the various states. Some were Old Federalists, others Old Republicans, but all saw Jackson as the inevitable presidential candidate, and the movement as the guarantor of their political fortunes. Tennessee furnished John Overton, planter and politician William B. Lewis, and Senators John Henry Eaton and Hugh Lawson White. Kentucky contributed two newspapermen, estranged friends of Clay, Amos Kendall and Francis Preston Blair. From Missouri came bluff and egotistical Senator Thomas Hart Benton, the earlier shooting affray forgotten in a political reconciliation. Pennsylvania provided Congressman James Buchanan. Isaac Hill and his *New Hampshire Patriot* lent vigorous support, as did the Albany *Argus,* organ of the New York Regency. A Washington coterie that included Van Buren, Benton, Calhoun, and his friend Duff Green (editor of the *United States Telegraph*) organized a central committee of correspondence, and similar committees in the various states helped establish pro-Jackson newspapers and provided orators who would blast Adams and Clay.

Organization in the States.   The way in which organization proceeded in the various states throws considerable light on the character of the Opposition. In Maryland Old Federalist Roger B. Taney became its leader. In Massachusetts David Henshaw, a Republican rebuffed by the Adams men, became a firm supporter of Jackson. So, too, did Theodore Lyman, Jr., a relative of Timothy Pickering of the Essex Junto of die-hard Federalists, and Harrison Gray Otis of Hartford Convention fame became a leading Jacksonian. Marcus Morton, leader of the Jacksonian ruralites in Massachusetts, became bitter in later years because Jackson appointed so many of these Old Federalists to office in the state. The Opposition in Maine contained a considerable infusion of Old Federalists, and the Jacksonian Portland *Argus* welcomed their support while denouncing the national administration as being Federalist to the core. Oliver Wolcott of Connecticut, a violent Federalist when he was Secretary of the Treasury under Washington and Adams, was now an equally violent Jacksonian.

In the Middle States, outside of New York, Federalists played a prominent role in the formation of the Opposition. In the southern and western states where Federalism had always been, or had become, weak or non-existent, the Republican party split into factions. There the growing Opposition party rallied around Jackson as a slaveholder, or as a bold western leader who would see to it that South or West, as the case might be, would have a fair deal. In Kentucky by 1828 many of the Jacksonians were men-on-the-make, jealous of the privileges of the "haves," and seeking privileges of their own. Similar restive elements flocked to the Opposition in all sections of the country.

These Opposition nuclei in the various states put great stress on states' rights, on the dangers that might emanate from a strong central government, and on the grievous wrong that had been done to the Hero of New Orleans. They operated through individual effort, through state and local committees of correspondence, through pamphlet literature, and by means of Jackson newspapers. By these means they sought to inculcate correct principles, Jacksonian principles, in the voting population. Careful efforts were also made to take the "right" side, which meant the popular side, on local issues.

Weakness of the Administration in Action. The Adams administration exposed itself to attack on many fronts. Its head, cold and phlegmatic in his public appearances, was subject to caricature as unfeeling and selfish, a leader who had no interest in the problems of the common man. His refusal to use his

position to reward others for service made virtue odious to
many who might, under different circumstances, have given
valuable support. He offered little aid to such skillful political
strategists as that rising politician, Thurlow Weed of New York,
or to such able leaders as Daniel Webster, of whom Adams had
a low opinion, and who might have been stimulated to real
activity as the administration's House leader had he been
promised further rewards.

It was ironic, the way in which Adams's high principles
worked to his disadvantage. The Creek Indians in Georgia provided an illustration of this melancholy fact. The Indian Springs
treaty, concluded under the Monroe administration with the
Creeks, deprived them of nearly 5,000,000 acres of their rich
cotton lands without decent recompense. Adams rightly regarded
it as fraudulent and ordered a new treaty negotiated, a decision
that stirred volcanic wrath among the Georgia whites. They
knew that the President was a high tariff man. They knew he
was wrong on slavery. He had sent Rufus King of New York,
whose denunciations of slavery in the Missouri Compromise
debates had enraged the South, as Minister to England. He was
proposing participation in an international meeting where a
slave revolt in San Domingo might well be on the agenda. Now
he wanted to deprive the Georgia whites of the Indian lands they
coveted, and the state threatened resistance to the federal government.

Adams persisted and the Indian Springs treaty was annulled.
Then new treaties were negotiated in 1826 and 1827 and in
these the Creeks did abandon their claims to the Georgia lands.
This ended the controversy, but Adams received no credit for
the outcome. Instead Georgia and the whole South now regarded him with a hearty dislike.

The Attack in Congress. The Opposition was quick to
detect the weaknesses of the Adams administration, and it
moved to take advantage of them by launching obstructive and
persistent attacks in the national legislature. The Panama Congress offered one such opportunity. Adams and Clay proposed
to increase the influence of the United States in Latin America
by sending delegates to a meeting of Central and South American
states at Panama, and the President sent the names of two dele-

gates to the Senate for confirmation. There followed three months of running debate, first in the Senate over confirmation and then in the House over the necessary appropriation. The Opposition evoked all manner of specters. Southerners denounced the Panama meeting because the international slave trade and the San Domingo slave revolt might come under discussion. Van Buren and others viewed it with alarm as an insidious means of increasing the power of the central government, and also as a menace to the sovereignty of the United States. (*See Reading No. 17.*) Before the debate ended, the Opposition had distorted and magnified the intentions of the administration beyond all reason. The delegates finally received Congressional confirmation, but one died en route to Panama and the other arrived after the Congress of the Latin American states had adjourned.

The attack on the administration's Panama Congress proposal was frustrating enough, but worse was to follow. The Opposition harassed the executive department by demands for special reports. It charged that Adams was corrupting the civil service. Van Buren characterized the administration as Federalist in tone and intent. Congressional oratory rang the changes on "bargain and sale" in both House and Senate. Constitutional amendments appeared, designed to safeguard the will of the people, or to prohibit a second presidential term. Another proposal would forbid the appointment of members of Congress to any federal office (save in the judiciary) during the term of their office and for two years thereafter, a "safeguard" blithely disregarded by Jackson after he became President. John Randolph capped the climax when he declared that "the bargain" was one between "Blifil and Black George . . . the Puritan with the black-leg." (*See Reading No. 18.*) Clay challenged the mad Virginian, and a duel took place in which neither man was hurt.

Politicians throughout the country copied these defamatory tactics, and their efforts bore fruit. In 1826, for the first time in history, the Congressional elections returned majorities in both houses hostile to the executive branch. The Jacksonians in the new Congress promptly formed committees that would promote the Hero's fortunes. Further harassment of Clay and Adams followed. Bills were introduced designed to transfer from the President to Congress much of the executive patronage. A whole series of House resolutions appeared denouncing corruption, indicting Adams for extravagance in the use of the public funds, and demanding retrenchment and reform. At the same time the solons ignored or ridiculed Adams's proposals for building a network of roads and canals across the country, for voyages of scientific discovery, for the promotion of agriculture, commerce, industry, and literature—works of national importance and beyond the competence and resources of any one state. Adams pointed out that Europe had over 130 observatories, he called them "lighthouses of the skies," whereas the United States had none. His opponents seized on that expression, making it a subject of derisory comment. In the eyes of these neo-Jeffersonians, such projects manifested an intent to build a national government of awesome power, one that would trample on the rights of the states to run their own affairs.

The zeal of the Opposition for protecting the country from the fell designs of the Administration had its ironic aspects, for of genuine national issues they had none. The Democratic party, as it was eventually to be called, was a hodge-podge of opinions on the tariff, internal improvements, public lands, the Bank of the United States, and other questions of the day. The basic objective of its leaders was simplicity itself. They were out to form a political party, elect a President, and enjoy the perquisites of power.

The Tariff of Abominations. One of the House committees appointed with political intent was that on manufactures, and the tariff bill that came from this body was designed primarily to ensure the election of Andrew Jackson. The master planners of this measure were Silas Wright of New York, who took a leading part on the committee in the House of Representatives, and Martin Van Buren in the Senate. They framed it to please the strong protectionist sentiment of the wool growers in New York, the hemp and sheep men of the West, and the iron manufacturing interests in Pennsylvania and the Empire State. High duties on molasses and sail duck were undisguised slaps at Adams's stronghold, as were to some extent the duties on wool and hemp.

The best evidence indicates that the architects of this "Tariff of Abominations," as the South called it, wanted this bill to pass. They believed that it was essential if Jackson were to carry northern and western states, and that the South would swallow the protectionist pill rather than abandon Old Hickory. Northern Jacksonians, Wright included, voted for some reductions of the duties on molasses and sail duck in order to placate New England industrialists. But the South Carolinians and other southerners voted steadily for the highest protective features, hoping that this would kill the measure by forcing New England to reject it. New England swallowed its resentment, the bill passed without the proposed reductions, and Calhoun began composing his *Exposition and Protest* justifying the right of nullification. He and many other southerners believed that Van Buren had betrayed them. It seemed apparent to them that the party the New Yorker was organizing would never meet their demands for a lower tariff, and they looked with deep suspicion on the Red Fox of Kinderhook.

The Campaign of 1828.   Outside of Congress the Democratic campaign of 1828 started at New Orleans on January 8 with a military revue in celebration of Jackson's victory over the British. This glorification set the pace for activities that became more and more frenetic as the autumn drew near. Jackson had declared that there were issues which involved the very framework of the government. He wanted constitutional amendments that would surely place the election of the President in the hands of the people, and that would prevent the President from appointing members of Congress to high office. But as the campaign progressed these were lost sight of in a grand vilification of the President and the Secretary of State.

By 1828 the Jackson party had built everywhere, save in New England, effective state organizations with committees which raised money for financing newspapers, for organizing parades, barbecues, rallies and dinners, and for providing unlimited supplies of hickory brooms, canes, sticks, poles, and trees. Through orations and newspaper editorials they portrayed their candidate as a protectionist in Pennsylvania, a low tariff man in the South, and everywhere as a Hero who would chase out of Washington the gambler who was at the head of the State De-

partment and that waster of the people's money in the White
House. Newspapers, pamphlets, platform speakers covered
Adams with abuse. He had ceded away Texas to Spain. He was
a Federalist. He was an apostate Federalist. He lived in splendor
and with kingly pomp. He had used government funds to buy
a billiard table and other gambling furniture, and then had installed them in the White House. As Minister to Russia he had
acted as a pimp for Emperor Alexander, and had actually procured an American girl for the royal pleasure.

Suffering under this torrent of censure, the Adams-Clay party
tried to take the offensive. Adams remained aloof but, spurred on
by Clay and Webster, the supporters of the administration under-
took fund raising, organized local and state committees and
conventions, and subsidized newspapers. Sheets supporting
Adams appeared in most of the states, but they were not
mouthpieces for a state party machine, as were the Albany
Argus and the Richmond *Enquirer,* and they found it much
easier to abuse the Hero than to extol the cold man in the
White House. Clay and Webster did some campaigning and
there were other stump speakers who glorified the American
System and the President's beneficent plans for the country,
but it was uphill work.

When it came to attacking the Opposition, the supporters of
Adams found that Jackson's stand on the tariff and internal
improvements was too ambiguous for effective assault, and in
their turn resorted to personal vilification. They declared that the
General was rash and headstrong; that his passions were beyond
his control. Coffin handbills lamented the six militia men:

> Oh! Did you hear the plaintive cry
> Born on the southern breeze?
> Saw you John Harris earnest pray
> For mercy, on his knees?

The climax of this abuse came with the charge that Old Hickory
and his wife had lived in sin before their marriage. Rachel
Donelson's first husband had been Captain Lewis Robards. The
marriage was an unhappy one, the couple separated and, on
news from across the mountains that Robards had obtained a
divorce, Rachel married Andrew Jackson. Then it developed

that there had been no divorce, one was promptly obtained, and the marriage ceremony had to be performed a second time. All this came out in explanations from the Jackson forces, accompanied by the charge that Adams and his wife had also had premarital relations.

The Antimasonic Excitement. For a time the Adams-Clay forces had prospects of carrying New York State. This was due to the Antimasonic excitement. In 1826 William Morgan of Batavia, New York, a brick and stone mason and member of the Masonic order, became involved in arguments with his lodge brethren. Argumentative, fond of whiskey, and in need of money, he determined to publish the ritual of the first three degrees—the Blue Lodge—of that secret fraternity. This aroused the bitter hostility of the craft. As Morgan's book, *Illustrations of Masonry,* was about to appear he was arrested on a false charge and lodged in the Ontario County jail in Canandaigua. Someone paid his debt and he left the jail a free man, only to be hustled into a yellow carriage and driven by relays of horses to Fort Niagara on the shores of the Niagara River. There all trace of him disappeared.

An investigation of Morgan's abduction was set on foot. When it developed that prominent Masons were obstructing the inquiry a great hue and cry developed. Indignant citizens declared that Masonry was an aristocratic, oathbinding system; that its members felt their fraternal obligations were superior to all others, even those of patriotic duty; that Masonry was subversive to true democracy. (*See Reading No. 19.*)

The excitement engendered by this affair spread from its focal point in western New York into the surrounding areas of the country. By 1828 Thurlow Weed, William Henry Seward, and others were directing its energies into political channels, and an Antimasonic party was in process of formation. This budding political movement bade fair to do great harm to the Jacksonian party in the state, for Jackson was a high Mason and Adams was free from any such taint.

Had the Adams-Clay forces and the Antimasons effected a working combination, as Weed wanted them to do, it would in all likelihood have carried the state. But many of the New York Adams men were members of the hated order, and so was the

Secretary of State. Genuine fusion proved impossible. The Anti-masons had no national ticket and Adams polled a heavy vote in western New York, but the Antimasonic and Adams-Clay parties ran separate state tickets, a sad handicap for both in the state election. The administration supporters also failed to capitalize on Democratic blunders in New York City. The result was that Van Buren became governor by a plurality vote, and Jackson carried the state with a 5,000 majority. This gave him about two-thirds of the state's electoral vote.

The Election of 1828. The national election of 1828 be-gan in September and lasted into November, the ballots being cast at different times in different states. It became evident at an early stage that Jackson was in the lead and this may have swelled his final victory, which was decisive.

Voter participation varied in amount, being light in some states but on the whole considerably better than it had been in 1824. Jackson had about 56 per cent of the popular votes cast. He carried Pennsylvania, had 5 of the 11 Maryland electoral votes, 20 out of the 36 in New York, and all of the states south and west of Maryland. This was doing very well for a campaign in which he had had no platform save vague promises about retrenchment and reform.

This election highlighted a distinct phase of party change and party formation. It was now clear what had become of the Old Federalists. In New England and New York a great majority of them had rallied to the Adams standard. In Pennsylvania, Maryland, and New Jersey they had divided their favors in fairly equal fashion between the two contending groups. In the South a preponderant majority had joined forces with the Jackson men. As for the two major parties that had appeared, the campaign had stimulated their organization in practically every state. There were still no platforms or designated party names, save those of their chief candidates, but each party had a national central committee together with a considerable num-ber of state and local committees of correspondence.

The Adams followers, who now were beginning to style themselves National Republicans, had shown some powers of organization, especially in the old northern states, but throughout the country they were demoralized by defeat and in the South and West the party broke up. The Jacksonians had a different story to tell. Nurtured by victory and patronage, they manifested great strength in the Middle States, especially in New York where Van Buren's Regency held control for the next twelve years. They also showed increasing power in New England, driving for control in both Maine and New Hampshire and demonstrating vitality in Rhode Island and Connecticut. In the southern and western states the Jacksonians held the field practically without a rival, a situation that, as events were to show, was conducive to factionalism.

Similarities in the Two Parties. Though the Democrats, as Jackson's followers now began to call themselves, had such a superior position, the ideological gulf between the rival groups in 1828 was more apparent than real. There had been much talk of states' rights and conjuring up of the ogre of a central government, but these were scarcely fundamental differences in party principle, for party positions differed from section to section. The Jacksonians had promised retrenchment and reform. They had made some effort to conjure up the shade of Jefferson. But, as Arthur Meier Schlesinger, Jr., has observed, the Congressional Opposition "had been confused and opportunistic, hiding a basic lack of ideas behind a smoke screen of parliamentary obstruction and campaign invective." [1] The orators on the hustings had been no better. Jackson's victory had been due to his popularity, the Adams lack of appeal, and the ability of the Jacksonians to use these and less creditable campaign materials in producing an emotional response from the voters. The electorate was told over and over again that Old Hickory was the candidate of the people; that Adams was the darling of the aristocracy. The response to these assertions demonstrated how important to politicians is skillful bidding, however sophistical it may be, for mass support. The question still remained as to what the Democrats would do, what their policies would be, once they grasped the reins of power.

The Dynamic American Society. The land in which Jacksonian Democracy had just won such a marked political triumph was filled with dynamic movement. Its population was increasing by leaps and bounds, due to the fertility of its sons

[1] A. M. Schlesinger, Jr., *The Age of Jackson* (Boston, 1945), p. 45.

and daughters and to the arrival, between 1828 and 1844, of half a million immigrants. Its people, a hodgepodge of nationalities mostly from western Europe, were energetic, optimistic, and imbued with a firm belief that their future (and through example that of the world as well) would be shaped by their own efforts and would be in accordance with the ideals of the American Revolution.

Southerners, like the rest of the population, were responsive to the profit motive. But, fettered socially and economically by slavery, they were becoming more and more traditional and conservative in outlook. The citizens in the northern part of the country were, by contrast, experimentalists and prolific in efforts to reform society. These varied from religious innovations and moral crusades such as the attack on Demon Rum to attempts at establishing Utopian communities. (*See Reading No. 20.*)

Americans, North and South, had some reverence, if little time, for culture. A Hudson River School of painters glorified the national landscape, especially in its wilder, romantic aspects. There was a classical revival, inspired by Jefferson, in architecture. Washington Irving, Ralph Waldo Emerson, Henry David Thoreau, Edgar Allan Poe, and others were creating a noble tradition in the field of literature. But the main interest in all sections of the country centered on economic achievement.

This was a period of enormous economic growth, with both North and South engaging in an energetic pursuit of material gain. Their land hunger seemed insatiable. The lure of rich soils in Louisiana, Texas, Iowa, Nebraska, Wisconsin, and Minnesota and the vision of what lay beyond these regions sent millions of Americans into the Middle West, the Southwest, and beyond the mountains to Oregon and California. In 1840 over one-third of the national population lived west of the Allegheny Mountains.

The urge to utilize space to its full extent (*See Reading No. 21.*) brought with it a transportation revolution that, in less than two generations, spanned the gap from flatboats and stage coaches to steamboats and railroads. It sent freight rates plunging downward, and quintupled the speed with which goods were carried across and up and down the continent. It also brought increasing demands from the New West, and to a lesser extent from the East as well, for cheap lands, internal improvements, and protective tariffs.

At the same time that millions of Americans began populating the western spaces, an urbanization movement also appeared. Cities and large towns increased and multiplied. Between 1820 and 1850 the population of Cincinnati leaped from 9,000 to 115,000, that of New York City from 123,000 to 515,000. And as urban and semi-urban centers developed, their opportunities for gain and their living problems increased in like proportion.

Both urban and rural America demanded easier and better ways of living and making profits. One result of this was an ever increasing supply of inventions—furnaces, hot and cold water systems, improved textile machinery, and a host of machine tools. The corporate form invaded the business world. America had its industrial revolution paralleling that of England, France, and the German states, with all the difficulties that this kind of development brought in its train.

The business cycle with its ups and downs, its inflations and depressions, came with the growth of industry. Nor did Americans share equally in the wealth which the resources of the country and their own efforts produced. The textile mills and iron manufacturing plants, the hundreds of banks and bankers, the growing number of established firms and ambitious newcomers, covered the land with enterprises of the most varied character. Many of these ventures failed, for the business risks in this period were very great. Many succeeded, some in fabulous fashion, and the wealthy class increased in numbers. The growing urban labor class, often working for starvation wages and living in squalor and deprivation, insisted more and more vehemently upon improvement in their condition in life. Laborers demanded better educational opportunities, a ten hour day, the right to unionize, and other changes that would improve their situation and open new opportunities for their children. The hopes and aspirations of the growing labor force had considerable influence on the course pursued by the leaders of Jacksonian Democracy.

Nor were the demands of the laboring class and the hardships of the rising entrepreneurs the only problems that beset an expanding America. The influx of foreigners, a majority of whom joined the party that claimed Jefferson and Jackson as its patron saints, promoted sharp nativist reactions among competitors with these newcomers. There were also sectional conflicts between East, West, and South over tariff policy, internal improvements, public lands policy, and slavery. There was contention over the rights and powers of the federal government, and over the extent of states' rights. There were sharp divisions of opinion over the kind of currency, specie or paper, that should provide the medium of exchange for agriculture, commerce, and industry.

The United States was the fortunate possessor of a vast territory rich in resources, a continental market with great potential for development. It was also a land full of economic and social problems, sectional rivalries, and diverse views as to the function and proper scope of government. Over this conglomeration of affluence, misery, and aspiration, statesmen with some vision and politicians with less were bent upon acquiring or maintaining power through the manipulation of the democratic process.

CHAPTER 3

Jacksonian Democracy, 1829–1837

Inauguration. On March 4, 1829, Andrew Jackson became the seventh President of the United States. His inaugural address, delivered in the open air before the Capitol and to an immense throng of wellwishers, pledged economy in government, respect for states' rights, and a "just and liberal" policy. He recognized the "high importance" of internal improvements and of the diffusion of knowledge, always provided that these objectives could be constitutionally pursued. He declared that there was need for reformation of the public service, which reformation he interpreted as the weeding out of the "unfaithful" and "incompetent." Few heard what he said, for he spoke in a very low voice, but that was not important. The crowd had come to see him and to pay tribute to one who had risen from humble beginnings to the highest eminence in the land.

The inaugural ceremonies at an end, the crowd moved down Pennsylvania Avenue to the White House, where a reception, unparalleled before or since, took place. The multitude surged into the mansion in quest of the President and of the provender that had been set out by the staff. Glass and china crashed and splintered, gentlemen's noses were bloodied, and ladies fainted. The punch and cakes were taken out on the lawn to prevent further damage, and the people followed the refreshments. Meanwhile the crowd pressing about the President within doors was so great that, to avoid physical injury, he made his escape by way of a back door to Gadsby's tavern. (*See Reading No. 22.*)

National Republicans professed horror at such goings on. The President's admirers declared that the significance of the affair lay in its democratic character. At last, they said, the people had come into their own.

An Inauspicious Beginning. The administration inaugurated in this spectacular fashion had in other ways an inauspicious beginning. The Cabinet was Jackson's own selection. Martin

Van Buren was Secretary of State and Samuel D. Ingham, a Pennsylvanian, was in the Treasury. John H. Eaton, Secretary of War, was an old Tennessee friend of the President. John Branch of North Carolina headed the Navy Department. John M. Berrien of Georgia was Attorney General, and "General" William T. Barry of Kentucky was Postmaster General. Jackson thought this was a superb body of public servants but, save for Van Buren, it was composed of nonentities and was destined to be of little use to the Chief Executive.

Calhoun was a problem of a different sort. He had been re-elected Vice President, but between the able and ambitious South Carolinian and his chief there was soon to be bad blood. Then, too, the foreign ministers at Washington were in a querulous mood, distrustful of this new head of the government, this military chieftain with the volcanic temper, the idol of "King Mob." There was also the matter of appointments.

Jackson was determined to reward his friends with office, and proceeded to bestow offices on those that he considered faithful supporters—Old Federalists as well as Old Republicans. Ritchie, who had been doubtful from the first, was disturbed by this scattering of political largesse in what he deemed indiscriminate fashion, and communicated his doubts to the Secretary of State. Van Buren himself had vainly protested against Jackson's determination to make his friend Samuel Swartwout who, it turned out, was a scoundrel, Collector of the Port of New York. Perturbed by his inability to convince the President of Swartwout's unfitness for the collectorship, and by the general course of events, Van Buren tells in his autobiography how he put on his hat and walked the streets of Washington until a late hour one night, debating with himself as to whether or not he should resign his post. The next morning he decided to stay on, trusting that his influence and that of other friends, together with Jackson's fundamental honesty and good sense, would yet save the credit of the administration. (*See Reading No. 23.*)

Retrenchment and Reform. Since retrenchment and reform had been the Jacksonian watchwords during the campaign, the administration made an effort to move in those directions. During 1829 and 1830 something like a million dollars was lopped off of Treasury expenditures. Diplomatic, civil, and miscellaneous expenses, lumped together on the government's balance sheet, suffered a similar reduction, as did costs in the Navy Department. These economies were of short duration; before Jackson's first term was over they had vanished. Expenditures in the executive department in 1833 were more than 20 per cent higher than they had been in 1828 under Adams. The cost of the military establishment showed a marked increase. The postal deficit under the incompetent administration of Postmaster General Barry jumped 275 per cent from 1828 to 1830.

Retrenchment proved to be only temporary, as was to be expected in a rapidly growing country; reform, also difficult to achieve, centered on appointments to office. Jackson summed up his views on officeholding in his first message to Congress. He declared that few men could "for any great length of time enjoy office and power without being more or less under the influence of feelings unfavorable to the faithful discharge of their public duties. . . . they are apt to acquire a habit of looking with indifference upon the public interests and of tolerating conduct from which an unpractised man would revolt." Offices thus held became a "support for the few at the expense of the many." Therefore rotation in office should be "a leading principle in the republican creed" and he recommended "a general extension of the law which limits appointments to four years." (*See Reading No. 24.*)

The practice of rewarding faithful supporters by appointments to office was already widely used in the state governments, but this had never been the case in the government at Washington. During Jackson's eight years in office there were over 1,000 removals, something above one-tenth of the total number of officeholders. This was not the drastic sweep of which his opponents accused him, but it did introduce a practice that became an integral part of national politics.

The spoils system, as it came to be known, had some practical justification. It was a means of ensuring faithful party allegiance, and its dictum that officeholding should be widely shared helped to identify the Democracy as the party of the people. There were undoubtedly some officeholders—gray old dodderers and fussy bureaucrats—who merited removal. Nevertheless rota-

tion in office, as it was euphemistically called, exalted party
loyalty over administrative efficiency as a principle of appointment, and established in the national government the practice
of turning out good public servants so that loyal henchmen, fit
or unfit, could be rewarded for their political services.

It is unlikely that the spoils system was of more value to the
health of the democracy than the appointment practices that
preceded it, even though it did remove barnacles from the ship
of state. Certainly it provided a marked contrast to the policy
of Jackson's predecessor in office who, between 1825 and 1829,
made only twelve removals, all for fraud or misconduct.

Identification with the Masses. The carefully inculcated
belief that the Democratic party, despite the presence in its
ranks of Old Federalists and wealthy men, was an emanation
from the grass roots, constituted one of the secrets of the party's
power. Other factors strengthened this legend. Jackson's father
was a Scotch-Irish pioneer farmer, and his son had a simple,
rural background. Old Hickory was the first President of whom
it might justly be said that he came entirely from humble (if
a Scotch-Irishman was ever humble) pioneer stock. He was
the first President who did not rise through high service in the
government at Washington to the most prestigious office in the
land. He was the first President familiarly known to the people
by a nickname. These were all valuable in identifying the Democracy as the party of the common man. Duff Green, in the
days when he was a supporter of the administration, never
tired of repeating in the *United States Telegraph* that Andrew
Jackson was "the candidate of the people." And the people, at
least a considerable majority of them, believed this to be true.

Jackson's political opponents circulated a story that, to their
minds, illustrated the stupidity of the popular faith in the President. According to this tale, the driver of a stage coach in the
interior of Pennsylvania who was something of a wag drew
up one day before a tavern. The knot of idlers raised the inevitable question, "What's news?" "Haven't you heard," said the
driver. "The General made his grand entry yesterday into
Philadelphia in a barouche drawn by four gray horses; and
the crowd pressing around him so as to obstruct his progress, he

just stepped out of the carriage, drew his sword, and run one fellow clean through the body."

"The darned fool," exclaimed one of the auditors; "why didn't he stand out of the general's way! " [1]

Factionalism. Despite the Democracy's attempt at identification with the masses, the party that rode to victory in 1828 under Jackson's banner did not by any means enjoy solid and harmonious support. Pennsylvania Calhounites and "Original" Jackson men warred with one another. Factionalism was rampant in the South and in the West. In New York, Massachusetts, and Pennsylvania the spread of Antimasonry and the appearance of workingmen's parties reflected desires for reform and dissatisfaction on that ground with both of the major parties. If Jacksonian Democracy was to remain dominant, it would need powerful leadership.

The Kitchen Cabinet. It was not long before signs appeared that Jackson would be more than a figurehead President. One of these signs was his so-called "Kitchen Cabinet." Due possibly to criticism of his early appointments, and guided by the canny comments of Van Buren, Old Hickory gathered about him an unofficial body of astute advisers. As the years went on this group varied in composition, but from time to time the Secretary of State, newspapermen Kendall, Blair and Isaac Hill, Taney, Senator Edward Livingston of Louisiana, and others gave advice on patronage and major policy questions, advice that Jackson used with benefit to himself and his party. The Kitchen Cabinet showed that the President was not afraid to seek counsel from shrewd and able men. Early in the administration the "Eaton malaria" gave him an opportunity to demonstrate that he was also a stubborn and resolute leader.

The Eaton Affair. John H. Eaton, Secretary of War, wealthy and a widower, had become infatuated with Margaret (Peggy) O'Neale Timberlake, a fascinating little brunette whose father kept a boarding house which Eaton frequented. Jackson stayed there for a time in 1824, and found that Peggy played the piano "delightfully," and that she entertained her pious

[1] A. Nevins, ed., *The Diary of Philip Hone,* 2 vols. (N.Y., 1927), I, p. 128. Reprinted with the permission of Dodd, Mead & Co.

mother every Sunday evening with sacred music. Peggy's husband, purser John B. Timberlake, was often at sea for long periods. On April 2, 1828, Timberlake died while on a Mediterranean cruise. His demise was apparently due to tuberculosis, but a rumor spread in Washington that he had committed suicide because his wife was having an amour with Senator Eaton.

There was no doubt of Eaton's infatuation with Peggy, but he was not altogether certain that he wanted to lead her to the altar. He consulted Jackson. The General replied that, if he loved Mrs. Timberlake, he should marry her. Indeed, he should do so forthwith, or else leave the O'Neale boarding house. Advised in this forceful fashion, Eaton decided on matrimony, and the wedding was set for January 1, 1829. On that day Democratic Congressman Churchill C. Cambreleng wrote about the affair to Van Buren. "Poor Eaton is to be married tonight to Mrs. T—! There is a vulgar saying of some vulgar man, I believe Swift, on such unions—about using a certain household —[sic] and then putting it on one's head." Cambreleng credited Swift instead of Montaigne, but the remark was an adequate measure of Washington society's reaction to the match. It was shortly after the marriage that Eaton accepted the post of Secretary of War.

The stories of Peggy's romantic past continued to float about but Jackson, mindful of the tales about Rachel and himself, refused to give them any credence. When the ladies of the Cabinet and his own niece, Emily Donelson, refused to recognize Peggy socially the President took up the cudgels on her behalf. He blasted the traducers, demanding proof of her immorality that they were unable to furnish. Peggy, he declared, was "chaste as a virgin."

The Eaton affair had widening repercussions. Floride Calhoun, wife of the Vice President, was one of the ladies who refused to call on Mrs. Eaton. Jackson, who at first thought Clay was attempting to disrupt the Cabinet by spreading the gossip, became more and more certain that Calhoun was at the bottom of the affair. But the President felt only gratitude toward Van Buren, a widower, who called on Peggy and invited her and her husband to dinner parties. The New Yorker's stock rose steadily. He learned to ride horseback so that he and the President might take early morning rides through Washington during which Eaton's troubles were discussed, and other matters as well. Tactfully the Red Fox gave advice on political procedures, and the President listened with growing respect and trust. Meanwhile it had become apparent that Old Hickory and his Vice President were far apart on grave matters of public policy.

Jackson's Differences with Calhoun. After the passage of the Tariff of Abominations in 1828, Calhoun had written his famous *South Carolina Exposition and Protest*. There he argued that the Constitution gave the power of taxation to the government solely for the purpose of raising revenue, and that any protection involved must be purely accidental. This being the case, the tariff of 1828 was obviously unconstitutional, imposed by the North because it had a majority in Congress. A remedy for this rank injustice, Calhoun declared, lay in the right of "interposition" by a state. In other words, where the Constitution was flouted by the national government, a state could interpose its authority and nullify the offending law. (*See Reading No. 25.*)

Calhoun's thinking on nullification differed from the President's. Jackson had a more limited view of states' rights than had the South Carolinian, and as a nationalist he loathed the doctrine of nullification.

The two men also differed on other fundamental points. Jackson was a moderate tariff revisionist, Calhoun an avowed enemy of protection. The President wished to pay off the national debt and then distribute the surplus revenue to the states in proportion to population. Calhoun would extinguish the debt but he opposed distribution, preferring to eliminate the surplus revenue by lowering the tariff. Jackson detested the Bank of the United States, but Calhoun took no stand in regard to that institution.

On all these points of difference between the President and Vice President, Van Buren was substantially in accord with his chief. At the close of 1829 Jackson wrote to his friend John Overton that Van Buren was open, candid, and manly, and also able and prudent. "I wish," the President added, "that I could say as much for Mr. Calhoun."

The Webster-Hayne Debate. Events now moved toward

two dramatic moments in American history. The first of these was the Webster-Hayne debate. South and West had a quasi-alliance seeking to promote a low tariff and cheap public lands policy. When, on December 29, 1829, Senator Samuel A. Foote of Connecticut proposed a resolution of inquiry as to the expediency of limiting the sale of public lands, a great debate began in the Senate. Benton denounced the proposal, declaring that the East wanted to retard the settlement of the West so that it could be sure of cheap labor for its factories. Senator Robert Y. Hayne of South Carolina supported Benton, his argument for cheap land merging into one for states' rights and a limitation of the national government's power.

Webster in reply to Hayne denounced the attack on the East and the extreme states' rights advocates, deplored sectional cleavage, and declared that the federal government was a fit instrument for developing the wealth and resources of the nation. Hayne, in his response, taunted Webster with New England's record in the War of 1812, assailed his nationalist viewpoint, and defended the doctrine of interposition. Then came the famous second reply to Hayne. Whatever New England had done in the past, said the Senator from Massachusetts, it was now seeking the national welfare. The federal government was a manifestation of the will of the American people, and the national interest was paramount to that of any state or section. The peroration, a magnificent apostrophe to nationalism, ended with the words "Liberty *and* Union, now and forever, one and inseparable." (*See Reading No. 26.*)

That night the two men met at a White House reception. "How are you this evening, Colonel Hayne?" said Webster. The South Carolinian smiled and replied, "None the better for you, sir."

The Jefferson Day Dinner.   Jackson had no love for Webster, but the doctrine of interposition stirred his fighting instinct and he soon found an opportunity to make this manifest. The South Carolinians sought to use the celebration of Jefferson's birthday on April 13, 1830, for a glorification of states' rights. They offered prepared toasts to the Virginia and Kentucky Resolutions, and to Georgia for its defiance of the Adams administration. When the time came for the volunteer toasts the

President threw down the gauntlet by proposing simply, "Our Federal Union. It must be preserved." The best that Calhoun could offer in response was a toast to "The Union—next to our liberty the most dear. . . ." The plans of the states' rights advocates had gone awry. (*See Reading No. 27.*)

Philip Hone, New York merchant and ardent National Republican, said later that this toast had been worth five hundred thousand votes for the President. "The most popular man we have ever known," Hone wrote in his diary. "Talk of him as the second Washington! It won't do now; Washington was only the first Jackson." [2]

The Jefferson Birthday confrontation fitted in with Van Buren's plans for succeeding Jackson in the White House. The New Yorker's project received a further impetus when Calhoun's enemies brought out evidence that, back in 1818 during a Cabinet meeting, Calhoun had urged censure for the General because of his conduct in the Florida campaign. Jackson confronted the Vice President with this evidence. The latter's long and labored reply, to the effect that this was a political intrigue by his enemies, did nothing to assuage Old Hickory's wrath. He now turned against Calhoun's supporters, and one of the first victims was Duff Green, editor of the *United States Telegraph*. Late in 1830 Francis Preston Blair was brought from Kentucky to edit a new organ for the administration, the Washington *Globe*. By one means or another, many of the *Telegraph* subscribers were induced to shift over to the *Globe*. The federal patronage was also readjusted, and not in favor of Calhoun's friends. Then in the spring of 1831 and in accordance with Van Buren's advice, Jackson reorganized his Cabinet. Van Buren and Eaton resigned, and the President asked Ingham, Branch, and Berrien, all pro-Calhoun, to follow suit. They were replaced, respectively, by Louis McLane in the Treasury, Levi Woodbury in the Navy Department, and Roger B. Taney as Attorney General. The War Department, formerly Eaton's domain, was now managed by Lewis Cass, and Edward Livingston was Secretary of State. Jackson named Van Buren Minister to England.

Calhoun's star was evidently on the wane, but it was equally

[2] *Ibid.*, p. 97.

apparent that there was dissension within the ranks of the Democracy. Calhoun broke openly with Jackson, and declared
that he would be a candidate for the presidency in 1832. He
and other advocates of states' rights viewed Van Buren and his
machinations with the deepest suspicion and dislike. Factional
dissension broke out in the Virginia Democracy, in Pennsylvania, and Mississippi, and even in Jackson's home state of
Tennessee. The party showed signs of disintegration, but its
leader was a determined and popular figure. It remained to be
seen whether or not he could hold the party together as an
effective political force.

The Recall of Van Buren. The Jackson administration
had to face opposition not only from dissidents in its own party,
but also from the forces led by Henry Clay who was sent by
Kentucky to the Senate in 1831. Clay's American System with
its credo of a national bank to regulate the currency, a protective tariff to stimulate manufactures, and a goodly public land
sales revenue to be distributed among the states for building
roads and canals, furnished the positive program of the National Republicans. In order to put this program into effect,
victory at the polls was essential, and they launched a vigorous
attack upon the Hero and all his works.

One of the first moves in this offensive was the rejection of
Van Buren as Minister to England. The narrow Democratic
majority in the Senate did not hold firm, enough supporters of
Calhoun joined with the National Republicans to produce a
tie vote on confirmation, and the Vice President then cast the
vote that called Van Buren back to the United States. The enemies of the Red Fox believed that this would cover him with
disgrace and ruin his political career. Benton heard Calhoun
exclaim, "It will kill him dead, sir, kill him dead. He will never
kick, sir, never kick." But never was prophecy more false. Rejection brought Van Buren home a martyr to political hatred.
It hardened Jackson's determination to support his friend, and
paved the way for his triumph at the 1836 Democratic national
convention.

Jackson's Indian Policy. Jackson's opponents thought
they had found another weak spot in his armor when they
attacked his Indian policy. The President protested his interest

in the red man's welfare. "Toward the aborigines of the country," he declared in his message to Congress in December, 1830, "no one can indulge a more friendly feeling than myself, or would go further in attempting to reclaim them from their wandering habits and make them a happy, prosperous people." Actually, he had no love for the Indians, and his beneficent plans for them consisted simply in removing the Cherokees, Creeks, Choctaws, Seminoles, and other tribes from the lands of their forefathers, lock, stock, and barrel to reservations west of the Mississippi.

In pursuing his Indian policy the President flouted decisions by the Supreme Court upholding the Cherokees in their efforts to retain their Georgia lands. According to report, Jackson said "John Marshall has made his decision: *now let him enforce it!*" (*See Reading No. 28.*) Whether or not he actually made this remark, it was in accord with his comment to his friend, John Coffee, that the Supreme Court's decision "has fell still born" and that, if the Indians resisted Georgia, the federal government would be unable to prevent their destruction.[3]

The forced migrations which Jackson sponsored constitute a disgraceful page in American history. Lack of adequate preparation, force, fraud, and terrible hardships characterized the removals. The Indians for the most part submitted silently to their fate, though some of the tribes took to the warpath. The Seminoles under their gallant young chief, Osceola, fought for years, and the government spent millions of dollars in their subjugation. In the end the white man had the lands he coveted.

Humanitarians, and especially religious sects such as the Methodists and Quakers, condemned this treatment of the Indians. Clay and other opponents of the President declared that it was a national disgrace and urged nationwide protests. But the outcries of moralists and politicians fell mainly on deaf ears. To most Americans the Indian was a nuisance or worse, and the sooner he was shoved out of the way the better for all concerned.

The Veto Power.   Jackson's attitude toward the veto power was another aspect of his decisive character that brought out-

[3] J. S. Bassett, ed., *Correspondence of Andrew Jackson,* 7 vols. (Wash., D.C., 1926–1935), IV, p. 430.

raged cries from his opponents. From 1789 to 1829 Presidents used the veto only nine times, and only three of these had involved important aspects of public policy. By the time Jackson had been in office two years he had vetoed four internal improvements bills. During his eight years as President he used the veto twelve times and in so doing justified his action on grounds of expediency as well as constitutionality.

Clay, Webster, and their followers bitterly attacked this use of the veto. They declared that "King Andrew" was subverting the foundations of the republic; that his attitude toward government was that of an arrogant "military Chieftain." If his use of the executive power was not checked, they said, the United States might find itself under an elective monarchy, or even a despotism.

These dire predictions wildly exaggerated the state of the nation. Jackson had no intention of becoming a despot, or of establishing despotic precedents. But it is true that his conception of his office, and his actions therein, had a significant impact on the character of the American government. Before 1829 the role of Congress had tended to eclipse that of the President. The legislative branch had been the driving force in pushing the country into the War of 1812. In the period after 1815 the struggles over the tariff, internal improvements, and slavery expansion had taken place in Congress, and had been fought over without reference to any presidential election. Before 1824 it had become established procedure to name presidential candidates in Congressional caucus. The House and the Senate had made Adams's term of office a lesson in futility. But now Jackson made the presidential veto a potent weapon, one which greatly increased executive control of governmental policy. It was a permanent change, for succeeding presidents never relinquished the power that he established. This was only one of the ways in which he made the presidency a formidable part of American political life.

Jackson's Internal Improvements Policy. Jackson's attitude toward internal improvements at national expense also demonstrated his independent attitude toward Congress, and drew the fire of his political opponents. Toward such improvements he took a position that was, to a considerable extent, ambivalent. He warned Congress that the national government must not attempt to construct or promote roads and canals in any way that limited the jurisdiction of the state or states within which such improvements lay. (*See Reading No. 29.*) Furthermore, it should never make appropriations for works of a purely local or state character, for to do so "would of necessity lead to the subversion of the federal system." Internal improvements, he felt, were apt to be wasteful of the people's money. They should not be allowed to interfere with the speedy extinguishment of the national debt and the reduction of taxes to the lowest point consistent with maintaining a proper state of defense. (*See Reading No. 30.*)

Thus far the President's arguments were consistent with those views on the economical and limited character of the federal government that were part and parcel of Democratic philosophy. They also harmonized with his loathing for Henry Clay's American System. At the same time he could not help recognizing the value to the nation of roads, canals, and river and harbor improvements; nor were his administrations backward in aiding such developments. More money was spent for them by the national government during his eight years in office than had been spent by all of his predecessors put together, and some of the projects that he approved were strictly local in character. The only saving grace in his position, so far as consistency was concerned, lay in his avoidance of any systematic plan for a comprehensive system of roads and canals, and his avowed concern lest the public revenues be wasted on pork barrel legislation. These aspects pleased the South, which felt no need for more roads and canals, but they scarcely pleased Henry Clay and his supporters.

The Maysville Road Veto. Among Jackson's vetoes of internal improvements bills, that of the Maysville road particularly galled his opponents. This road was some sixty miles in length, stretching from Lexington, Kentucky, Clay's home town, to Maysville on the Ohio River. The veto, lengthy and labored, centered its argument on waste and unconstitutionality, but its inspiration was clearly political. Its wordiness smacked of Van Buren, who heartily approved it and probably had a hand in its composition. The road was so short that, as the Red Fox remarked, eliminating its improvement would alienate only a small number of voters. New York and Pennsylvania, which financed their own improvements, liked the veto, and it stood as a symbol of the Jacksonian Democratic dogma that the activities of the national government should be on a limited scale, as distinguished from National Republican extravagance.

The Tariff of 1832. There was one bill approved by the President with which the National Republicans could not find a great deal of fault, for it originated in a House committee headed by a prominent member of their own party. John Quincy Adams had not renounced political life after his defeat for reelection, and his constituents had sent him to Congress. There he had been appointed chairman of the committee on manufactures. Adams was not an extreme protectionist, as was apparent when the bill drafted under his guidance reached the floor of the House. The tariff of 1832 avoided the worst features of its predecessor, and reduced the general level of duties to about that of the tariff of 1824. Advocates of high protection, Clay in particular, viewed it with disfavor, but moderate men thought it a good bill. On July 14, 1832, Jackson signed it into law. He believed that the South would find it acceptable but in this, as will be seen, he was mistaken.

Nicholas Biddle's Bank. While the tariff bill made its way through Congress, another issue of great importance took the center of the political stage. The second Bank of the United States had been chartered in 1816 with a twenty year span of life. Its capital was $35,000,000, which made it the largest corporation in America and one of the largest in the world. It could issue bank notes up to the amount of its capitalization, and was obligated to serve as a depository for the funds of the national government.

The Bank had been badly handled under its first president, William Jones, and had fallen into great popular disfavor as a result of its foreclosure policy during the panic of 1819, but since that time it had risen in public esteem. This was partly due to the policies of Jones's successor, Langdon Cheves, but mainly to those of the man who became its president in 1823. Nicholas Biddle was then thirty-seven years old. His family was prominent in Philadelphia and he bade fair to add luster to the family name. Brilliant in his studies at the University of Pennsylvania and at Princeton, he was admitted to the bar but turned his attention to literature, diplomacy, politics, and finally to banking, which absorbed more and more of his attention. In 1819 President Monroe made him a director of the Bank of the United States, and four years later he became its president.

Biddle was witty, urbane, charming, and rather astonishingly naive. There was also more than a touch of arrogance in his makeup, but his management of the Bank's affairs was wise and statesmanlike.

The Bank was by no means a monopoly in its field, but it occupied a position of great importance. It issued about one-fourth of the country's bank notes and, through its power of discount and its policy of calling on the state banks to redeem their currency issues, it exercised major control over the volume of credit and the character of the currency available throughout the country. Biddle exercised this power with a view to establishing sound credit and monetary stability, and used the Bank's efficient exchanges in helping to move the crops and generally to facilitate commercial operations.

The Bank was not only a valuable but also a potentially dangerous institution, for the terms of its charter did not provide effective governmental regulation. It customarily made loans to public figures, a practice that might easily lend itself to grave abuses. Biddle took care to distribute its favors with reasonable judgment, but there was no disguising the power that a determined Bank president could wield. He told a Senate investigating committee in 1832 that there were very few banks that the Bank of the United States could not have destroyed, but that it had aided many, and that many had been saved by its efforts. This was undoubtedly true, but this frank acknowledgment of its power convinced more than one good Democrat that its charter must not be renewed.

The Bank's Enemies. No such institution could long exist, beneficent though its operations might be, without acquiring enemies. Farmers, businessmen, and speculators sometimes chafed at its restrictive credit policies. Bankers primarily inter-

ested in profits disliked the control it exercised. Eastern workingmen, having had experience in being paid with depreciated
bank notes, disliked all banks. And Biddle's arrogance helped
to bring the Bank into disfavor. (*See Reading No. 31.*)

The Bank's most powerful enemy was the President of the
United States. Jackson's early experiences as a land speculator
had been unfortunate, and he had emerged from them deeply
suspicious of banks, bankers, and paper money. This enmity
now centered on the Bank of the United States, for he heard
it had played politics in the 1828 election. He held it to be a
monopoly, one dangerous to liberty, and his messages to Congress had manifested his distrust. (*See Reading No. 32.*) There
is evidence that he always wanted to destroy the Bank, but was
at first held back by some of his advisers.

For the Bank had friends, or at least non-enemies, in high
Democratic circles. All of Jackson's reshuffled Cabinet, save
Attorney General Taney, were friendly to what Jackson called
"the Monster." So was James Alexander Hamilton, a trusted
adviser of the President; and Van Buren and the New York
Regency were reluctant to see open warfare on this powerful
institution, which was extremely popular in the important state
of Pennsylvania.

The Bank Asks for a Recharter.   There was no question as
to where Pennsylvania stood. In the spring of 1832 that state's
legislature unanimously adopted a resolution of confidence in
the Bank, both National Republicans and Democrats coming
to its support. This attitude on the part of the Keystone State
played a large part in the Bank's decision that spring to ask for
a recharter. Biddle, who felt that Jackson meant to destroy the
Bank, was also urged to immediate action by Clay and Webster.
Pennsylvania was an important state and Jackson was on the
verge of a campaign for election. He would not dare to veto
lest he lose the state. So argued the politicians.

A bill providing for a fifteen year recharter was taken up,
late in May, in the Senate. On June 11 it passed that body, and
three weeks later passed the House by 107 to 85. In the Senate
the Bank had practically solid support in New England and,
save for New York and divided New Jersey, in the Middle
Atlantic states. The Northwest and Southwest divided. Only the

South, which feared the concentration of power above the Mason and Dixon line, was strongly opposed.

The Veto. Passage of the recharter roused all of Jackson's fighting instinct. (*See Reading No. 33.*) The Bank, he said, was trying to kill him. Very well, he would kill it. He called Amos Kendall, Taney, Andrew J. Donelson, and Levi Woodbury to his aid, and they drew up the veto message that, on July 10, 1832, went down to the Senate.

The message detailed various objections to the bill renewing the Bank's charter. It toadied to foreigners. Its modifications of the preceding charter were valueless. It was unconstitutional. The fundamental argument, the one freighted with political appeal, came at the end of the message. It contained, in brief, the *raison d'être* of the Democratic party as conceived by the Jackson administration. The Bank, it said, represented privilege, monopolistic privilege, which worked for the benefit of the few and for the disadvantage of the many. The object of good government was to remove such privileges and to prevent the granting of new ones. This would result in equality of opportunity for all. (*See Reading No. 34.*)

On Friday, July 13, 1832, the Senate sustained the veto by a vote of 22 for passage to 19 against, and thus the Bank was projected into the presidential campaign.

The Campaign of 1832. There were three tickets in the field in 1832, the first campaign in which nominations were made by national party conventions. Clay was the standard bearer for the National Republicans. The Antimasonic party, which had spread out from New York into New England, Pennsylvania, and Ohio, nominated William Wirt, a scholarly Virginia lawyer. Jackson's renomination was a foregone conclusion and the Democratic convention met primarily to choose his running mate. Old Hickory wanted Van Buren, and to ensure his selection the Jacksonians prevailed on the convention to adopt a rule that the nomination had to be by a two-thirds majority. No other candidate for second place had anything like that number of supporters, and the rule ensured Van Buren's nomination. From then on the two-thirds rule became traditional Democratic practice in nominating both presidential and vice presidential candidates.

The campaign was a spirited affair. The Democrats were well organized, their central committee in Washington supervising an effort that extended down into the counties and towns of the states. Subsidized newspapers excoriated Clay, Wirt, and the Bank, and local committees distributed literature and organized parades and barbecues. The central theme of all these efforts was that the Democracy was leading the people's fight against aristocracy and monopoly. This was linked with an appeal for support of the valiant chieftain, their leader in the fray. The National Republicans used much the same type of organization, but their approach to the voters was along different lines. They contended, so they declared, for the national welfare and for prosperity, and against despotism and dictatorship. The Bank itself was an issue only in areas where it was definitely unpopular. Where the opposite was the case, Democratic speakers declared that it would be rechartered with the necessary amendments if Jackson were reelected. The President himself was the Democracy's best issue.

Significance of the 1832 Election. In the election Clay carried Massachusetts, Rhode Island, Connecticut, Maryland, Delaware, and Kentucky. Wirt had Vermont. The rest went for Jackson, who had approximately 55 per cent of the popular vote of the nation. It was a decisive victory and his opponents were downcast, but there was a fly in the Democratic ointment. The President's popular majority was slightly less than it had been in 1828, the only vote of a reelected President in American history to show a decline.

Jackson's great personal popularity had given him a second term, but significant cracks were beginning to appear in the structure of the Democracy. The pro-Bank memorials sent to Congress in 1832 far outnumbered those against the "Monster," an indication that there was considerable mistrust of the war against the Bank on the part of both state banks and of the people. Among many southerners the treatment of Calhoun—one of their own—still rankled, and in the South and West there was deep-seated dislike of Van Buren. Alabama, Georgia, North Carolina, Virginia, and other states showed distinct signs of unhappiness at the prospect of this wily northerner inheriting the mantle of the Hero.

Nullification. Immediately after the election of 1832 came a crisis over the tariff. South Carolina was in a state of high excitement. Resentment over the tariff of 1832 contributed to this state of mind. Another important cause was fear lest the stability of the South's social structure be violently disturbed by attacks upon slavery.

The dread of slave revolts was always present in the South of that period. For South Carolinians the memory of Denmark Vesey and the uprising he had tried to organize in Charleston in 1822 was still fresh. The terror that event had aroused had been reenforced by the appearance in 1831 of William Lloyd Garrison's *Liberator,* and by the Virginia slave revolt that same year led by Nat Turner. South Carolina was in a mood to bid defiance to majority rule, if such were to be imposed upon them by a section of the country that understood neither their needs nor their fears.

The state threw away its vote in 1832 on John Floyd of Virginia, and believers in Calhoun's doctrine of nullification dominated the state government. On November 19, 1832, a convention called by Governor James Hamilton met at Columbia. Nullifiers outnumbered Unionists by five to one. The convention declared that on February 1, 1833, the tariffs of 1828 and 1832 would become null and void, so far as South Carolina was concerned. It prohibited appeal of its action to the Supreme Court of the United States, and asserted that attempts to coerce the state would be forcibly resisted and would result in its organizing a sovereign government independent of the Union. (*See Reading No. 35.*)

President Jackson felt that the tariff could well be lowered below that established in 1832. (*See Reading No. 36.*) His administration helped Congressional leaders to draft a bill that would bring protection down some 50 per cent by 1834. But the South Carolina threat to the Union made Jackson furious. His "Proclamation to the People of South Carolina," one of the most dramatic state papers in American history, warned them that their course of action could only end in disaster. "Disunion by armed force is *treason*," said the President. "Are you really ready to incur its guilt?" (*See Reading No. 37.*) At his instigation a Force Bill passed Congress providing military and other measures for meeting resistance to federal laws. Van Buren, always cautious, urged giving up the military provisions of this measure, but Old Hickory refused to budge. (*See Reading No. 38.*)

Henry Clay, relishing his role of Great Pacificator that he had earned in the 1820 controversy over Missouri, led the way out of the present crisis with the Compromise Tariff of 1833. This provided for a gradual lowering of the duties in the existing tariff that were over 20 per cent. By 1842 all duties would be reduced to that level. This measure passed, together with the Force Bill, and Jackson signed both on March 2, 1833. South Carolina's position had not been supported by the other southern states, and the hotheads at Columbia decided to accept the olive branch offered by Congress. The state legislature nullified the Force Bill but accepted the new tariff, and the country breathed a sigh of relief. (*See Reading No. 39.*)

Jackson had threatened dire punishment of the nullifiers. (*See Reading No. 40.*) Calhoun, who had resigned as Vice President and was sent up to Washington as a United States Senator, thought that the President might hang him. There had been no rash action, however, and the country as a whole approved the course taken by the national government. Only extreme states' righters harbored a lasting grievance; the military provisions of the Force Bill drove them out of the Democratic party. John Tyler of Virginia was one of these and Calhoun, too, parted company for several years with the Democracy.

The Bank Again. Removing the Deposits. The nullification crisis in no way lessened the President's animosity toward the Bank of the United States. He determined to withdraw the federal deposits in that institution; that is, to stop making federal deposits in it while he continued to draw on those already there in meeting the expenses of the federal government. The deposits, he said, were not safe, and Biddle would use them to force a recharter. It was clear that the action he contemplated would greatly curtail the Bank's power.

Jackson pushed this project against difficulties. The House of Representatives declared by a vote of 110 to 46 that the public deposits were safe in the Bank. All of the Cabinet save Roger Brooke Taney opposed removal. Two secretaries of the treasury, Louis McLane and William J. Duane, had to be dispensed with before the President found a man who agreed with his policy. Then Taney became Secretary of the Treasury, and certain banks that came to be known as "Pet Banks" were selected to receive the deposits. Needless to say, an overwhelming majority of the banks so favored were in the hands of loyal Democrats.

Biddle's Counterattack. The removal of the deposits disturbed public confidence in the Bank and made the whole monetary situation unstable. It also threatened the Bank with destruction. Biddle, who had not lost his hopes of recharter, felt much alarmed. To meet the President's move he began curtailing the Bank's discounts and calling in its loans. This policy of contraction heightened an already considerable monetary crisis which went on into the spring of 1834, each side blaming the other as it developed. Biddle and his supporters, hoping that contraction and the accompanying crisis would force the President to abandon his attack on the Bank, carried curtailment beyond the degree that was necessary to protect the institution. They found that their action was not only proving fruitless but was also lessening the Bank's popularity, and Biddle abandoned curtailment in the summer of 1834.

In December, 1834, a Senate investigating committee headed by John Tyler made a report approving the Bank's policy and operation, but it was too late to affect the outcome of the struggle. Biddle had gone down to defeat before his redoubtable adversary.

Significance of the Bank War. Although the effort to renew the Bank's charter ended in failure, the struggle had significant consequences. It was another step in the increase of executive power that took place under Jackson's leadership, for he had successfully defied majority opinion in both houses of Congress and had thus fortified the principle of executive independence.

The Bank war also represented a stage in the movement of Jacksonian Democracy toward a specie currency. Suspicious of all note issues, Jackson wanted the Pets to stop the issuance of bank notes up to five dollars, and eventually up to twenty dollars, in value. The New York Democracy passed a law, later repealed by the Whigs, that removed bills less than five dollars from circulation. In a number of other states there were similar restrictions by Democratic legislatures on paper currency.

Finally, the Bank war, together with the hard money leanings of the administration, produced dissension within the ranks of the Democracy. In Pennsylvania, Virginia, Mississippi and other states Bank Democrats lost faith in their party and began to look for another political haven. This was one factor in the creation of a powerful opposition, the Whig party, that began to materialize in 1834.

Opinions differ as to whether or not the destruction of the Bank of the United States was harmful to the national economy. Some argue that the Bank's restraining credit expansion in the interest of monetary stability retarded economic growth; that credit expansion by the state banks, though often wasteful, made for a rapid development of the nation's resources. Others maintain that the destruction of the Bank ended a promising beginning in that central banking, which is so important to the national economy as a means of regulating bank credit; that it prolonged an unstable currency situation, thus fostering a boom and bust economy; and that Jackson's bank policy, while representing an effort to please both the workingmen and other hard money advocates, actually aided and abetted only local banking interests whose main aspiration was profit for themselves.

Jackson's Supreme Court Appointments. The President's enemies felt that his war against the Bank stigmatized him as an autocrat whose whims made him a menace to society. They also had dark forebodings because it became Jackson's lot to appoint no less than seven members to the Supreme Court, including the Chief Justice.[4] They charged that political motives of the basest sort inspired these appointments, and that the "new" Court would undo the work of Chief Justice John Marshall in building a strong national Union.

Some color was lent to these charges by the sectional character of the appointments, for all save two of the appointees came from the slaveholding states. The Court did become more cog-

---

[4] One of these, William Smith of Alabama, appointed March 3, 1837, declined the appointment because he wanted to remain politically active as a Jacksonian Democrat. President Van Buren appointed in his place John McKinley, also of Alabama.

nizant of states rights than had previously been the case, but it still firmly upheld national sovereignty. The most significant change under Chief Justice Taney was an increased emphasis on the social and economic, rather than the constitutional, aspects of the cases that came before him. This was strikingly evidenced in a legal battle that involved transportation developments.

The Charles River Bridge Case.   The Charles River Bridge Company owned and operated a toll bridge across the Charles River. Massachusetts proposed to construct a toll-free bridge close by. The Bridge Company claimed that its charter gave it monopoly rights, and that the state's proposal was an impairment of contract.

Taney's decision represented the majority opinion of the Court and was against the Company. His main thesis was that, where exclusive privileges had not been specifically granted, community rights were superior to property rights. This decision was of vital importance to the development of means of transportation, not only in Massachusetts but throughout the country. Also, by ruling against monopoly on the part of one company, it opened the door to the competitive corporation capitalism that became one of the hallmarks of the American economy. (*See Reading No. 41.*)

The Censure of the President.   During the latter part of Jackson's second term his adversaries continued their attacks upon him and his policies. They painted alarming pictures of ruin and desolation made imminent by this irresponsible tyrant, but their efforts were largely in vain. Their one real triumph came in March, 1834, when Clay succeeded in getting the Senate to pass resolutions censuring Jackson for removing the deposits, and for assuming power not granted to him by the Constitution or the laws of the country. Jackson vigorously protested this affront (*See Reading No. 42*) and it proved to be a hollow victory. The 1834 elections increased the Democratic majority in the House and gave that party a majority of two in the Senate. In January, 1837, the Democrats expunged the resolutions of censure from the Senate records.

Jacksonian Foreign Policy.   Three other aspects of Jackson's second term—the administration's attitude toward foreign affairs, toward slavery, and toward inflation—merit consideration. First in regard to foreign affairs, the President exhibited both cautious diplomacy and a strong nationalistic bent. These were manifested in his handling both of trade with the West Indies, and of debts owed by foreign countries to the United States.

Britain had closed the West Indies to American ships, and Clay and Adams had been unable to obtain a reversal of this policy. Jackson's first administration took up the problem anew. After a year of fruitless negotiation the President was ready to retaliate by a non-intercourse law directed against "Canaday." At that point, however, the efforts of diplomats on both sides of the Atlantic prevailed. Congress passed a law granting new trading privileges to British ships and Britain responded in kind. The trade with the West Indies was now unrestricted.

The French problem involved an indemnity of 25 million francs that the two nations had agreed was due to the United States for losses suffered by its citizens during the Napoleonic wars. When the French Chamber of Deputies did not make the necessary appropriations, Jackson threatened reprisals. This aroused Gallic pride and resulted in a tense situation. The French Chambers finally passed the appropriations, conditional on a satisfactory explanation of the President's threats. His advisers prevailed upon him to include in his next message to Congress a disavowal of any intention to menace France. French sensitivity was then appeased, and payment of the indemnity began in 1836. (*See Reading No. 43.*)

Still other aspects of foreign affairs demonstrated the nationalism in Jackson's foreign policy. As an expansionist he tried hard to interest Mexico in selling Texas to the United States. Twice the President tried to buy that province, for which he was willing to pay $5,000,000, but the Mexicans were obdurate. Threats of reprisals and the occasional appearance of an American frigate in a foreign port were means used in collecting indemnities from countries other than France for losses suffered during the Napoleonic wars. Like a later President, Jackson knew the value of speaking softly and also the advantages in carrying a big stick.

Slavery and the Right of Petition.   Jackson's foreign policy was based to a considerable extent upon the concept of national pride. This was much more difficult to utilize in handling the rising tumult over slavery, which arrayed North against South. The abolitionist movement grew steadily in the North during the early 1830s, sparked by the activities of Benjamin Lundy, William Lloyd Garrison and the American Antislavery Society. Petition was a favorite weapon of the movement, and petitions for the abolition of slavery in the District of Columbia, where Congress had jurisdiction, flooded both House and Senate. Southerners wanted the national legislature to refuse altogether to receive these documents, which would have been tantamount to denying that Congress had any authority to act. The course taken in the Senate, largely due to Van Buren, recognized the right of that body to receive petitions and refer them to a select committee with instructions to report back that Congress ought not to interfere in any way with slavery in the District. In the House the offensive documents were received and immediately tabled. By these means the Democracy sought, not too successfully, to quiet the fears of the South for the safety of its peculiar institution. But the refusal to give due consideration to the requests of constituents fostered abolitionism and alarmed many advocates of free speech who were not violent opponents of slavery.

The Specie Circular. Abolitionism was not the only portent of coming troubles. During the middle 1830s the country experienced a speculative boom of major proportions. An air of undue optimism prevailed in East and West, North and South. Credit expansion, fostered by the Pet Banks, was rampant, public land sales rocketed and speculators reaped rich harvests. Well over $100,000,000 of foreign capital flooded into the country, invested in roads, canals and state bank securities. Everywhere there was talk of fortunes being made overnight, especially in land. Everywhere there was inflation.

The administration, at first complaisant, finally awakened to the danger of this situation, and in 1836 took what it hoped would be remedial action, a proposal that would also further the President's plans for a hard money currency. On July 11, 1836, the Specie Circular directed all government agencies to receive only gold and silver in payment for public lands. Hand in hand with this act went another one to distribute the expected surplus in the federal treasury that would come with the approaching extinction of the national debt.

The Specie Circular did serve as a check to inflation. It also cast doubt on the value of all paper money and stimulated a demand for gold and silver, the supply of which was already inadequate for the country's needs. General disquiet ensued. Banks began calling in their loans, money became tight, and the mood of the country changed from one of optimism to one of alarm. Such was the developing situation as the President's second term drew to a close.

The Significance of Jacksonian Policies. Andrew Jackson's eight years in the White House were of lasting importance to the country he loved and to the party he led. By his vetoes, by maintaining his right as well as that of the Supreme Court to interpret the Constitution, by refusing to bow to the will of Congress on the Bank issue, by his sturdy foreign policy, he elevated the presidency to a position of great prestige and importance. His nationalism, exhibited in the nullification crisis and in the conduct of foreign affairs, helped to strengthen the Union and to prepare the way for expansionist Democratic policies during the ensuing decade. His doubtful contributions were on the financial side, for his policies toward the Bank of the United States and hard money were anything but constructive. His distrust of banks was myopic and, as Bray Hammond remarks, his Specie Circular was a step toward "an exclusively metallic currency such as Europe had had in the Middle Ages." But these errors of judgment were honestly committed in the name of the people's welfare and helped to give his party an invaluable reputation as the true defender of the common folk, their shield against the grasping greed of the "aristocrats," their guide in seeking the affluence to which they aspired. (*See Reading No. 44.*)

The Two-Party System. The Democrats. During Jackson's two terms in office a well-defined and well-developed two-party system again took form in the United States. The Jacksonian Democracy, or the Democracy as it termed itself, and its opponent, the Whig party, became clearly defined as the major political organizations in the nation. These two giants confronted one another in the political arena for nearly twenty years.

The Democratic party proclaimed its devotion to equality of opportunity for all and saw government's function as that of establishing and maintaining such equality. Always with an eye to economy in government, Democrats believed that in Washington they should play the part of passive policemen, opening the door of opportunity for all, but keeping within very narrow limits any attempt to foster national prosperity by governmental action. (*See Reading No. 45.*)

Many diverse elements went to make up the Democratic party. Attracted by its repeated expressions of devotion to equality, expressions almost revivalistic in their fervor, libertarian idealists enlisted under its banner where, paradoxically enough, they found themselves cheek by jowl with politicians on the make. Nor was this the only example of Democratic diversity. The party contained pro- and anti-tariff, pro- and anti-internal improvements and pro- and anti-Bank men; it claimed the allegiance of aristocratic planters and of southern yeomen, of bankers, businessmen and northern farmers; and it had a special appeal for entrepreneurs who were seeking a place in the sun (a large element in a society which viewed America as primarily a land of economic opportunity).

Whether or not Jacksonian Democracy enlisted the support of the working class is still a matter of dispute among historians, and much has been said, pro and con, on the subject by present day scholars. Nothing definite is likely to come out of this discussion, at least for a long time. To one observer at least the most likely supposition is that urban workingmen moved at various times into and out of the Democratic party, attracted by Jackson's denunciation of "monopolistic" corporations and the profession of devotion to equality of opportunity, but repelled by the avidity with which Democratic state legislators chartered corporations and by the inability of the party to find effective legislative remedies for the workingman's complaints.

As for Old Hickory, he said repeatedly that his great source of strength lay in the rural areas, not in the towns and cities. (*See Reading No. 46.*) There is little or no evidence that he thought of himself as a special champion of the workingman. On one occasion he played the role of strikebreaker on behalf of a company of which his old friend, John H. Eaton, was president. Jackson's aim was to open the door of opportunity for industrious folk of all classes. If the privileges and favors bestowed by government were sternly restricted, he felt that it would be possible for all to become capitalists. Both he and his party were respectful of states' rights, moderately interpreted, and preferred to leave to state governments such positive legislation as was necessary for the general welfare.

There were weaknesses in a party so variously constituted and with such a program of action. The qualified adherence to states' rights angered extremists in that category. The war on the Bank alienated Bank Democrats in many states, particularly so in Pennsylvania. Dislike and distrust of Van Buren as a sly, slippery northerner, the enemy of Calhoun, was a divisive factor in the South and produced much discontent in that section. Another important weakness stemmed from a dichotomy in the Democratic viewpoint. On the one hand Democrats looked back with yearning to the simple agrarian principles of early Jeffersonian days. On the other hand they encouraged a pursuit of wealth that drove society steadily toward the goals of an industrial and a financial capitalism that showered profits on a prosperous minority of the population.

The Two-Party System. The Whigs. As the Democratic party went from one triumph to another in the early 1830s, the inadequacy of the opposing political groups became more and more apparent. National Republicanism, cast in a minority role, was demoralized by its defeats in 1828 and 1832. Antimasonry was too narrow an issue on which to build a national political organization. Workingmen's parties in the eastern cities were local movements whose projects lacked capital, whose key principles were stolen for the use of larger organizations, and whose life was in general short. If those who professed to fear Democratic policies in national affairs were not to remain forever helpless, if the "outs" were ever to become the "ins," a new political organization national in scope was a necessity. The Whig party was the answer of this opposition to Jacksonian rule.

The Whig party as a recognized political movement came to

life in the year 1834. Most of the National Republicans, a majority of the Antimasons, and an increasing number of dissatisfied Democrats trooped into its ranks. A large proportion of the laboring class usually voted the Whig ticket. Fights between Democratic factions in the states, together with local issues divisive in character, often swelled Whig strength. The party was a heterogeneous group of individuals whose common tie was opposition to "King Andrew," and whose name, "Whig," indicated a devotion to middle class values that the followers of the "tyrant" supposedly lacked.

The Whigs in general were optimistic as to the social and economic future of the United States. They accepted political democracy, that is to say, universal manhood suffrage, as an established fact, but regarded the franchise as a privilege rather than a right. They were therefore apt to be suspicious of the common herd. There was a saying among them that Whigs knew one another by the instinct of gentlemen. They believed that all who worked in whatever category of labor—bankers and hod carriers, textile mill owners and ditch diggers—had an essential harmony of interest. Whigs had a vision of the possibilities of American economic development that was more compelling than that held by the Democrats and, again unlike their rivals, they believed that government, national as well as state and local, should be a constructive agent in promoting the growth of the national economy.

Whiggery quickly developed great strength in Vermont, Massachusetts and Rhode Island; it sprang to vigorous life in the Middle States. The same was true in the South, where urban business and banking interests, with allied planters, controlled its destiny. The first four presidential election years in which Whiggery functioned, 1836–1848, saw them carry 27 slave states while the Democrats carried 26, gain a 2.4 per cent advantage in the total slave states votes cast for President, and maintain a comparable advantage in the number of slave states Congressmen. The Whigs also quickly displayed great strength in the western part of the country, in Tennessee and Kentucky, and in the Old Northwest.

Common Characteristics of Whigs and Democrats. The Whig and Democratic parties had their differences, but they also had many things in common. Both owed their existence to energetic and able leaders who found presidential contests extremely valuable aids to party formation. The outstanding men in both camps had a love of power, a zest for the excitement of political contest, the adulation of the crowds, the heady wine of victory, together with more or less of a desire to do something for the welfare of locality, state and nation. Both parties were capitalistic, both accepted political democracy as a going concern and both, from time to time and place to place, evidenced concern for the lot of the common man. Both trumpeted great principles and expressed great fear of the opposition, but as the *Democratic Review* remarked in 1837,[5] there was not that hostility of opinions and principles that the violence of party warfare seemed to indicate. Professor Benson in his study of Jacksonian Democracy in New York State concludes that there was no fundamental distinction between the two parties in sources of leadership, voting support, and claims to voter support. The struggle in New York was chiefly over office and only secondarily over final goals. Professor McCormick in *The Second American Party System* declares that in New Jersey and Pennsylvania as well as in New York the spoils of office exerted a powerful influence in party struggles. Such was the opinion in 1832 of Massachusetts Democrat Robert Rantoul. Supreme Court Justice Joseph Story, writing to Francis Lieber in 1836, thought that sheer political partisanship, indifferent to social and economic issues, had become a threat to freedom; that it was "establishing a system of despotism of opinion fatal to all true ambition, & a corrupt influence & eagerness for office destructive of all liberty."

[5] *Democratic Review,* Vol. I, p. 1.

CHAPTER 4

The Turning Point

The 1836 Presidential Contest. The presidential campaign of 1836 was a dull and eventless affair. There was no doubt as to the Democratic standard bearer. It was Jackson's choice, Martin Van Buren, unanimously nominated on May 20, 1835, in a national convention at Baltimore. The Whigs, not yet well organized nationally, spurned a single nomination and adopted the strategy of putting forward sectional candidates who bade fair to have popular support. The Massachusetts legislature nominated Webster. In the South it was Hugh Lawson White, a Democratic defector who detested Van Buren. The Whig western candidate was the sixty-three-year-old William Henry Harrison, who had been more or less of a hero in the War of 1812.

The campaign was practically without issues save the overriding one of approval or rejection of Van Buren. In an effort to curry favor in the South, the Red Fox opposed distribution of land sale proceeds. He also opposed abolition of slavery in the District of Columbia without the South's consent and emphasized that he was against any interference with the peculiar institution of the slave states.

The election showed that Van Buren was considerably more popular in New England than Jackson had been, and had practically the same strength as Old Hickory in the Middle Atlantic states. In the slave states the Whigs had a popular majority of 243 out of 425,629 votes cast. Van Buren lost South Carolina, Georgia and Tennessee, carried Mississippi by some 500 votes and Louisiana by less than 300. In the Old West he was weak against Harrison, who carried Ohio and Indiana, making in that area a better showing than had Jackson in the 1828 campaign. The election as a whole gave the Little Magician a popular majority of only 25,688 out of 1,505,290 votes cast. The Democratic party was now confronted by a vigorous political opponent.

The Panic of 1837. President Martin Van Buren, fifty-five years old and veteran of many a hard fought political campaign, had now reached the goal of his desire. He pledged that he would follow in the footsteps of Democracy's great leader, and looked forward to a happy term of office that might last for eight years. Less than a month after his inauguration, however, America was in the throes of a depression that turned his dream into a nightmare.

The speculative surge in land investment and business enterprises, and the over-expansion of note issues characterizing the middle 1830s came to an end. The Specie Circular had destroyed public confidence in the nation's economic situation. Flush times disappeared when an English depression sent the price of cotton downward and prompted Old World investors to liquidate their holdings in American bank and canal stocks. Land prices collapsed and business failures mounted into the hundreds, and then the thousands. Banks suspended specie payments. Unemployment spread. The United States was in the grip of a depression that lasted, with some periods of relief, until 1843.

Van Buren and the Depression. Van Buren's answer to the depression was mainly negative in character, as befitted the Democracy's concept of the function of government. He refused to ask for the repeal of the Specie Circular, so it remained on the books until May of 1838. He refused to take any substantial steps toward alleviating the crisis, holding that such was not the function of the central government. Such suggestions as he made to the special session of Congress assembled in September, 1837, were for the purpose of relieving the embarrassments of the government itself, though he did make it clear that he had postponed the payment of bonds for duties by the merchant importers. Suffering individuals and communities in general were told not to expect relief by direct governmental action. (*See Reading No. 47.*)

The Independent Treasury Bill. Where the government's relation to banking was concerned, Van Buren took an attitude that was conservative in some respects, radical in others. Like Jackson, a hard money man at heart, and confronted by the part the Pet Banks had played in fostering inflation, Van Buren proposed that the government withdraw from any direct connection with banks and banking by keeping its revenues in its own vaults. This Independent Treasury bill, introduced in Congress in 1837 by Van Buren's supporters, contained a "specie clause" providing for a gradual elimination of bank notes receivable by the government. After January 1, 1841, the federal government could receive and pay out only specie, or specially authorized notes and paper.

Effect of This Monetary Policy. The Independent Treasury became a fundamental objective of the Van Buren administration. It not only continued the Jacksonian hard money policy, but also catered to the sensibilities of the so-called Loco Foco elements in New York, Pennsylvania and other states who opposed all "monopolies," including banks, and demanded a specie currency. Moreover it pleased states' rights advocates, since it separated the national government from any connection with the state banks.

The Independent Treasury bill was finally passed by Congress and Van Buren signed it on July 4, 1840. As events proved, it had none of the destructive effects feared by its opponents but, joined as it was with the depression, it had a significant impact on the Democratic party. Many Democrats opposed it—some because they feared the specie kept in the government's treasuries would hamper banks in supporting their loans; others because they disliked its fostering of a hard money policy. In New York State the party split, Conservative Democrats moving toward and finally into the Whig ranks, Loco Focos moving into closer cooperation with the Democracy. The Democratic defections were especially noticeable among the well-to-do in New York City, where many Tammany bank directors and merchants became Whigs. In Pennsylvania and Virginia there was the same story of defections by conservative-minded Democrats. In the Old Northwest, Democrats divided on the financial policies adopted by the Jackson and Van Buren administrations, and the financial uncertainties of the times brought many of the more prosperous citizens in that region into the Whig party. The Democracy seemed more than ever to identify with the common man, but reliance upon the loyalty of the masses was destined for a rude awakening.

Democratic Land Policy. Democratic land policy also indicated to some extent the party's desire to champion the aspirations of ordinary folk. As a means of passing the Independent Treasury bill, the Van Buren administration joined forces with western advocates of cheap land and of a preemption policy that safeguarded the rights of squatters on the public domain. Little progress was made toward lowering of land prices, but preemption bills became law in 1838 and again in 1840. There is no evidence, pro or con, that they had any effect on the state of the national economy.

The Slavery Question. While the Democrats' preemption bills endeared them to the squatters on the public lands, they pleased neither speculators nor those in East and West who wished to devote land revenues to the promotion of internal improvements. It was also difficult to devise a policy toward slavery that would please everyone. The South was powerful in Congress, and Van Buren felt that he had to propitiate that section. Congressional gag rules remained in force until the next decade. Slavery and slave auctions continued in the District of Columbia. The President uttered some platitudes about the iniquity of trade in human beings, but the administration proposed no remedial legislation and federal insistence upon denying the right of search gravely hampered British efforts to stop the international slave trade. The Red Fox's encouragement of the union of southern planters with the "plain Republicans" of the North compelled him to show at least complacency toward the constitutional principles of the nullifiers, as well as toward less radical protagonists of southern rights.

Canadian-American Troubles. Van Buren found the nation beset by external as well as internal difficulties. In the field of international affairs the attention of the United States centered on Canada, where religious difficulties, Anglo-French jealousies and the resentment of pioneer farmers over the power and exactions of the large landed proprietors brought on in 1837 an armed rebellion. This was quickly suppressed, but there was much sympathy south of the border for the rebels, especially after December, 1837, when the *Caroline*, an American steamer used by the insurgents, was seized by Canadian militia, taken out into the Niagara River, set on fire and sunk. In this affray a United States citizen lost his life.

Subsequent to the *Caroline* incident a number of citizens south of the Great Lakes and the St. Lawrence River enlisted with the rebels, and there were raids across the border attended with considerable bloodshed. Excitement among the citizenry increased and Van Buren felt compelled to warn against invasions of a friendly country. He also asked reparations for the *Caroline*. These were refused and hot tempers flared when, in November, 1840, a Canadian deputy sheriff, Alexander McLeod, boasted that he had killed the American on the *Caroline*. McLeod was thrown into the Lewiston, New York, jail, to be tried for murder in the New York courts.

Great Britain vigorously protested the seizure of McLeod. The British government was also at loggerheads with the United States over the Maine-Canadian boundary, where the so-called "Aroostook War" over disputed territory broke out between citizens of Maine and New Brunswick. Anglo-American relations were at a low point as Van Buren's term of office came to an end.

The Campaign of 1840. The marked deterioration of Anglo-American relations was a factor in the 1840 presidential campaign, a contest which was well under way before the close of 1839. Clay wanted the Whig nomination, but the politicians passed him over for William Henry Harrison, who was a military hero of sorts and had made a brave showing in the 1836 presidential contest. The Democrats nominated Van Buren (there was no alternative) at their national convention and dispersed in a gloomy mood. Delegations of antislaveryites from six northern states met in Albany to form the Liberty party and to nominate an ex-slaveholder, James G. Birney of Kentucky, for the nation's highest office.

The Whigs and the Liberty party had no platforms. The Democrats endorsed the Independent Treasury and declared their opposition to a national bank, high tariffs and internal improvements at federal expense.

In the ensuing campaign the Whigs profited by the Democratic example set in 1828. They exalted the military record of Harrison and denounced Van Buren as an extravagant spendthrift who wasted the people's money. Harrison, they declared, was one of the common folk. He lived in a log cabin (it was actually a comfortable farm house), drank cider, and extended a hospitable welcome to all comers. Log cabins appeared everywhere, and every Whig orator who could do so with any semblance of truth boasted that he had lived in one. Webster publicly regretted that he had not been born in such a humble abode. There were Whig bands and parades, barrels of cider, and countless orations harping on the theme that the Whig party was the party of the common man and would bring back national prosperity. (*See Reading No. 48.*)

The Democrats vilified Harrison, praised the Independent Treasury, and lauded Van Buren for establishing a ten-hour day for federal employees (a move made in 1840 with a view to the election). But the depression hung like an incubus over their heads. During 1838 and 1839 Democratic control in state after state had vanished as the voters blamed the party in power for the hard times. The party was also weakened along the northern border by defections caused by Van Buren's impartial attitude toward the frontier difficulties.

A Significant Election. The outcome of the election was a Whig landslide of monumental proportions. Harrison won 234 of the electoral college votes, as compared with 60 for Van Buren. The Whig hero carried 19 of the 26 states, including every northern state save New Hampshire and Illinois, and seven states in the South. His party had majorities in both House and Senate. All this had taken place in the midst of an unprecedented outpouring of the electorate. Nearly 80 per cent of the eligible voters of the nation had gone to the polls, a far greater proportion of the electorate than had cast their ballots in 1828.

The election of 1840 had several significant aspects. While the Liberty party made a miserable showing, polling only 6,225 votes and failing to carry a single county, it marked the appearance of a sectional movement, clear and distinct, in the arena of national politics. The campaign also demonstrated that the Whig party was now a well-organized, national entity, one that could make effective use of conventions and of central and local committees, a party that had sent the Democracy down to humiliating defeat. For the election had exploded the Democratic claim that it, and it alone, was the party of the common people. It might still boast with confidence that it held within its ranks a somewhat smaller number of the rich and well-born than did its great opponent, but for the next decade Whigs and Democrats would have the allegiance of a substantially equal number of voters.

CHAPTER 5

The Transformation

Disillusionment. The crushing defeat of 1840 was a great shock to the Democracy. The *Democratic Review* confessed that before that election it had believed the result would be a complete dissolution of the Whig party. And then had come the deluge! Party leaders began to question the old shibboleths. Robert J. Walker, the able Senator from Mississippi, was openly scornful of the hard money dogma. Orestes Brownson, New England reformer, intellectual and Democrat, declared that for three presidential terms the people had, presumably, ruled, and during that time paper money and corporations had become firmly established. What fundamental difference, he asked, was there between the principles of Thomas Jefferson and John Quincy Adams? Brownson called for a new constitutional party, its nucleus to be the small states, the slaveholding states, and "the real friends of Equal Rights and Social Progress." The Democrats in the states, he asserted, had fought neither against banks nor paper money. They had been as anti-democratic as the Whigs themselves. Southern Democrats, for their part, became impatient with the Van Buren doctrine that Loco Focos and southern planters constituted an effective political union. Everywhere the leaders of the party began looking for new slogans and new aims.

Democratic Problems. A changing national situation complicated the problems of the Democracy. Leaders of the southern wing of the party were alarmed for the safety of slavery. They demonstrated its profitability by the rising gap between the cost of raising slaves and their price; its necessity by the ever-present specter of rebellions. But new, free states were coming into the Union and Van Buren, whom they mistrusted, was still the titular head of the Democracy. These men felt, strongly that control of the party was essential to their peace and security. With that control they could protect states' rights and could limit the national government's power to inflict upon them either social or economic injury.

Different aims and aspirations stirred the northern Democracy. There Democrats preached the rights of man (though chiefly of white men), and the maintenance of equality of opportunity; there Loco Focoism, as represented by William Cullen Bryant's New York *Evening Post,* exerted a powerful influence. Northern Democratic leaders, too, were conscious that the changes produced by the industrial revolution, especially in the field of transportation, demanded positive governmental action at a level beyond the capacity of individual states. Many of them and their followers wanted protective tariffs and internal improvements at national expense, both of which were abhorrent to their southern brethren.

The westerners among these northern Democrats felt no concern for the Negro, free or slave, but proclaimed their devotion to individual liberty, private initiative and agrarianism. The doctrine of free soil for free men appealed to people in the Great Lakes region, and the western Democracy in general was eager for territorial expansion.

Expansion. As the Democracy strove to rally from defeat, both its southern and western leaders turned to expansion, recognizing it as a movement with great popular appeal. They invoked pride in the American future, the need of both farmers and laborers for more land, the argument that natural frontiers like the Rio Grande and the Pacific were vital as guards against British designs, a belief in the necessity of national growth. Expansion was, as John L. O'Sullivan said in 1845 in the *Democratic Review,* the nation's Manifest Destiny. (*See Reading No. 49.*) Many Whigs were of this same mind, but it was the Democratic party that became the chief political champion of this movement.

The Whigs Pave the Way to Expansion. The Whigs, ironically enough, prepared the way for this Democratic expansionist drive. President Harrison died just a month after entering office, and Vice President John Tyler moved into the White House. Tyler, always a Democrat at heart, had left that party because Jackson trampled on states' rights in the South Carolina nullification crisis. His states' rights scruples now in-

volved him in a quarrel with Clay over the reinstitution of a
national bank. Two presidential vetoes ruined Clay's bank
project and spread dissension among the Whigs. By the fall of
1841 the *Democratic Review* was gloating that the Whigs had
demonstrated their utter incapacity to govern, and that there
was rising "on the crumbled ruins of the Whig party" a firmer,
stronger, loftier Democracy.

After the break with Clay, Tyler began to move back into
the Democratic party by the same states' rights road he had
used to leave it. At the same time, with the aid of Secretary
of State Daniel Webster, he cleared the way for expansion.
McLeod's acquittal in the New York courts and an informal
expression of regret by the British over the sinking of the
Caroline settled that dispute, and the Webster-Ashburton treaty
of 1842 provided a compromise adjustment of the boundary
troubles between Canada and the United States. Tense relations
with Great Britain disappeared in an atmosphere of harmonious
cooperation, and Tyler felt free to devote himself to an expansionist project in which he was deeply interested.

Texas. As part of the American westward push, some
30,000 citizens of the United States had moved into the Mexican
province of Texas. Mexico had abolished slavery, but Mexican
rule over Texas was lax, and many of the Texans owned slaves.
By 1836 it became apparent that the Mexican government intended to exert a firm control over the province north of the
Rio Grande, and the Texans rose in revolt. Under the leadership
of Sam Houston, the so-called Lone Star State established its
independence, an independence that the United States recognized, but that Mexico refused to grant. Texas proposed annexation to the United States while Van Buren was President,
but no definite steps were then taken. The state proposed it
again in March, 1842.

Tyler was held back from taking action by Secretary of State
Webster's lack of interest in the project, but Webster resigned
in May, 1843. The President then appointed as head of the
State Department Abel P. Upshur of Virginia, an ardent an-
nexationist. Upshur died, February 28, 1844, in the explosion
of a cannon on the battleship *Princeton,* and Tyler put in his
place John C. Calhoun, who also was avid for annexation.

Calhoun and the West-South Alliance.   Calhoun was at this time pushing for cooperation between South and West in a great expansionist movement. Democratic leaders in the Old Northwest wanted the Oregon country, where Great Britain and the United States had been in joint occupation since 1818, and in the western states had arisen a formidable demand for "Fiftyfour forty or fight," that is, for all of Oregon up to the Alaska panhandle. An even more fervent demand for Texas came from the South.

Calhoun sought to combine the two movements, but at the same time that he sent the Texas treaty to the Senate he also sent to the British Minister in Washington, Richard Pakenham, a strong defense of slavery. (*See Reading No. 50.*) Both documents appeared in the Senate and in the New York *Evening Post*. This linked Texas and slavery expansion together in the public mind, the Senate rejected the treaty, and Texas became the great issue in the approaching presidential contest.

The Election of 1844.   Up to this point it had looked as though Clay and Van Buren would head the Whig and Democratic tickets, and both published letters deploring annexation as likely to produce war with Mexico. The Whig convention unanimously nominated Clay, but southern Democrats, aided by delegates from the Old Northwest, revolted against Van Buren. The Democratic convention was deadlocked until the ninth ballot, when it nominated the first dark horse in presidential history, James K. Polk of Tennessee, on a platform calling for "the re-occupation of Oregon and the re-annexation of Texas." The Liberty party was again in the field, once more nominating James G. Birney.

The campaign was full of vicious attacks and counterattacks, but Texas was the chief issue. Clearly Polk was an expansionist: Clay was not in any immediate sense. As southern Whigs began defecting to Polk on the Texas issue, Clay began writing letters softening his stand on annexation. These helped him in the South but hurt him in crucial New York State, where antislavery Whig voters moved into the Birney column and so gave that state to Polk. With New York went the election.

Significance of the 1844 Election.   The election of 1844 showed the two major parties very evenly balanced in the popular vote: only 1.4 percentage points separated the leading candidates. It heartened the Liberty party men, for Birney polled 61,699 votes. The Democratic party had shown great strength in the South and West, and this encouraged Tyler and Calhoun to hasten annexation. Congress passed a joint resolution to that effect and on March 3, 1845, the United States invited Texas to enter the Union.

The Democrats indeed seemed triumphant and, on the surface, harmonious. Down to 1845, while there was some splitting on internal improvements, Congressional Democrats had in general followed party lines in voting on bank, tariff and land policy issues. But there were disquieting omens. Van Buren and his followers were bitter over his rejection in 1844. The northern reformist wing of the party was becoming restless under increasing southern domination. Faction was obvious in many northern states, especially in New York where the Democracy split into Barnburners and Hunkers, the former being the Van Burenite wing, conservative on economic questions but opposed to slavery expansion, the latter taking opposite viewpoints. And Thomas Hart Benton, long a standard bearer of Jacksonian Democracy, broke with his party's leadership on the annexation of Texas. (*See Reading No. 51.*)

The New Democracy. The Democratic party in the middle 1840s was both like and unlike the Democracy of the previous decade. It opposed high tariffs and the distribution of land sales, and continued to denounce a national bank. But the bank was now a dead issue; the administration took no interest in imposing a specie currency on the country; Polk was more dogmatically opposed to internal improvements at national expense than Jackson had ever been; and the chief of state was a vigorous advocate of expansionism, especially of the southern variety.

The New President and His Problems. Dignified by nature, tenacious of beliefs, secretive, a past master of the art of dissimulation, James K. Polk devoted himself with dogged perseverance to the task of being President. He loathed the Whigs and their ideas and regarded himself as a good Democrat. This he was, according to his lights, but it was his misfortune to preside over the Democracy when the rivalries of ambitious men, local factions and, worst of all, sectional animosity were working to undermine the national party constructed by Jackson and his supporters.

One evidence of internal dissension quickly appeared. The Cabinet was not constructed in accordance with Van Buren's suggestions, and Polk made William Learned Marcy, a Hunker, Secretary of War. This did much to alienate the northern wing of the party, where Van Buren's influence was paramount. But despite the acrimony thus engendered Polk laid down an ambitious plan of action for his administration.

The Aims of the President.   Polk's plans were extensive and were, to an astonishing extent, fulfilled. He told his Secretary of the Navy, George Bancroft, that he meant to settle the Oregon question with Great Britain; to acquire California and a large district on the Pacific Coast; to reduce the tariff to a revenue basis; and to restore the Independent Treasury which the Whigs had repealed during the Tyler administration. Save for the tariff objective, all this was accomplished before he left office, but with great cost to the Democratic party.

The twenty-ninth Congress with which Polk had to work had a Democratic majority of fifty in the House and six in the Senate, but the latter was nominal due to intra-party divisions, to the superior quality of Whig leadership and to the presence of Calhoun who was still White House conscious. Despite Senate storm signals, however, Polk drove toward both his foreign and domestic goals.

Domestic Measures.   Reestablishing the Independent Treasury, which the Whigs had abolished in 1841, was an easy matter; the necessary bill passed both Houses by a strictly party vote. The tariff question, however, was full of sharp, prickling thorns.

The tariff of 1846 accorded in general with the interests of planters and farmers who had immense quantities of cotton and wheat to dispose of in foreign markets, and who could scarcely afford retaliation by imposing high duties on European goods. It lowered duties, especially on iron and wool, but did so in modest fashion. Even so the new iron and wool rates roused such Democratic ire in New York, Pennsylvania, and Ohio that Congressman William Lowndes Yancey read those states out of the Democratic church. Other Democrats, too, were upset by the measure. Senator John M. Niles from Connecticut thought it a miserable bill. So did Thomas Hart Benton, who voted for it only because it rid the country of the tariff of 1842, and New England Democrat Gideon Welles confided to his diary that it was a financial absurdity. But despite the engendered discontents Polk felt free to move ahead with his expansionist plans.

The Fate of the South-West Alliance.   Calhoun had obtained an informal alliance of southern and western Democrats to push for the "re-occupation" of Oregon and the "re-annexation" of Texas. In his inaugural Polk declared that the American title to Oregon was "clear and unquestionable," a statement much resented in Great Britain. In December, 1845, he asked Congress for a resolution authorizing him to give Britain a year's notice abrogating the 1818 agreement of joint occupation. Congress did so, but only after it became evident that the Democratic expansionists of the Old Northwest were much more avid for all of Oregon than were Calhoun and the southern Democrats.

Polk gave notice, but he did not, as he had intimated he would, continue to look John Bull "straight in the eye." His plans for expansion in the Southwest were closer to his heart and he had no desire for a war on two fronts. The treaty with Great Britain arranged in 1846 provided for a division of Oregon at the 49th parallel of latitude. The Senate ratified it by a vote of 41 to 14, disregarding the fiery opposition of Democratic expansionists from the Old Northwest.

The Oregon compromise was not the only disappointment in store for the western Democrats. They wanted a graduation bill providing systematic reductions in the price of unsold public lands. Such a bill appeared in Congress with Polk's blessing. Southern Democrats supported it only in order to gain western votes for the tariff of 1846. Once the tariff bill became law, enough southern Democrats deserted graduation to secure its defeat in the House. Nor was this all. Western Democrats were now anxious for internal improvements at federal expense and such a bill passed Congress in July, 1846. Polk vetoed it on the ground that it was pork barrel legislation, clearly unconstitutional under a strict interpretation of the Constitution.

The South-West coalition was now a thing of the past, western Democrats moved toward cooperation with the Northeast, and the Whigs fished in troubled waters by pointing out that southern men and southern policy were gaining altogether too much influence in the Democratic party. Gideon Welles felt there were stronger manifestations every day that the party was on the verge of dissolution. The northern wing was beginning to resent its wrongs, and Welles viewed with pleasure the steadily rising storm.[1]

War with Mexico. While these portentous events were taking place the country became involved in war with Mexico. Texas became part of the Union at the beginning of 1846, Mexico threatened war, and Polk ordered General Zachary Taylor and an army of several thousand men to advance into the Lone Star State as a safeguard against invasion. Taylor advanced to the south side of the Nueces River, the boundary of Texas as a Mexican province. Texas declared that the Rio Grande was its southern boundary and Polk supported this claim. At the same time, through John Slidell, envoy extraordinary and minister plenipotentiary to Mexico, the President tried to obtain a settlement of American claims in Mexico, a recognition of the Rio Grande boundary, and the purchase of New Mexico Territory and all or part of California. Slidell's mission was fruitless, and as this became apparent, Polk ordered Taylor to advance to the Rio Grande; he did so and blockaded the river.

By the beginning of May, 1846, Polk definitely had decided that armed conflict with Mexico was inevitable. Then news came that there had been an encounter between Mexican and American forces east of the Rio Grande, and Polk asked Congress to declare war, alleging that American blood had been shed "upon the American soil." Congress complied and on May 13, 1846, came the American proclamation of war.

Course of the War. The House and Senate voted war appropriations by overwhelming majorities, but the Whigs were critical of the conflict and many Democrats were unhappy. It was the southern Democracy that had been avid for the struggle, and Van Buren's followers were bitter in spirit. Benton, too, thought it an unjust war. (*See Reading No. 52.*) Even Calhoun

[1] Gideon Welles, "Diary," (Huntington Library), July 31, 1846.

was doubtful, fearing lest the South be damaged by identification with a war of aggression. Such forebodings were justified by forthcoming events.

The course of the war was a series of triumphs for the armies of the United States. California fell easily into American hands. Taylor won a series of victories in northern Mexico. General Winfield Scott, marching overland from Vera Cruz, captured Mexico City in September, 1847, and effective Mexican resistance was at an end. By the treaty of Guadalupe Hidalgo, signed on February 2, 1848, Mexico recognized the Rio Grande boundary and ceded New Mexico Territory and California, receiving in return $15,000,000 and the assumption of American claims amounting to $3,250,000. The Polk administration had gained an empire in the Southwest for the United States, but in doing so had prepared the way for the disruption of the Democratic party and of the Union itself.

The Rising Spirit of Sectionalism. In August, 1846, Polk had asked Congress for an appropriation of $2,000,000 to be used in negotiating a treaty with Mexico. He obviously had California and other possible territories in mind, and immediately the question of slavery extension into such new territories came to the fore. It remained a burning question throughout the conflict and into the years that followed.

The extension of slavery into the new territories was clearly a sectional issue. Southerners, both Whigs and Democrats, were now committed to the defense and perpetuation of slavery. In the North there was a corresponding increase of antislavery feeling. This was not based on a belief that blacks should be given all the rights and privileges of white men. The great majority of white northerners had no interest in giving the blacks social and economic equality with themselves. There was a widespread belief, North as well as South, that blacks were basically inferior to whites. The antislavery movement was in part a moral revulsion against making slaves of those who were, after all was said and done, human beings. It arose also out of the repugnance of free labor to compete with slave labor, and out of a desire to promote northern economic aims by increasing the number of free states and their representation in Congress. This antislavery movement manifested itself both in propagandistic attacks on the South's "peculiar institution," and in opposition to the extension of slavery into any new territories of the Union.

As the Mexican War went on and it became apparent that most southern expansionists wanted Cuba and all of Mexico, there was an increasing northern reaction. "Conscience" Whigs in Massachusetts became stridently vocal. A combination of Whigs and abolitionists wrested control of New Hampshire from the Democrats. In New York State the Seward-Weed wing of the Whig party became more and more openly antislavery and championed suffrage for the free blacks. Nor was this movement confined to Whigs and abolitionists. Northern Democrats, bitter over Oregon, over the tariff and over three vetoes by Polk of internal improvements bills, were in no mood to support the extension of slavery in order to please the South. The Van Buren wing of the party said so openly and vehemently. In New York State even the anti-Van Buren Hunkers, who did not want to agitate the slavery question, opposed the extension of slavery into the new territories. The same spirit manifested itself among the Democrats in other northern states. They became convinced that growing antislavery sentiment in the North necessitated a guarantee that the war was not being fought for the purpose of extending slavery.

The Wilmot Proviso. Polk's request for the $2,000,000 appropriation provoked a marked reaction among embittered northern and western Democrats. Several of them met in consultation and selected one of their number, David Wilmot of Pennsylvania, to offer an amendment to the resolution of appropriation. This was the famous Wilmot Proviso, which Gideon Welles called a "Jefferson Ordinance" because it utilized the language of the Jeffersonian prohibition of slavery in the Old Northwest Territory that had appeared in the Ordinance of 1787. It provided that, save for punishment of crime, no slavery or involuntary servitude should ever exist in any territory that might be acquired from Mexico.

The amended resolution passed the House but failed in the Senate. The Proviso never became law but, as Seward was to say later in the Senate, it was a specter that would not disappear. It

symbolized the sectional strife over slavery and slavery extension
that eventually split the Democracy and ensured the election of
Abraham Lincoln and the coming of the Civil War.

Dissension and Discord.   As the Mexican War drew toward
its close and the election of 1848 came into view, the Democratic
party found itself in a sad state of division and discord. Northern
Democrats distrusted their southern brethren and differed among
themselves, some standing by the Wilmot Proviso while others,
represented by Lewis Cass of Michigan and Stephen A. Douglas
of Illinois, were willing to see slavery expand if free soil could
keep pace with it. Jealousy and discord also pervaded Democratic ranks in other ways. In Massachusetts and New York factions feuded over control of the party organization. In Pennsylvania the followers of James Buchanan and George M. Dallas,
both of whom longed for the presidential nomination, were bitter
rivals in a party deeply split over the tariff. There was much
hatred of President Polk. Benton and the Van Burenites disliked
and distrusted him. Francis Preston Blair was wroth because
Thomas Ritchie's Washington *Union* supplanted the Washington
Globe as the administration's organ. The New York *Evening
Post* fulminated against the war and the annexation of territory,
while Robert Barnwell Rhett of the Charleston *Mercury* voiced
the South's stand for states' rights and the expansion of slavery
without let or hindrance. The one hope for a Democratic triumph in the election was that the Whig party, faction-ridden and
divided over slavery, was in an equally chaotic condition.

The Free Soil Movement.   In an attempt to smooth over
discord, the nominating conventions of both major parties engaged in fence-straddling performances. The Whigs nominated
Zachary Taylor, a Louisiana slaveholder but also a military hero.
The Democrats nominated Lewis Cass, a thorough-paced Michigan conservative who was fearful of angering the South. Both
parties in their platforms pussyfooted on slavery.

There was also a third party, an amalgam of Democrats and
Whigs, that took the name of Free Soil and that absorbed the
Liberty party. Born out of opposition to slavery extension, dislike
of Cass, distrust of Taylor, the desire of Van Burenites for revenge, and the determination of the Barnburners to triumph over
the Hunkers in New York State, the Free Soil party was frankly

and wholly sectional. The old Jacksonian Martin Van Buren headed the ticket (*See Reading No. 53*) and old Jacksonians F. P. Blair and Gideon Welles were leaders in the movement. Whig Charles Francis Adams, son of John Quincy Adams, was its candidate for Vice President. Its motto was, "Free soil, free speech, free labor and free men," but its concern was for white, not black, labor. The party's platform straddled on the tariff but championed internal improvements at federal expense, a position that appealed to western Democrats outraged by Polk's vetoes.

The Election of 1848. There were no great issues dividing the two major parties and the outcome showed them very evenly balanced in popular strength, the Whigs having a national plurality of only 138,625 votes. Eight slave and seven free states went for Taylor, seven slave and eight free states for Cass, who was mistrusted in the South on account of his advocacy of popular sovereignty and who had marked strength only in the Old Northwest. Van Buren, denounced by the Democrats as "the Judas Iscariot of the Nineteenth Century," carried no states, but polled some 10 per cent of the total vote. His greatest appeal to the voters was in New York, Pennsylvania and New England.

The election settled nothing, its chief result being an increase in sectional cleavage over the extension of slavery. Gideon Welles, surveying the result, felt that, while the Democratic party organization had demonstrated strength, it was now thoroughly devoid of principle and was "to all intents and purposes dissolved."

The Compromise of 1850. Before Taylor had been in the White House a year, contention over slavery brought on a major crisis. Quarrels between North and South over slave status in the territories acquired from Mexico, over the rendition of fugitive slaves, and over slavery in the District of Columbia convulsed both Congress and the country. A formidable secession movement developed in the South, and when Congress met in December, 1849, the dissolution of the Union with an accompanying civil war seemed not only possible but probable.

It was under these circumstances that Henry Clay, supported by Webster, proposed the terms of settlement that have become known as the Compromise of 1850. These included the admission of California as a free state and the organization of the remaining territories acquired from Mexico without reference to slavery; the adjustment of a boundary dispute between Texas and New Mexico territory; the abolition of the slave trade in the District of Columbia; and a more effective and stringent fugitive slave law. A long debate ensued over these proposals. Men such as William Henry Seward in the North and John C. Calhoun in the South argued against compromise, though for different reasons. Taylor, who wanted to resolve difficulties by having both New Mexico and California organized as states, was cool to Clay's proposal and for months its passage appeared doubtful. Then Taylor's death brought Vice President Millard Fillmore, a friend of Clay's proposal, into the White House. Democrat Stephen A. Douglas, an energetic and skillful parliamentarian, took over from the aging Kentuckian the burden of marshaling the Compromise measures through Congress. By the autumn of 1850 they had become law.

California came in as a free state, but the Compromise was in general more favorable to the South than to the North. Slavery was still lawful in the District of Columbia, the territories acquired from Mexico were open to slavery, and the new fugitive slave law was hailed in the South and execrated in the North. Though credit has to go to Clay and Webster for proposing main features of the settlement, the Democratic party was chiefly responsible for its passage. Democrats had originated most of its proposals before Clay combined them as a compromise; Douglas was more responsible than anyone else for marshaling the various bills through Congress; and Democrats supplied most of the votes that made them law. (*See Reading No. 54.*)

The Election of 1852. The country breathed a sigh of relief with the passage of the Compromise of 1850. It seemed evident that, together with the Compromise of 1820 that had settled the status of slavery in the Louisiana Purchase, it had eliminated any further possibility of conflict over slavery in the territories of the Union. Despite continued northern dissatisfaction with the fugitive slave law, people in general regarded the 1850 settlement as a "finality." This attitude became strikingly apparent in the election of 1852, an event that also demonstrated the extent to which southern influence had become predominant in the Democratic party.

Beset by half a dozen aspirants for the presidential nomination in 1852, the Democratic national convention turned to a dark horse, Franklin Pierce of New Hampshire. The party platform, frankly pro-southern, pledged allegiance to states' rights, endorsed the Compromise of 1850 with specific commendation for its fugitive slave law, and deplored the efforts "of the abolitionists and others" to make Congress interfere with slavery where it already existed. Most of the Democratic Free Soil bolters of 1848 now came back into the party, feeling that its preservation and victory were paramount considerations. As Van Buren wrote later, Democrats had seen the "destructive tendencies of slavery agitation" and were "resolved to avoid them in the future." For the time being they patched up their quarrels and united behind Pierce.

The election itself appeared to justify the Democratic determination to avoid trouble over slavery. The Whigs nominated General Winfield Scott, a friend of that ardent antislaveryite Seward. Since Scott himself was suspected of Free Soil learnings, the result of the contest was an overwhelming Democratic victory. Pierce carried every section of the country, and only four states—Massachusetts, Kentucky, Tennessee and Utah—were in the Scott column. The Democracy was now supreme in the nation and particularly so in the South where Whigs by the thousands deserted their party, never to return.

But there were two great flaws in the Democratic triumph. Southern dominance in the party's counsels was now unmistakable, and the man it had put in the White House was a pusillanimous leader. Pierce's admirers had dubbed him "Young Hickory," a sad misnomer. Charming in personality but weak of will, Pierce was under the influence of two men in his Cabinet—Secretary of War Jefferson Davis and Attorney General Caleb Cushing—whose predilections were all in favor of the South. Once again old Jacksonian Unionists such as F. P. Blair, Benton and Van Buren became deeply disturbed, convinced that since the time of Polk, false leaders had taken control of the Democracy. That their fears had substance became evident before the Pierce administration was two years old.

The Kansas-Nebraska Bill. In January, 1854, Stephen A. Douglas reported out of the committee on territories in the

Senate a bill for the organization of the territories of Kansas and Nebraska. These constituted a major portion of the Louisiana Purchase, and had been declared forever free by the Compromise of 1820. Why Douglas decided to devote his remarkable ability to pushing this measure through the Senate remains something of a mystery, but it is probable that his land speculations, his interest in a transcontinental railroad, and his desire to further his presidential aspirations by pleasing the South were his chief reasons. The Kansas-Nebraska bill in its final form specifically repealed the Missouri Compromise, leaving it to the people of the territories whether or not they should have slavery. Douglas's superb generalship and the power of the presidential patronage (for he had the support of Pierce) pushed the bill through Congress and it became law in the spring of 1854.

The bill was a southern triumph, for it opened to slavery an area from which it had been excluded by national legislation. This, together with continued southern insistence that slaveholders had a right to take their human property into all the territories of the Union, produced an explosion of wrath among the antislavery forces of the North. (*See Reading No. 55.*) It led directly to the formation of the Republican party, into which trooped antislavery Whigs, Democrats and reformers of all kinds, responding to the social, economic and moral challenges that were implicit in the measure. Thousands of northern Democrats, under such leaders as the Blairs of Maryland and Missouri, Salmon P. Chase of Ohio, Gideon Welles of Connecticut and Preston King of New York, left the Democracy for this new political organization.

The Election of 1856. Though weakened by these defections from its ranks, the Democracy struggled to maintain itself as a national entity. In 1856 it nominated for President James Buchanan of Pennsylvania, an old Jackson Democrat but destitute of Old Hickory's capacity for leadership. The Democrats regarded Buchanan as especially available because as Minister to Great Britain, he had had no connection with the Kansas-Nebraska bill, and having been long in the political limelight, had the Jacksonian aura. They felt that they had the South securely in their grasp and that Old Public Functionary, as Buchanan was called, would command the most northern votes. However, they disregarded the fact that he was indecisive, suspicious and stubborn, a crafty middle-of-the-roader who was completely un-inspired. The platform endorsed the Kansas-Nebraska bill and declared for decision on slavery by the people of a territory when it was admitted as a state.

The Republicans nominated a dashing western explorer, John C. Frémont, and asserted that the territories must be kept free soil. The American party (a mushroom growth due to popular dislike of the millions of foreign immigrants) had hoped to win the presidency in 1856, but now split over slavery extension. Thus the North Americans accepted Frémont as their standard bearer, while the South Americans joined the Whig remnant in nominating Millard Fillmore on a platform vaguely promising popular sovereignty in the territories.

The outcome of the election demonstrated the weakness of the South Americans and of the Whigs, for Fillmore carried only Maryland. Buchanan won on account of heavy support from northern financial centers fearful that Republicanism meant civil war, of appeals to national feeling against the sectional Republicans, of promises of order and of a conservative approach to current problems, and of the use of money in buying votes in critical states. It was significant, however, that the Republicans had shown great strength in the North. Had they carried Pennsylvania and either Indiana or Illinois, Frémont would have been in the White House. The Democratic party had indeed elected a president, but there was no real unity between its northern and southern wings, and again the contest had settled no great public question.

The Dred Scott Decision.   Two days after Buchanan's in-auguration, Chief Justice Taney, in one of the most significant cases that has ever come before the Supreme Court, handed down the Dred Scott decision. It stated that Congress could not interfere with slavery in the territories, and a majority of the court joined Taney in declaring the Missouri Compromise un-constitutional. The Republicans raged against this pronounce-ment, for it invalidated their contention that Congress had the power to prevent slavery extension. And within the Democratic party there was much difference of opinion on the question of whether or not the people of a territory could exclude slavery from within their limits.

Growing Disorganization of the Democratic Party. More than slavery was fracturing the Democracy. Partly because of weak leadership in the White House, the party lacked a strong national setup and, save when confronted by the demands of a presidential campaign, thirty-one state organizations went their separate ways. Nor were these state organizations able to maintain harmony within their own ranks. All kinds of feuds consumed their energies and wasted their strength. The New York Democracy with its never-ending squabbles between the Hard Shells and the Soft Shells, and between Tammany and Fernando Wood in New York City, was a prime example of such contentions. Pennsylvania was little better off. Intra-party feuding was general throughout the West, save in Illinois where Douglas held a tight rein, and in one southern state after another tidewater interests versus those of the frontier, and Unionists versus states' righters, were involved in constant bickering.

Nationally as well as locally the Democracy now had deep political divisions. Douglas, its one great statesman, and his followers in the North, had to contend with the hostility of a South which rejected his doctrine that the people of a territory should decide the slavery question for themselves. Southern Democratic Unionists, and there were many of them, were on the defensive in regard to slavery, fearful of northern economic power and population growth, and at odds with northern Democrats over tariff policies, over free land for settlers, and over internal improvements at national expense. More and more southern Democrats were turning an attentive ear to the siren song of southern nationalism, even to the counsels of such fire-eaters as Robert Barnwell Rhett of South Carolina and William Lowndes Yancey of Alabama, who openly preached secession.

The situation in Kansas, where the free soil and proslavery settlers were hopelessly at odds over the government of the Territory, deepened the divisions in the ranks of the Democracy. When an unrepresentative and disreputable constitutional convention drew up the Lecompton constitution, protecting the slave property already in Kansas, and it was ratified in a fraudulent referendum, Buchanan determined to accept it as a means of ending controversy and bringing Kansas in as a state. This made a travesty of popular sovereignty; Douglas refused to cooperate, and the resultant feud between the supporters of Douglas and Buchanan split the northern Democracy wide open. (*See Reading No. 56.*)

The Democracy's woes were increased by financial conditions. A short but sharp financial panic in 1857 was of course blamed on the party in power and helped to deplete Democratic ranks in the Congressional elections of 1858. Evidences of graft and corruption, unearthed by a Republican investigating committee, spread abroad an impression that the federal government was dishonest and frayed the party's hold on the electorate.

The parlous situation of the Democracy became more than ever apparent in April, 1860, when the party's national convention assembled in Charleston, South Carolina. The southern radicals there were hostile to Douglas, frightened by Republicanism and embittered by the specter of slave revolts conjured up in 1859 by John Brown's raid on Harper's Ferry. They demanded a platform guaranteeing full southern rights in the territories, and when this was refused, the delegates from eight of the fifteen slave states walked out of the convention. The Douglas men could not rally two-thirds of those remaining, and after fifty-seven ballots the members recessed to assemble again in Baltimore on June 18. There desperate efforts at compromise were vain. Again the bulk of the southern delegates, together with a scattering of northerners, withdrew. What had once been the party of Andrew Jackson was now split into a northern and southern wing. (*See Reading No. 57.*) Each wing put its own ticket in the field, and Lincoln was elected as a minority president.

Why It All Came About. The Jacksonian Democratic party rose to triumph in 1828 partly as a result of social and economic dissatisfactions, partly out of the schemes and plans of ambitious politicians, partly because these politicians found a leader who had powerful popular appeal. With Andrew Jackson as President the party was strongly national at the same time that it served sectional and class interests in balanced and restrained fashion. It also derived strength from its iterated and reiterated

claim that it was true to the great Jeffersonian principles of
liberty, equality of opportunity, justice for all, and reverence for
agrarian simplicity.

Despite internal dissensions and confused economic policy,
Jacksonian Democracy remained predominant for some ten
years, sheltering itself behind the invincible popularity of its
leader, and aided by the weakness and division of the political
opposition. Jackson's strong nationalism and the conviction that
he represented the spirit and the values honored on the frontier
appealed to the people. Party policies were skillfully handled,
and there was enough of a leftward swing to capture at least
part of the rising labor vote. The party also had the great advantage of economic prosperity and the absence of any great and
divisive sectional conflict.

There was, however, a fundamental contradiction between the
principles and practices of the Jacksonian Democracy. While it
claimed devotion to agrarian values and to the great principles
of liberty and equality for all, it became more and more devoted
to satisfying the acquisitive aspirations of an aggressive and
materially-minded populace. Federal expenditures for internal
improvements increased markedly during Jackson's two terms.
The hard money fetish, though accepted as gospel by both Jackson and Van Buren, was an idle dream, for specie alone could
not satisfy the demands of a rapidly growing economy for an
adequate medium of exchange. The party destroyed the Bank of
the United States in the name of equality of opportunity, and
professed to view banks and bank paper with suspicion. In the
states, however, it chartered one bank after another. Confronted
by the conflict between its philosophy and the realities of economic life, the Democratic party took refuge in fostering a free,
competitive capitalism that, it was hoped, would benefit the
laborer, the farmer, and the rising entrepreneurial class.

During the administration of Martin Van Buren the Jacksonian
dream of continued ascendancy in political affairs vanished in
the panic and resultant depression of 1837. Crushing political
defeat in 1840 spread distrust and dismay among the party
faithful. Faced by the increasing intransigence of the South in
defense of slavery and states' rights; confronted by a Whig party
that, despite its misadventures in 1841, remained an equal com-

petitor for the suffrages of the nation, the Democrats sought new slogans and new goals. This necessity was all the more compelling because the Bank, the tariff and internal improvements either disappeared or became intra-party rather than inter-party issues. The new Democratic cry was expansion, a slogan that met with special favor in the South. Many Whigs also favored expansion, and where national party principles were concerned, the differences between Whigs and Democrats became nominal.

By the early 1850s the national political contests had become naked struggles for power, with slavery expansion the chief issue in the public mind. The Whig party lost its hold on the South in the election of 1852, and that section's influence on the Democracy became ever more powerful. The rise of Republicanism accentuated sectional differences over human bondage. The aims and ideals of Jacksonian Democracy were no longer potent forces and the party, faced by the increasing conflict over slavery extension and influenced more and more by its southern element, moved toward the split in 1860 that ensured the election of Abraham Lincoln and brought on the Civil War. Save as a political tradition still dear to the hearts of many mid-nineteenth century Americans, Jacksonian Democracy had disappeared.

Part II
READINGS

The Constitution Opens the Door to Political Parties *

These are the passages in the Constitution that helped to promote national party formation in the United States. That part of the second selection which relates to the opening of the certificates of the presidential electors was later repeated in the Twelfth Amendment to the Constitution.

Article I, section 2. The House of Representatives shall be composed of Members chosen every second Year by the People of the several States, and the Electors in each State shall have the Qualifications requisite for Electors of the most numerous Branch of the State Legislature.

Article II, section 1. Each State shall appoint, in such Manner as the Legislature thereof may direct, a Number of Electors, equal to the whole Number of Senators and Representatives to which the State may be entitled in the Congress: but no Senator or Representative, or Person holding an Office of Trust or Profit under the United States, shall be appointed an Elector.

[The Electors shall meet in their respective States, and vote by Ballot for two persons, of whom one at least shall not be an Inhabitant of the same State with themselves. And they shall make a List of all the Persons voted for, and of the Number of Votes for each; which List they shall sign and certify, and transmit sealed to the Seat of the Government of the United States, directed to the President of the Senate. The President of the Senate shall, in the Presence of the Senate and House of Representatives, open all the Certificates, and the Votes shall then be counted.]

* There are many reproductions of the Constitution of the United States. These excerpts follow that published in 1935 by the Office of Education, United States Department of the Interior.

Composition of the First National Parties.
A Nineteenth Century View*

This is an account by a conservative historian of the way in which social classes divided over the policies of Hamilton. While the account is, in the main, judicious, the indication that all the southern planters opposed Hamilton's plans is an over-simplification. The author, Richard Hildreth (1807–1865), was an editor, a novelist, a moralist and a lawyer as well as an historian. He began planning his History of the United States *as an undergraduate at Harvard. A competent craftsman, Hildreth rests his fame chiefly on this work.*

The body of lawyers attached to these tribunals, essential, indeed, to their operation, and from among whom the supply of judges was exclusively drawn, associated together under certain rules for their own benefit, and possessing that invaluable juridical knowledge which to the great mass of the people was a mystery, constituted a sort of separate and superior order in the state. The education and habits of this class were by no means such as to incline them to ultra-democratical ideas. The usage, indeed, of trials by jury introduced something of democracy into the administration of justice; but the jury was, for the most part, in strict subordination to the court; and the lawyers, as a body, inclined strongly to the opinion that, however the people might be trusted with the election of representatives and of a few local officers, they would do well, in political as in legal matters, to rely with pretty implicit confidence on those whom they had chosen as their attorneys, without venturing themselves upon any very direct interference with the management of affairs.

Of the same opinion were the clergy and the leading members

* Hildreth, Richard, *The History of the United States of America,* 3 Vols. (New York, 1851–1852), I, 346–348.

of the great religious sects. Indeed, the theological doctrine of the natural depravity of mankind, and that goodness is only to be found in the regenerate, could not be reconciled, without some difficulty, with the theory of the capacity of mankind to govern themselves. The existence of a select class of church members, raised by spiritual gifts above the ordinary level, would naturally harmonize with the idea of a select class also in secular matters, to whose superior wisdom and virtue the administration of affairs might more safely be intrusted.

The merchants and capitalists, mostly men who had raised themselves by their own superior energy and sagacity to a position above the vulgar level, were little disposed to descend again to that level on questions of political concernment; and this feeling would naturally exist, to a still stronger degree, among the large landed proprietors of the Middle States and the slave-holding planters of the South.

The classes above enumerated might be considered as constituting the natural aristocracy of the Union and the states, disposed, from their superior education and social position, to regard the chief direction of public affairs as properly appertaining to them, and not inclined to give to the democratic principle any further extension than it had already attained; indeed, disposed perhaps somewhat to curtail it.

What might be called the natural democracy of the Union consisted of the great body of small land-holders, the mass of the free inhabitants, men who cultivated their own farms with their own hands; in virtue of that inherent power which superior wealth, knowledge, and social position every where carry with them, and which no formal declaration of equality can ever take away, swayed, indeed, in all the states, to a very great extent, by the classes above enumerated; but still watching with jealous eyes every thing which tended to curtail their political rights, or which seemed to look like special legislation for the benefit of particular classes.

It would, however, be a very great mistake to suppose that the line of separation between the political parties of the Union, either at this or at any other period, at all coincided with the above classification into a natural aristocracy and a natural democracy. The same thing has happened in the United States which has happened in all other communities; the great political divisions have arisen not so much from any direct contest between the principles of aristocracy and democracy, as from the factions into which the natural aristocracy has split; the democracy chiefly making itself felt by the occasional unanimity with which it has thrown itself into the scale of one or other of such contending factions. Generally speaking, however, no such unanimity has been perceptible, each faction of the natural aristocracy having on most occasions been able to carry with it a majority at least of that section of the natural democracy most immediately within the circle of its influence.

In the division of parties which took place on the question of the funding system and the general policy of the new federal government, the lawyers, the clergy, the merchants and capitalists, the great land-holders in the Middle States, almost all the educated and intelligent men of the North, united quite generally in favor of Hamilton's measures; and their influence had been sufficient, thus far, to give to those measures the support of the Northern States. South of the Potomac the planters were all-powerful, while the other sections of the natural aristocracy counted in those states for little or nothing in comparison; and as the planters were generally opposed to the funding system, they had little difficulty in carrying those states into an opposition to the federal administration, an opposition into which the outcry so loudly raised in those states against the Constitution itself was by this time pretty generally merged.

Hamilton on the Role of the National Government*

Alexander Hamilton (1757–1804) contributed greatly to the strength and stability of the United States in its early days under the Constitution. He came of humble origins: John Adams called him "the bastard brat of a Scotch pedlar." But the tenor of his thought was aristocratic. He believed that those who possess means and ability should rule the country. His broad constructionist views of the Constitution and his vision of the national government's great role are exemplified in these comments on Jefferson's inaugural message in 1801.

. . . . In addition to objects of national security, there are many purposes of great public utility to which the revenues in question might be applied. The improvement of the communications between the different parts of our country is an object well worthy of the national purse, and one which would abundantly repay *to labor* the portion of its *earnings,* which may have been borrowed for the purpose. To provide roads and bridges is within the direct purview of the Constitution. In many parts of the country, especially in the Western Territory, a matter in which the Atlantic States are equally interested, aqueducts and canals would also be fit subjects of pecuniary aid, from the general government. In France, England, and other parts of Europe, institutions exist supported by public contributions, which eminently promote agriculture and the arts. Such institutions merit imitation by our government; they are of the number of those which directly and sensibly recompense *labor* for what it lends to their agency.

To suggestions of the last kind, the adepts of the new school

* Hamilton, Alexander, *Works,* H. C. Lodge, ed., 12 Vols. (New York, 1904), VIII, 262–264.

have a ready answer: *Industry will succeed and prosper in proportion as it is left to the exertions of individual enterprise.* This favorite dogma, when taken as a general rule, is true; but as an exclusive one, it is false, and leads to error in the administration of public affairs. In matters of industry, human enterprise ought, doubtless, to be left free in the main; not fettered by too much regulation; but practical politicians know that it may be beneficially stimulated by prudent aids and encouragements on the part of the government. This is proved by numerous examples too tedious to be cited; examples which will be neglected only by indolent and temporizing rulers, who love to loll in the lap of epicurean ease, and seem to imagine that to govern well, is to amuse the wondering multitude with sagacious aphorisms and oracular sayings.

What has been observed is sufficient to render it manifest that, independent of the extinguishment of the debt, the revenues proposed to be yielded up would find ample and very useful employment for a variety of public purposes. Already in the possession of so valuable a resource; having surmounted the difficulties which, from the opinions and habits of our citizens, obstruct, in this, more than in any other country, every new provision for adding to our public income; certainly without a colorable pretence of their being a grievous or undue pressure on the community—how foolish will it be to resign the boon, perhaps in a short time to be compelled again to resort to it; and for that purpose to hazard a repetition of the obstacles which have been before encountered and overcome,—obstacles which gave birth to one insurrection, and may give birth to another! Infatuated must be the councils from which so injurious a project has proceeded!

But admitting the position, that there is an excess of income which ought to be relinquished, still the proposal to surrender the *internal* revenue is impolitic. It ought to be carefully preserved, as not being exposed to the casualties incident to our intercourse with foreign nations, and therefore the most certain. It ought to be preserved, as reaching to descriptions of persons who are not proportionately affected by the impost, and as tending, for this reason, to distribute the public burden more equitably. It ought to be preserved, because if revenue can really be

spared, it is best to do it in such a manner as will conduce to
the relief or advancement of our navigation and commerce.
Rather let the tonnage duty on American vessels be abolished,
and let the duties be lessened on some particular articles on
which they may press with inconvenient weight. Let not the
merchant be provoked to attempt to evade the duties by the
sentiment that his ease or interest is disregarded, and that his
capital alone is to be clogged and incumbered by the demands
of the Treasury. . . .

Jefferson's Political Principles in 1799*

As the text of this book shows, Jefferson's ideas in regard to political practices and principles varied considerably during the course of his life. However, in this letter to Elbridge Gerry, January 26, 1799, he professes a "political faith" from which he declares he will never stray.

I do then, with sincere zeal, wish an inviolable preservation of our present federal constitution, according to the true sense in which it was adopted by the States, that in which it was advocated by it's friends, & not that which it's enemies apprehended, who therefore became it's enemies; and I am opposed to the monarchising it's features by the forms of it's administration, with a view to conciliate a first transition to a President & Senate for life, & from that to a hereditary tenure of these offices, & thus to worm out the elective principle. I am for preserving to the States the powers not yielded by them to the Union, & to the legislature of the Union it's constitutional share in the division of powers; and I am not for transferring all the powers of the States to the general government, & all those of that government to the Executive branch. I am for a government rigorously frugal & simple, applying all the possible savings of the public revenue to the discharge of the national debt; and not for a multiplication of officers & salaries merely to make partisans, & for increasing, by every device, the public debt, on the principle of it's being a public blessing. I am for relying, for internal defence, on our militia solely, till actual invasion, and for such a naval force only as may protect our coasts and harbors from such depredations as we have experienced; and not for a standing army in time of peace, which may overawe the

* Jefferson, Thomas, *Writings*, P. L. Ford, ed., 10 Vols. (Washington, 1896), VII, 327–329. Jefferson to Elbridge Gerry, January 26, 1799.

public sentiment; nor for a navy, which, by it's own expenses and the eternal wars in which it will implicate us, will grind us with public burthens, & sink us under them. I am for free commerce with all nations; political connection with none; & little or no diplomatic establishment. And I am not for linking ourselves by new treaties with the quarrels of Europe; entering that field of slaughter to preserve their balance, or joining in the confederacy of kings to war against the principles of liberty. I am for freedom of religion, & against all maneuvres to bring about a legal ascendancy of one sect over another: for freedom of the press, & against all violations of the constitution to silence by force & not by reason the complaints or criticisms, just or unjust, of our citizens against the conduct of their agents. And I am for encouraging the progress of science in all it's branches; and not for raising a hue and cry against the sacred name of philosophy; for awing the human mind by stories of raw-head & bloody bones to a distrust of its own vision, & to repose implicitly on that of others; to go backwards instead of forwards to look for improvement; to believe that government, religion, morality, & every other science were in the highest perfection in ages of the darkest ignorance, and that nothing can ever be devised more perfect than what was established by our forefathers. To these I will add, that I was a sincere well-wisher to the success of the French revolution, and still wish it may end in the establishment of a free & well-ordered republic; but I have not been insensible under the atrocious depredations they have committed on our commerce. The first object of my heart is my own country. In that is embarked my family, my fortune, & my own existence. I have not one farthing of interest, nor one fibre of attachment out of it, nor a single motive of preference of any one nation to another, but in proportion as they are more or less friendly to us. But though deeply feeling the injuries of France, I did not think war the surest means of redressing them. I did believe, that a mission sincerely disposed to preserve peace, would obtain for us a peaceable & honorable settlement & retribution; and I appeal to you to say, whether this might not have been obtained, if either of your colleagues had been of the same sentiment with yourself.

These, my friend, are my principles; they are unquestionably

the principles of the great body of our fellow citizens, and I
know there is not one of them which is not yours also. In truth,
we never differed but on one ground, the funding system; and
as, from the moment of it's being adopted by the constituted
authorities, I became religiously principled in the sacred discharge of it to the uttermost farthing, we are united now even
on that single ground of difference.

Crawford as a Loose Constructionist*

Crawford made this speech urging recharter of the first United States Bank on February 11, 1811. He introduced the necessary bill and in his introductory remarks declared that the Bank was "an institution of twenty years standing, the good effects of which had been universally experienced, whose influence on the public prosperity was admitted by all. . . ."

Mr. President, it is contended by those who are opposed to the passage of this bill, that Congress can exercise no power by implication, and yet it is admitted, nay, even asserted, that Congress would have power to pass all laws necessary to carry the Constitution into effect, whether it had given or withheld the power which is contained in the following paragraph of the 8th section of the 1st article: "to make all laws which shall be necessary and proper for carrying into execution the foregoing powers and all other powers vested by this Constitution in the Government of the United States or in any department or officer thereof." If this part of the Constitution really confers no power, it at least, according to this opinion, strips it of that attribute of perfection which has by these gentlemen been ascribed to it. But, sir, this is not the fact. It does confer power of the most substantial and salutary nature. . . .

The Secretary of the Treasury has informed you that he conceives a bank is necessary to the legitimate exercise of the powers vested by the Constitution in the Government. I know, sir, that the testimony of this officer will not be very highly estimated by several honorable members of this body. I am aware that this opinion has subjected him, and the committee also, to the most invidious aspersions; but, sir, the situation of that officer, independent of his immense talents, enables him to form a more

* *Annals of Congress,* 11 Cong., 3 sess., 137, 142.

correct opinion than any other man in the nation of the degree of necessity which exists at the present time for a national bank, to enable the Government to manage its fiscal operations. He has been ten years at the head of your Treasury; he is thoroughly acquainted with the influence of the bank upon your revenue system; and he has, when called upon, declared that a bank is necessary to the proper exercise of the legitimate powers of the Government. His testimony is entitled to great weight in the decision of this question, at least with those gentlemen who have no knowledge of the practical effects of the operations of the bank in the collection, safe-keeping, and transmission of your revenue. In the selection of means to carry any of your Constitutional powers into effect, you must exercise a sound discretion; acting under its influence, you will discover that what is proper at one time may be extremely unfit and improper at another. The original powers granted to the Government by the Constitution can never change with the varying circumstances of the country, but the means by which those powers are to be carried into effect must necessarily vary with the varying state and circumstances of the nation. We are, when acting to-day, not to inquire what means were necessary and proper twenty years ago, not what were necessary and proper at the organization of the Government, but our inquiry must be, what means are necessary and proper this day. The Constitution, in relation to the means by which its powers are to be executed, is one eternal *now*. The state of things now, the precise point of time when we are called upon to act, must determine our choice in the selection of means to execute the delegated powers.

Jackson's Inclination to Violent Procedures*

Andrew Jackson's high temper made him prone to violent action. Peril to the nation as well as personal insults roused in him a combative instinct that not infrequently expressed itself in dire threats, which he was capable of carrying into execution. Here are two illustrations of this quality of his mind and character. The first is from a letter to James Monroe, January 6, 1817, written shortly after Monroe's election to the presidency. The second is a reminiscence by a friend and supporter, James A. Hamilton of New York. The incident Hamilton relates occurred early in January, 1828, when Hamilton, as a representative of the Tammany Society of New York, was en route with Jackson and his party to New Orleans and a grand celebration of the General's victory there over the British in 1815.

1. Jackson to Monroe, January 6, 1817. I have read with much satisfaction that part of your letter on the rise, progress and policy of the Federalist. It is in my opinion a Just exposition—and I am free to acknowledge, had I commanded the military Department where the Hartford convention met, If it had been the last act of my life, I should have hung up the three principle leaders of the party, I am sure an independant court martial would have condemned them under the 2nd section of the act establishing rules and articles for the government of the army of the u.s. These kind of men altho called Federalist, are really monarchrist, and traitors to the constituted Government. . . .[1]

2. Reminiscence by James A. Hamilton. The steamer Pocahontas was chartered by citizens of New Orleans to convey

* [1] Jackson, Andrew, *Correspondence*, J. S. Bassett, ed., 7 Vols. (Washington, D.C., 1926–1935), II, 272–273.

the General and his party from Nashville to that city. She was fitted out in the most sumptuous manner. The party was General and Mrs. Jackson, two gentlemen with their wives, a young lady, Miss B——, Governor Samuel Houston, Wm. B. Lewis, Robert Armstrong, and others, and the New York delegate. The only freight was the General's cotton-crop.

During the voyage we stopped at the different towns on the river, at the most of which the people were assembled; and at the principal ones, committees addressed the General, to whom he made appropriate replies. In the course of the voyage an event occurred, which I repeat, as it is suggestive of character. A steamer of greater speed than ours, going in the same direction, passed us, crossed our bow; then stopped and let us pass her; and then passed us again in triumph. This was repeated again and again, until the General, being excited by the offensive course, ordered a rifle to be brought to him; hailed the pilot of the other steamer, and swore that if he did the same thing again he would shoot him. As I believed the General was in earnest, and as such an outrage could not be of service to our cause, I went below and stated to Mrs. Jackson what had occurred; she said mildly, "Colonel, do me the favor to say to the General I wish to speak to him." I did so. He went to the cabin with me, and remained there in chat with her.[2]

[2] Hamilton, James A., *Reminiscences* (New York, 1869), 69–70.

Senator Jackson on Public Policy*

This is a letter from Jackson to one of his supporters, Dr. L. H. Coleman of Warrenton, North Carolina, dated April 26, 1824. Jackson was at this time in the United States Senate. Though the letter begins with a disclaimer of ambition for office, it shows his desire for the presidency. When published, its reference to the tariff made Henry Clay shake his head, stamp his foot, and exclaim, "Well, by God, I am in favor of an injudicious tariff."

Sir: I had the honor this day to receive your letter of the 21st instant and with candor shall reply to it. My name has been brought before the nation by the people themselves without any agency of mine: for I wish it not to be forgotten that I have never solicited office, nor when called upon by the constituted authorities have ever declined where I conceived my services would be beneficial to my country. But as my name has been brought before the nation for the first office in the gift of the people, it is incumbent on me, when asked, frankly to declare my opinion upon any political or national question pending before and about which the country feels an interest.

You ask my opinion on the Tariff. I answer, that I am in favor of a judicious examination and revision of it; and so far as the Tariff before us embraces the design of fostering, protecting, and preserving within ourselves the means of national defense and independence, particularly in a state of war, I would advocate and support it. The experience of the late war ought to teach us a lesson; and one never to be forgotten. If our liberty and republican form of government, procured for us by our revolutionary fathers, are worth the blood and treasure at which they were obtained, it surely is our duty to protect

* Jackson, Andrew, *Correspondence,* III, 249–251.

and defend them. Can there be an American patriot who saw the privations, dangers, and difficulties experienced for the want of a proper means of defense during the last war, who would be willing again to hazard the safety of our country if embroiled; or rest it for defense on the precarious means of national resources to be derived from commerce, in a state of war with a maratime power which might destroy that commerce to prevent our obtaining the means of defense, and thereby subdue us? I hope there is not; and if there is, I am sure he does not deserve to enjoy the blessing of freedom.

Heaven smiled upon, and gave us liberty and independence. That same providence has blessed us with the means of national independence and national defense. If we omit or refuse to use the gifts which He has extended to us, we deserve not the continuation of His blessings. He has filled our mountains and our plains with minererals—with lead, iron, and copper, and given us a climate and soil for the growing of hemp and wool. These being the grand materials of our national defense, they ought to have extended to them adequate and fair protection, that our own manufactories and laborers may be placed on a fair competition with those of Europe; and that we may have within our own country a supply of those leading and important articles so essential to war. Beyond this, I look at the Tariff with an eye to the proper distribution of labor and revenue; and with a view to discharge our national debt. I am one of those who do not believe that a national debt is a national blessing, but rather a curse to a republic; inasmuch as it is calculated to raise around the administration a moneyed aristocracy dangerous to the liberties of the country.

This Tariff—I mean a judicious one—possesses more fanciful than real dangers. I will ask what is the real situation of the agriculturalist? Where has the American farmer a market for his surplus products? Except for cotton he has neither a foreign nor a home market. Does not this clearly prove, when there is no market either at home or abroad, that there is too much labor employed in agriculture? and that the channels of labor should be multiplied? Common sense points out at once the remedy. Draw from agriculture the superabundant labor, employ it in mechanism and manufactures, thereby creating a home market for your breadstuffs, and distributing labor to a most profitable account, and benefits to the country will result. Take from agriculture in the United States six hundred thousand men, women, and children, and you at once give a home market for more breadstuffs than all Europe now furnishes us. In short, sir, we have been too long subject to the policy of the British merchants. It is time we should become a little more *Americanized,* and instead of feeding the paupers and laborers of Europe, feed our own, or else in a short time, by continuing our present policy, we shall all be paupers ourselves.

It is, therefore, my opinion that a careful Tariff is much wanted to pay our national debt, and afford us the means of that defense within ourselves on which the safety and liberty of the country depend; and last, though not least, give a proper distribution to our labor, which must prove beneficial to the happiness, independence, and wealth of the community.

This is a short outline of my opinions, generally, on the subject of your inquiry, and believing them correct and calculated to further the prosperity and happiness of my country, I declare to you I would not barter them for any office or situation of a temporal character that could be given me.

I have presented you my opinions freely, because I am without concealment, and should indeed despise myself if I could believe myself capable of acquiring the confidence of any by means so ignoble.

I am, sir, very respectfully, your obedient servant.

Choice of a President by the House of Representatives*

The Constitution originally provided (Article II, section 1) that the person having the greatest number of electoral votes should, if he had a majority, be President, and that the person with the next highest number of votes should be Vice President. If more than one had a majority and an equal number of votes, the House of Representatives should choose one of them by ballot for President. This was unsatisfactory. It almost assured that the President and Vice President should have differing viewpoints and, if the President died, there would be an automatic change of policy without a popular mandate. The situation became acute in 1800, when Jefferson and Burr had the same number of electoral votes. The result was the Twelfth Amendment, which was ratified in time for the election of 1804.

The Electors shall meet in their respective States and vote by ballot for President and Vice-President, one of whom, at least, shall not be an inhabitant of the same State with themselves; they shall name in their ballots the person voted for as President, and in distinct ballots the person voted for as Vice-President, and they shall make distinct lists of all persons voted for as President, and of all persons voted for as Vice-President, and of the number of votes for each, which lists they shall sign and certify, and transmit sealed to the seat of the government of the United States, directed to the President of the Senate;— The President of the Senate shall, in the presence of the Senate and House of Representatives, open all the certificates and the votes shall then be counted;—The person having the greatest number of votes for President, shall be the President, if such

* The Twelfth Amendment of the Constitution of the United States.

number be a majority of the whole number of Electors appointed; and if no person have such majority, then from the persons having the highest numbers not exceeding three on the list of those voted for as President, the House of Representatives shall choose immediately, by ballot, the President. But in choosing the President, the votes shall be taken by states, the representation from each state having one vote; a quorum for this purpose shall consist of a member or members from two-thirds of the states, and a majority of all the states shall be necessary to a choice. And if the House of Representatives shall not choose a President whenever the right of choice shall devolve upon them, before the fourth day of March next following, then the Vice-President shall act as President, as in the case of the death or other constitutional disability of the President.— The person having the greatest number of votes as Vice-President, shall be the Vice-President, if such number be a majority of the whole number of Electors appointed, and if no person have a majority, then from the two highest numbers on the list, the Senate shall choose the Vice-President; a quorum for the purpose shall consist of two-thirds of the whole number of Senators, and a majority of the whole number shall be necessary to a choice. But no person constitutionally ineligible to the office of President shall be eligible to that of Vice-President of the United States.

Clay Describes the Effort to Enlist His Support*

On January 8, 1825, Clay wrote this letter to Francis P. Blair describing in lighthearted fashion the way in which he was being courted by the friends of the three candidates for the presidency. There is much that is ironical in this missive. Clay was about to make the greatest political mistake of his career, and Blair was shortly to become one of his bitterest political enemies.

The expression "tears in his eyes" is an allusion to the affliction suffered by John Quincy Adams, a chronic watering of the eyes.

MY DEAR SIR,—My position in relation to the friends of the three returned candidates is singular enough, and often to me very amusing. In the first place they all believe that my friends have the power of deciding the question, and then that I have the power of controlling my friends. Acting upon this supposition, in the same hour, I am sometimes touched gently on the shoulder by a friend, for example, of General Jackson, who will thus address me, "My dear Sir, all my dependence is upon you, don't disappoint us, you know our partiality was for you next to the hero; and how much we want a Western President." Immediately after a friend of Mr. Crawford will accost me, "The hopes of the Republican party are concentrated on you, for God's sake preserve it. If you had been returned, instead of Mr. Crawford, every man of us would have supported you to the last hour. We consider him and you as the only genuine Republican candidates." Next a friend of Mr. Adams comes with tears in his eyes, "Sir, Mr. Adams has always had the greatest respect for you, and admiration of your talents. There

* Clay, Henry, *Private Correspondence,* C. Colton, ed. (New York, 1855), 109–110.

is no station to which you are not equal. Most undoubtedly
you are the second choice of New England, and I pray you
to consider seriously whether the public good and your own
future interests do not point most distinctly to the choice which
you ought to make." How can one withstand all this disinterested
homage and kindness? Really the friends of all three gentlemen
are so very courteous and affectionate that I sometimes almost
wish that it was in my power to accommodate each of them,
but that being impossible, we are beginning to think seriously
of the choice which we must finally make. I will tell you then
that I believe the contest will be limited to Mr. Adams and General Jackson. Mr. Crawford's personal condition precludes the
choice of him if there were no other objection to his election.
As the only alternative which is presented to us it is sufficiently
painful, and I consider whatever choice we may make will be
only a choice of evils. To both of those gentlemen there are
strong personal objections. The principal difference between
them is that in the election of Mr. Adams we shall not by the
example inflict any wound upon the character of our institutions,
but I should much fear hereafter, if not during the present
generation, that the election of the General would give to the
military spirit a stimulus and a confidence that might lead to
the most pernicious results. I shall, therefore, with great regret
on account of the dilemma in which the people have placed us,
support Mr. Adams. My friends are generally so inclined. What
has great weight with me is the decided preference which a
majority of the delegation from Ohio has for him over General
Jackson. If, therefore, Kentucky were to vote for the General
it would probably only have the effect of dividing our friends,
without defeating ultimately the election of Mr. Adams. Three of
the four States favorable to Mr. Crawford are believed to prefer
Mr. Adams to the General. Virginia is one of them. I am inclined to think that nearly three-fourths of our delegation have
yielded to the influence of these views, and will vote for Mr.
Adams. My friends entertain the belief that their kind wishes
toward me will in the end be more likely to be accomplished by
so bestowing their votes. I have, however, most earnestly en-
treated them to throw me out of their consideration in bringing
their judgments to a final conclusion, and to look and be

guided solely by the public good. If I know myself, that alone has determined me. Your Representative is inclined to concur with us in these sentiments and views, and if they should meet your approbation, as I know he has great respect for your opinions, I would be glad if you would by the return mail address a letter to him to strengthen him in his inclination. Be pleased to show this letter to Crittenden alone.

Adams's Account of His Conversations with Clay*

Note the careful way in which Adams relates these conversations. Apparently he made no outright offer to Clay of the State Department or anything else in return for the latter's influence in the election. Nevertheless it must have been clear to both men that the good understanding between them would result in a close working relationship. These conversations took place on January 9 and 29, 1825.

Jan. 9.—Mr. Clay came at six, and spent the evening with me in a long conversation explanatory of the past and prospective of the future. He said that the time was drawing near when the choice must be made in the House of Representatives of a President from the three candidates presented by the electoral colleges; that he had been much urged and solicited with regard to the part in that transaction that he should take, and had not been five minutes landed at his lodgings before he had been applied to by a friend of Mr. Crawford's, in a manner so gross that it had disgusted him; that some of my friends also, disclaiming, indeed, to have any authority from me, had repeatedly applied to him, directly or indirectly, urging considerations personal to himself as motives to his cause. He had thought it best to reserve for some time his determination to himself: first, to give a decent time for his own funeral solemnities as a candidate; and, secondly, to prepare and predispose all his friends to a state of neutrality between the three candidates who would be before the House, so that they might be free ultimately to take that course which might be most conducive to the public interest. The time had now come at which he might

* Adams, John Quincy, *Diary*, A. Nevins, ed. (New York, 1928), 335–336, 338. Reprinted with the permission of Allan Nevins.

be explicit in his communication with me, and he had for that purpose asked this confidential interview. He wished me, as fast as I might think proper, to satisfy him with regard to some principles of great public importance, but without any personal considerations for himself. In the question to come before the House between General Jackson, Mr. Crawford, and myself, he had no hesitation in saying that his preference would be for me.

Jan. 29.—On my return home, Mr. Clay came in, and sat with me a couple of hours, discussing all the prospects and probabilities of the Presidential election. He spoke to me with the utmost freedom of men and things; intimated doubts and prepossessions concerning individual friends of mine, to all which I listened with due consideration. He was anxious for the conciliation of Webster and Louis McLane, and expressed some jealousy as from Webster of the persons by whom he supposed me to be surrounded.

I told him the sources of Webster's anxieties, and my own earnest desire to conciliate him; the manner in which my overtures had been received by him, and my own high opinion of his talents and capacities for service.

Jackson's Reaction to "The Bargain"*

Nothing could demonstrate more effectively Old Hickory's rage and chagrin over being, as he felt, cheated out of the presidency in 1824 than the letter to Samuel Swartwout, written on February 22, 1825, from which the following excerpt is taken.

Mr. Clay never yet has risked himself for his country, sacrificed his repose, or made an effort to repel an invading foe; of course his "conscience" assured him that it was altogether wrong in any other man to lead his countrymen to battle and victory. He who fights, and fights successfully must according to his standard be held up as a "Military Chieftain": even Washington could he again appear among us might be so considered, because he dared to be a virtuous and successfull soldier, an honest statesman, and a correct man. It is only when overtaken by disaster and defeat, that any man is to be considered a safe politician and correct statesman.

Defeat might to be sure have brought with it one benefit, it might have enabled me to escape the notice and animadversions of Mr. Clay, but considering that by an opposite result, my country has been somewhat benefitted, I rather prefer it even with the opprobrium and censure which he seems disposed to extend. To him thank god I am in no wise responsible, there is a purer tribunal to which in preference I would refer myself— to the Judgment of an enlightened patriotic and uncorrupted people—to that tribunal I would rather appeal whence is derived whatever reputation either he or I are possessed of.

By a refference there, it will be ascertained that I did not solicit the office of President, it was the frank and flattering call of the freemen of this country, not mine, which placed my

* Jackson, *Correspondence,* III, 279–280.

name before the nation; when they failed in their colleges to make a choice, no one beheld me seeking thro art or management to entice any representative in Congress from a conscientious responsibility to his own, or the wishes of his constituents. No midnight taper burnt by me; no secret conclaves were held, or cabals entered into, to persuade any to a violation of pledges given, or of instructions received. By me no plans were concerted to impair the pure principles of our Republican institutions, or to frustrate that fundimental one which maintains the supremacy of the people's will; on the contrary, having never in any manner either before the people or Congress in the slightest manner interfered with the question, my conscience stands void of offence, and will go quietly with me, heedless of the insinuations of any, who thro management may seek an influence, not sanctioned by merit.

John Quincy Adams on Party Strife, March 4, 1825 *

In the years following the War of 1812 many men hoped that a general state of political harmony could be achieved. Those believing that partisanship, at least on the national level, was unnecessary, were known as "amalgamationists." Adams was one of them, as he demonstrated in this inaugural address. Like Jefferson in 1801, he had a vain hope that his administration would be unmarked by party strife.

. . . . Of the two great political parties which have divided the opinions and feelings of our country, the candid and the just will now admit that both have contributed splendid talents, spotless integrity, ardent patriotism, and disinterested sacrifices to the formation and administration of this Government, and that both have required a liberal indulgence for a portion of human infirmity and error. The revolutionary wars of Europe, commencing precisely at the moment when the Government of the United States first went into operation under this Constitution, excited a collision of sentiments and of sympathies which kindled all the passions and imbittered the conflict of parties till the nation was involved in war and the Union was shaken to its center. This time of trial embraced a period of five and twenty years, during which the policy of the Union in its relations with Europe constituted the principal basis of our political divisions and the most arduous part of the action of our Federal Government. With the catastrophe in which the wars of the French Revolution terminated, and our own subsequent peace with Great Britain, this baneful weed of party strife was uprooted. From that time no difference of principle, connected

* Richardson, James D., comp., *Messages and Papers of the Presidents,* 10 Vols. (Washington, D.C., 1899), II, 295–297.

either with the theory of government or with our intercourse with foreign nations, has existed or been called forth in force sufficient to sustain a continued combination of parties or to give more than wholesome animation to public sentiment or legislative debate.

Ten years of peace, at home and abroad, have assuaged the animosities of political contention and blended into harmony the most discordant elements of public opinion. There still remains one effort of magnanimity, one sacrifice of prejudice and passion, to be made by the individuals throughout the nation who have heretofore followed the standards of political party. It is that of discarding every remnant of rancor against each other, of embracing as countrymen and friends, and of yielding to talents and virtue alone that confidence which in times of contention for principle was bestowed only upon those who bore the badge of party communion. . . .

John Quincy Adams on Internal Improvements, December 6, 1825 *

Adams was a statesman with a vision of growth and development for his country. His policies as Secretary of State under President Monroe paved the way for the expansion of the United States to the Pacific Coast, and he believed that it was imperative to bind the nation together by a great system of internal transportation. This passage from his first message to Congress expresses his conviction that the creation of such a system was a function of the national government.

. . . . Upon this first occasion of addressing the Legislature of the Union, with which I have been honored, in presenting to their view the execution so far as it has been effected of the measures sanctioned by them for promoting the internal improvement of our country, I can not close the communication without recommending to their calm and persevering consideration the general principle in a more enlarged extent. The great object of the institution of civil government is the improvement of the condition of those who are parties to the social compact, and no government, in whatever form constituted, can accomplish the lawful ends of its institution but in proportion as it improves the condition of those over whom it is established. Roads and canals, by multiplying and facilitating the communications and intercourse between distant regions and multitudes of men, are among the most important means of improvement. But moral, political, intellectual improvement are duties assigned by the Author of Our Existence to social no less than to individual man. For the fulfillment of those duties governments are invested with power, and to the attainment of the end—the progressive improvement of the condition of the gov-

* Richardson, *Messages and Papers,* II, 311–313.

erned—the exercise of delegated powers is a duty as sacred and indispensable as the usurpation of powers not granted is criminal and odious. Among the first, perhaps the very first, instrument for the improvement of the condition of men is knowledge, and to the acquisition of much of the knowledge adapted to the wants, the comforts, and enjoyments of human life public institutions and seminaries of learning are essential. So convinced of this was the first of my predecessors in this office, now first in the memory, as, living, he was first in the hearts, of our countrymen, that once and again in his addresses to the Congresses with whom he cooperated in the public service he earnestly recommended the establishment of seminaries of learning, to prepare for all the emergencies of peace and war—a national university and a military academy. With respect to the latter, had he lived to the present day, in turning his eyes to the institution at West Point he would have enjoyed the gratification of his most earnest wishes; but in surveying the city which has been honored with his name he would have seen the spot of earth which he had destined and bequeathed to the use and benefit of his country as the site for an university still bare and barren.

In assuming her station among the civilized nations of the earth it would seem that our country had contracted the engagement to contribute her share of mind, of labor, and of expense to the improvement of those parts of knowledge which lie beyond the reach of individual acquisition, and particularly to geographical and astronomical science. Looking back to the history only of the half century since the declaration of our independence, and observing the generous emulation with which the Governments of France, Great Britain, and Russia have devoted the genius, the intelligence, the treasures of their respective nations to the common improvement of the species in these branches of science, is it not incumbent upon us to inquire whether we are not bound by obligations of a high and honorable character to contribute our portion of energy and exertion to the common stock? The voyages of discovery prosecuted in the course of that time at the expense of those nations have not only redounded to their glory, but to the improvement of human knowledge. We have been partakers of that improvement and owe for it a sacred debt, not only of gratitude, but of equal or proportional exertion in the same common cause. Of the cost of these undertakings, if the mere expenditures of outfit, equipment, and completion of the expeditions were to be considered the only charges, it would be unworthy of a great and generous nation to take a second thought. One hundred expeditions of circumnavigation like those of Cook and La Pérouse would not burden the exchequer of the nation fitting them out so much as the ways and means of defraying a single campaign in war. But if we take into the account the lives of those benefactors of mankind of which their services in the cause of their species were the purchase, how shall the cost of those heroic enterprises be estimated, and what compensation can be made to them or to their countries for them? Is it not by bearing them in affectionate remembrance? Is it not still more by imitating their example—by enabling countrymen of our own to pursue the same career and to hazard their lives in the same cause?

In inviting the attention of Congress to the subject of internal improvements upon a view thus enlarged it is not my design to recommend the equipment of an expedition for circumnavigating the globe for purposes of scientific research and inquiry. We have objects of useful investigation nearer home, and to which our cares may be more beneficially applied. The interior of our own territories has yet been very imperfectly explored. Our coasts along many degrees of latitude upon the shores of the Pacific Ocean, though much frequented by our spirited commercial navigators, have been barely visited by our public ships. The River of the West, first fully discovered and navigated by a countryman of our own, still bears the name of the ship in which he ascended its waters, and claims the protection of our armed national flag at its mouth. With the establishment of a military post there or at some other point of that coast, recommended by my predecessor and already matured in the deliberations of the last Congress, I would suggest the expediency of connecting the equipment of a public ship for the exploration of the whole northwest coast of this continent. . . .

Van Buren "Explains" His Views on the Tariff in 1827*

This account by Van Buren illustrates not only his skill in ambiguity but also the pride he took in using that particular device.

. . . . The annual petition of the manufacturers to Congress for increased protection, presented at the previous session, resulted in the report of what was called the Woollens' Bill. Having promised to accompany a friend on a visit to the Congressional Cemetery, I was absent from the Senate when the Bill was reached and rejected by the casting vote of Vice President Calhoun. My absence was assumed to have been intentional and was made the ground for the usual newspaper vituperation, according to which my delinquency was greatly aggravated by my accompanying Gen. Hamilton and Col. Drayton to South Carolina at the close of the session. Whilst at Charleston I received a letter from Comptroller Marcy urging my immediate return to arrest the use that our opponents were making of the materials with which I had thus supplied them. Having had some experience of his propensity to *croak,* and being withal not ready to comply with his unreasonable request, I replied that if my standing at home was not sufficient to protect me against such assaults it was not worth preserving and that I should not hasten my return for such a purpose. On my way homewards I learned at West Point from a reliable authority that the Tariff champion Mallary had informed his friends that it was the intention of the Protectionists to denounce my course at a State Tariff Convention which was to meet at Albany within

* Van Buren, Martin, *Autobiography,* J. C. Fitzpatrick, ed., American Historical Association, *Annual Report for the Year 1918,* 2 Vols. (Washington, D.C., 1918), II, 169–171.

a week or two, and that my old friend the Patroon had agreed
to preside at the meeting. I immediately determined to face
the assemblage and to speak for myself, but without communi-
cating my intention to a single friend.

To the very able exposition of the system and the persistent
assaults upon its injustice and impolicy by the New York Evening Post, the country is more indebted for its final overthrow,
in this state at least, than to any other single influence.

On the morning of the Tariff meeting at the Capitol I sent
for my friends Benjamin Knower and Charles E. Dudley, and
for the first time informed them of my intentions and asked
them to accompany me. They vehemently remonstrated against
the proposed step and told me that they had been reliably informed of the intention to pass a vote of censure upon my
course in regard to the Woollens Bill, and that altho' there would
be many of my political friends at the meeting, a very large
majority would be enemies who would avail themselves of my
presence to make the proceeding more humiliating. I agreed
with their opinion as to the meditated assault, but observed that
it would not be contained in the Report of the Committee, as
well to save the feelings of my friends at the Commencement as
because the managers would know that Gen. Van Rensselaer
would not make himself a party to such a Report by a Committee
of his appointing, and that as the censure, for these reasons,
would doubtless be reserved for a motion to amend, at the close
of the proceedings, if I could unexpectedly appear before them
after the organization of the meeting I would take my chance
for what was done afterwards. They still objected, but were of
course willing to go with me, and after ascertaining, by a mes-
senger dispatched for that purpose, that the assemblage was organized for its work we repaired to the Capitol.

My appearance occasioned evident surprise. The good Patroon
who presided asked me to take a seat by his side, which I respectfully declined, and chose an eligible position in the crowd.
At the end of every speech the eyes of the assemblage were
directed towards me, but I waited until every one had spoken
who desired to do so, and I then addressed the meeting for
nearly two hours. Some of the speeches previously made contained or insinuated enough to justify me in regarding myself

as accused of delinquency in the matter of the Woollens Bill and thus to open the whole subject. I was listened to throughout with silent but respectful attention. During the whole time my friend Knower sat directly before and with his eyes fixed upon me, and when I spoke of the injustice that had been done to me he was so much moved as to attract the attention of the meeting. He was then extensively engaged in the purchase of wool, but being a Republican of the old school and withal a singularly upright man and sincere friend, those fine qualities had not yet been affected by the ardent pursuit of money. At a later period he separated from many of his early friends, myself among the rest, in consequence of their anti-tariff opinions, but a short time before his death he addressed me a letter replete with the sentiments and the spirit of his best days.

At the close of my speech Mr. J. Townsend a son-in-law of Judge Spencer and a rich manufacturer, expressed a desire to pass a vote of thanks to me for it, but some of his more sagacious associates, who did not think as favorably of its probable effect, interfered and overruled him. The meeting dissolved without anything being further said or done, and we moved down State Street from the Capitol with every indication of exultation on the part of my friends at its *dénouement,* and of dejection on the other side.

Mr. Knower came to me in the evening and told me that, on his way home from the Capitol, Mr. Wood, one of his wool buyers and a sensible man, said to him—"Mr. Knower! that was a very able speech!" "Yes, very able!" he answered. "Mr. Knower!" again said Mr. Wood, after a considerable pause,—"on which side of the Tariff question was it?" "That is the very point I was thinking about when you first spoke to me, Mr. Wood!" replied Knower.

I have frequently been told and have always believed that I rendered much service to the cause of truth by that speech, but this conversation between two intelligent and interested men would seem to indicate that directness on all points had not been its most prominent feature.

Jefferson on the Necessity of Change, July 12, 1816*

In retirement Jefferson took a more philosophical attitude toward political problems than had been the case when he bore the heat and burden of political battle. This excerpt from a letter to Samuel Kercheval, written from Monticello, indicates his conviction that it is necessary to adapt political principles to changing circumstances.

Some men look at constitutions with sanctimonious reverence, and deem them like the ark of the covenant, too sacred to be touched. They ascribe to the men of the preceding age a wisdom more than human, and suppose what they did to be beyond amendment. I knew that age well; I belonged to it, and labored with it. It deserved well of its country. It was very like the present, but without the experience of the present; and forty years of experience in government is worth a century of book-reading; and this they would say themselves, were they to rise from the dead. I am certainly not an advocate for frequent and untried changes in laws and constitutions. I think moderate imperfections had better be borne with; because, when once known, we accommodate ourselves to them, and find practical means of correcting their ill effects. But I know also, that laws and institutions must go hand in hand with the progress of the human mind. As that becomes more developed, more enlightened, as new discoveries are made, new truths disclosed, and manners and opinions change with the change of circumstances, institutions must advance also, and keep pace with the times. We might as well require a man to wear still the coat which fitted him when a boy, as civilized society to remain ever under the regimen

* Jefferson, Thomas, *Writings,* A. A. Lipscomb, ed., 20 Vols. (Washington, D.C., 1903–1904), XV, 40–44.

of their barbarous ancestors. It is this preposterous idea which
has lately deluged Europe in blood. Their monarchs, instead of
wisely yielding to the gradual change of circumstances, of favor-
ing progressive accommodation to progressive improvement, have
clung to old abuses, entrenched themselves behind steady habits,
and obliged their subjects to seek through blood and violence
rash and ruinous innovations, which, had they been referred to
the peaceful deliberations and collected wisdom of the nation,
would have been put into acceptable and salutary forms. Let us
follow no such examples, nor weakly believe that one generation is not as capable as another of taking care of itself, and of
ordering its own affairs. Let us, as our sister States have done,
avail ourselves of our reason and experience, to correct the
crude essays of our first and unexperienced, although wise, virtuous, and well-meaning councils. And lastly, let us provide in
our Constitution for its revision at stated periods. What these
periods should be, nature herself indicates. By the European
tables of mortality, of the adults living at any one moment of
time, a majority will be dead in about nineteen years. At the
end of that period then, a new majority is come into place; or,
in other words, a new generation. Each generation is as independent of the one preceding, as that was of all which had gone
before. It has then, like them, a right to choose for itself the
form of government it believes most promotive of its own happiness; consequently, to accommodate to the circumstances in
which it finds itself, that received from its predecessors; and it
is for the peace and good of mankind, that a solemn opportunity
of doing this every nineteen or twenty years, should be provided by the Constitution; so that it may be handed on, with
periodical repairs, from generation to generation, to the end
of time, if anything human can so long endure. It is now forty
years since the constitution of Virginia was formed. The same
tables inform us, that, within that period, two-thirds of the
adults then living are now dead. Have then the remaining third,
even if they had the wish, the right to hold in obedience to their
will, and to laws heretofore made by them, the other two-thirds,
who, with themselves, compose the present mass of adults? If
they have not, who has? The dead? But the dead have no rights.
They are nothing; and nothing cannot own something. Where

there is no substance, there can be no accident. This corporeal globe, and everything upon it, belong to its present corporeal inhabitants, during their generation. They alone have a right to direct what is the concern of themselves alone, and to declare the law of that direction; and this declaration can only be made by their majority. That majority, then, has a right to depute representatives to a convention, and to make the Constitution what they think will be the best for themselves. But how collect their voice? This is the real difficulty. If invited by private authority, or county or district meetings, these divisions are so large that few will attend; and their voice will be imperfectly or falsely, pronounced. Here, then, would be one of the advantages of the ward divisions I have proposed. The mayor of every ward, on a question like the present, would call his ward together, take the simple yea or nay of its members, convey these to the county court, who would hand on those of all its wards to the proper general authority; and the voice of the whole people would be thus fairly, fully, and peaceably expressed, discussed, and decided by the common reason of the society. If this avenue be shut to the call of sufferance, it will make itself heard through that of force, and we shall go on, as other nations are doing, in the endless circle of oppression, rebellion, reformation; and oppression, rebellion, reformation, again; and so on forever.

These, Sir, are my opinions of the governments we see among men, and of the principles by which alone we may prevent our own from falling into the same dreadful track. I have given them at greater length than your letter called for. But I cannot say things by halves; and I confide them to your honor, so to use them as to preserve me from the gridiron of the public papers. If you shall approve and enforce them, as you have done that of equal representation, they may do some good. If not, keep them to yourself as the effusions of withered age and useless time. I shall, with not the less truth, assure you of my great respect and consideration.

Two Accounts of Why Van Buren
Became a Jackson Supporter*

Here are two accounts of Van Buren's decision to support Jackson for President. The first is by Van Buren himself and the second is by a contemporary New York politician and historian, Jabez D. Hammond, who was a careful and judicious observer. Hammond's political history of New York State from 1789 to 1848 is one of the best original sources on that subject.

1. My views in regard to the then next Presidential election were formally asked by that estimable man and inflexible old Republican, Judge William Smith, of South Carolina in an interview which I had with him at Boston, within three months after the commencement of Mr. Adams's Administration. I informed him that as Mr. Crawford was removed from further competition by the state of his health my next candidate would be Andrew Jackson. To his questions in regard to the probability of success and to the safety with which we might rely on the General's present political opinions—his confidence on the latter point having been shaken by the famous letter to Mr. Monroe and by the incidents of the last election,—I answered that by adding the General's personal popularity to the strength of the old Republican party which still acted together and for the maintenance of which the Judge and myself had been strenuous colaborers, we might, I thought, be able to compete successfully with the power and patronage of the Administration, then in the zenith of its prosperity; that we had abundant evidence that the General was at an earlier period well grounded in the principles of our party, and that we must trust to good fortune and

* Van Buren, *Autobiography,* 198–199; Hammond, Jabez D., *The History of Political Parties in the State of New York,* 3 Vols. (Cooperstown and Syracuse, 1845–1852), II, 211.

to the effects of favorable associations for the removal of the rust they had contracted, in his case, by a protracted non-user and the prejudicial effects in that regard of his military life.

Pleased with these views the Judge asked my consent to speak of them freely as coming from me, which was readily given, and he entered upon their support with characteristic spirit. It was at my suggestion that Gen. Jackson afterwards offered to Judge Smith a seat on the Bench of the Supreme Court of the United States, which he declined.

2. Mr. Van Buren, and several others, leading men of the old Crawford party at Washington, had, by this time, come to the conclusion to support Gen. Jackson for the next presidency in opposition to Mr. Adams. The strong popular vote which, in despite of the efforts of the Adams, Clay and Crawford parties, the general had received at the last election, probably had much effect in inducing them to come to this conclusion. It furnished, ready formed, a large capital which the Crawford party saw they could add to their own, simply by consenting to receive it. They knew too, that the chivalric bravery of General Jackson, his brilliant success in the late war, and the many popular and fascinating points in his character, would, when supported by such a compact, disciplined association as was the Crawford party in many of the states of the Union, render this extraordinary man irresistible as a candidate before the people. If he was not a learned lawyer and civilian, he was at any rate a man of a clear discriminating mind, and if he was subject to rashness and precipitancy, they thought they could surround him with friends and advisers who would keep him within due bounds. True, the Crawford men in this state had, in 1824 and 1825, manifested the utmost horror at the least prospect of his election, and Mr. Crawford himself was known to have expressed very unfavorable opinions of him, but a better knowledge of the man, and above all, a kind of political necessity, had materially changed their views.

Van Buren on the Panama Congress*

These are excerpts from two speeches that Van Buren made in the United States Senate on January 16 and on March 14, 1826. He invokes isolationism and unconstitutionality as arguments against participation in the Panama Congress. His reasoning makes strange reading today.

We have been invited to unite in a Congress thus constituted. The Executive asks our consent to his acceptance of that invitation. What are the limits contained in the invitation, and the restriction prescribed in the proposed acceptance? They consist in this, and in this *only:* that the United States shall not be called upon to do any act, during the continuance of the *present* war between Spain and the other States, which will conflict with our neutral obligations. If there be any other restriction or limitation, I call upon gentlemen to point it out. I affirm that there is none. I do not ask gentlemen for the suggestions or opinions of those either within or without doors. I appeal to the documents by which we are to judge now, and by which we shall be judged hereafter. If no other is pointed out, I shall assume that none exists. We are then invited to become a member of the proposed Congress, and of this *Confederacy of American States.* If the views of the Executive are not such as the documents import, why, in the communications made to us, are we not specially advised upon this point? But we are not without evidence of the most explicit character. We have called upon the Executive for information. Among other things sent us, are extracts from the correspondence between Mr. Clay and Mr. Poinsett, our Minister at Mexico. When the declarations of one of our Ministers, bearing distinctly upon a question before the Senate, made directly and officially to a foreign Government, is sent to us by the Executive, without explanation or disavowal, I

* *Register of Debates,* 19th Cong., 1 sess., 240–241, 246, 253–254.

know not how we are to avoid the conclusion, that the Minister has spoken a language authorized by his Government. More especially must that be the case when the declaration of the Minister, instead of being disavowed by his Government, is substantially in accordance with the declarations of its official organ, the Secretary of State. If this assumption be correct, much light, as to the views of our Government, may be derived from the correspondence before referred to, between Mr. Poinsett and Mr. Clay. In the letter of the former to the latter, of the 28th September, 1825, we find the following sentiments: "I first objected to the exception in favor of the American Nations, formerly Spanish possessions, on the ground that no distinctions ought to be made between any of the members of the Great American Family. That Great Britain having consented to such a provision ought not to influence the American States, because the Republics of America were united by *one and the same interest,* and that it was the interest of the European Powers to cause such distinctions to be made, as would divide it into small confederacies, and, if possible, to prevent us from uniting, so as to present one front against the attempts of Europe, upon our Republican Institutions." And afterwards still more explicitly, as follows: "I then recapitulated the course of policy pursued towards the Spanish colonies, by our Government, which had so largely contributed to secure their independence, and declared what *further* we were willing to do to *defend their rights and liberties;* but that this could only be expected from us, and could only be accomplished, by a *strict union of all the American Republics,* on terms of perfect equality and reciprocity; and repeated that it was the obvious policy of Europe to divide us into small confederacies, with separate and distinct interests; and as manifestly ours *to form a single great Confederacy, which might oppose one united front to the attacks of our enemies.*"

So far from disapproving the sentiments thus avowed by Mr. Poinsett, in his letter of the 28th September, Mr. Clay, in his despatch to Mr. Poinsett, of the 9th of November, holds the following language: "Again the United Mexican Government has invited that of the United States to be represented at the Congress of Panama, and the President has determined to accept the invitation. *Such an invitation has been given to no European*

*Government, and ought not to have been given to this, if it is
not to be considered as one of the American Nations.*" It is,
therefore, fair to conclude, that the language of Mr. Poinsett to
the Mexican Government was authorized by his own; and if
this be conceded, the views of the Executive must be such as I
have contended. With these views, ought we to join a Congress
thus constituted? I contend we ought not if we could, and that
the power to do so is not conferred by the Constitution. . . .

It is, then, the design of the Executive to enter into an agreement at the Congress, (it is not material for the present in what
form,) that if the powers of Europe make common cause with
Spain, or otherwise attempt the subjugation of Spanish America,
we shall unite with the latter, and contribute our proportion to
the means necessary to make resistance effectual: and further,
that we shall bind ourselves, at that Congress, as to the manner
in which we shall resist any attempts, by the European Powers,
to colonize any portion of this Continent. This design has been
fully, frankly, and explicitly stated to the Spanish American
States, and to us. Is the Senate of the United States willing to
sanction a measure of that description? I care not for the present
whether it be by treaty or by act, decree, or ordinance of the
Congress. Will you, in any shape or form, preliminary or final,
give to it your sanction? Upon this subject at least, we have had
"thoughts that breathe." In the confidence that I do not mis-
understand them, I will venture to affirm that there is not a
member on this floor who will avow his willingness to enter into
such a stipulation. If mistaken, I desire to be corrected. No—I
am not. Whatever may be his views, no one, within these walls,
is yet prepared to give his sanction to such a measure—a measure
by which the peace of the country is to be exposed to a contingency beyond the control of our Government—by which the
great question of peace or war will be taken from the Representatives of the People—by which, instead of retaining that freedom
of action which we now possess, we shall bind ourselves, in a
certain event, to pursue a certain course, whatever those, to
whom the government of the country may then have been committed, shall think the honor or interest of the country may require—by which, in the language of the Father of his Country,
we "shall quit our own to stand on foreign ground." No—thank

Heaven—a policy so opposite to all the feelings of the American People; so adverse, as I firmly believe it to be, to its true interests, has no friend, at least no advocate on this floor. If, by any act of ours, we contribute to its adoption, it will be, (and I derive infinite satisfaction from the conviction,) through a mistaken belief that the measure of which I speak is not contemplated by the Executive. . . .

I will now, Mr. President, call the attention of the Senate to another view of this subject, to a question of the gravest character, and most deeply affecting the dearest interests of the country—a question growing out of considerations which have heretofore occupied the best minds, and interested the purest hearts our country has produced: "WOULD IT BE WISE IN US TO CHANGE OUR ESTABLISHED POLICY UPON THE SUBJECT OF POLITICAL CONNEXIONS WITH FOREIGN STATES?" The President has said, that, "to form alliances," is not among the motives of our attendance at the Congress. But what description of alliance does he mean? They are of various kinds, and of different extent. We are, at that Congress, to stipulate in some form, (and I care not in what,) that we will resist any attempt at colonization, by the Powers of Europe, in this hemisphere, (or within our own borders if you please,) and that, in the event of any interference on their part, in the struggle between Spain and the Spanish American States, we will make common cause with the latter in resisting it. To this end we have been invited, and upon these points we have promised that our Ministers shall have *full powers*. We must do this, or the whole affair becomes empty pageantry; which, though it may be the offspring of personal ambition, will assuredly terminate in national disgrace. Call it an "alliance," or whatever name you please, it is a *political connexion,* at war with the established policy of our Government. And is this a light matter? Sir, when it is proposed to subvert a fundamental principle in our foreign policy, in the support of which we stand ALONE among all the nations of the earth—which, commencing with our Government, is endeared to the People, and upon whose deep foundations has been erected the magnificent superstructure of unequalled national prosperity—it surely becomes those entrusted with the management of affairs, to pause, and weigh, with scrupulous exactness, the importance of the step.

John Randolph's Attack Upon
Adams and Clay, March 30, 1826*

Randolph, an extreme advocate of states' rights, bitterly opposed the Adams-Clay administration. Eccentric if not half mad, he was also eloquent and possessed great powers of sarcastic invective. He regarded Thomas Jefferson as a defector from the states' rights doctrine and referred to him as "St. Thomas of Cantingbury." Randolph was once asked who was the greatest orator he had ever heard. "A Negro slave, sir," he replied. "She was a mother, and her rostrum was the auction block."

. . . . Mr. R. repeated what he had then said, in reference to the message of the President. Who made him a judge of our usages? Who constituted him? He has been a professor, I understand—I wish he had left off the pedagogue when he got into the Executive Chair. Who made him the *censor morum* of this body? Will any one answer this question?—Yes or no?—Who?—Name the person. Above all, who made him the searcher of hearts, and gave him the right, by an inuendo black as hell, to blacken our motives?—blacken our motives—I did not say that, then—I was more under self command; I did not use such strong language—I said if he could borrow the eye of Omniscience himself; and look into every bosom here—if he could look into that most awful, calamitous, and tremendous of all possible gulfs, the naked unveiled human heart—stripped of all its coverings of self love—exposed naked as to the eye of God—I said if he could do that, he was not, as President of the United States, entitled to pass upon our motives, although he saw and knew them to be bad. I said, if he had converted us to the Catholic Religion, and was our Father Confessor, and every man in this House at the footstool of the confessional had confessed a bad motive to

* *Register of Debates*, 19 Cong., 1 sess., 401.

him, by the laws of his Church, as by this Constitution, above the law and above the church, he, as President of the United States, could not pass on our motives, though we had with our own lips told him our motives, and confessed they were bad. I said this then, and I say it now. Here I plant my foot—here I fling defiance right into his teeth, before the American People. Here I throw the gauntlet to him and the bravest of his compeers, to come forward and defend these miserable dirty lines: "Involving a departure, hitherto, so far as I am informed, without example, from that usage, and upon the motives for which, not being informed of them, I do not feel myself competent to decide!" Amiable modesty! I wonder we did not, all at once, fall in love with him; and agree, *una voce,* to publish our proceedings—except myself—for I quitted the Senate ten minutes before the vote was taken. I saw what was to follow—I knew the thing would not be done at all, or would be done unanimously. Therefore, in spite of the remonstrances of friends, I went away, not fearing that any one would doubt what my vote would have been, if I had staid. After twenty-six hours' exertion, it was time to give in. I was defeated, horse, foot, and dragoons —cut up—and clean broke down—by the coalition of Blifil and Black George—by the combination, unheard of till then, of the puritan with the black-leg. . . .

Thurlow Weed on the Masonic Order, April 15, 1828 *

Born in 1797, the son of a poor carter in the Catskill Mountains' region, Thurlow Weed grew up in the rural areas of eastern and central New York State. He became a newspaper apprentice in 1811, and subsequently a journeyman printer and country editor who lived a hand-to-mouth existence. In 1821 he moved to Rochester, New York, where he developed talents as a political manager. After Morgan's abduction, Weed became editor of the Anti-Masonic Enquirer. *This excerpt is a good example of his hard-hitting editorial style.*

We have observed all, and participated in some of the conflicts of opinion which have agitated this state for the last eighteen years. We have seen much of the zeal and heat of party. We have witnessed the madness and violence of faction. All these things have passed like clouds which occasionally, for a brief moment, obscure the bright heavens from our view. The passions which provoke these strifes, are soon subdued, and then all is calm and peaceful again. Not so with Free Masonry. The victim who incurs that *"vengeance,"* is instantly marked out for persecution and ruin. His reputation, property, and if the offence be of sufficient magnitude, his liberty and life are jeopardized. There is a temper and ferocity in the principles of masonry which causes humanity to shudder. Its oaths and rites mock all the duties of civilization. Its ceremonies and injunctions tend to unbridle the worst passions of our nature. It converts men who are peaceful and honest in every other respect, into turbulent and venomous wranglers. There is no tie, either of business, friendship or religion, that masonry will not sunder. There is no duty to society, to our country or to God, that it does not violate.

* *The Anti-Masonic Enquirer, April 15, 1828.*

The public will probably never learn the extent of the wrongs and injustice that masonry has inflicted upon the country. Few men, we venture to say, have passed thro' life, without feeling the blow of a mystic, concealed hand. The first evidence that we received of the relentlessness of masonry, was from a man whom we highly esteemed. It was a few days after Morgan's abduction. He remarked with peculiar emphasis, that Doct. Backus *"had better let the Morgan affair alone if he did not wish to loose his business and be ruined"* This opened our eyes. We knew that it was a masonic sentiment, and not the language of his own heart. Soon afterwards we learned with some surprise, that a clergyman, at a masonic festival, had given the following toast:—*"The enemies of Freemasonry—may they find a grave six feet due east and west, and six feet deep."* Illustrations of this nature came under our observation daily, and they soon led us to a correct understanding of masonry. The means by which they vindicated and sustained their Institution was now obvious. Its opponents were marked. Slander, persecution, oppression and ruin was their allotted fate. The mystic banditti acted together, and no individual arm could resist them. But the alarm is now general. The overt act has finally been committed. The principles, character and aims of Free Masonry are known. The people have heard the testimony and passed sentence upon the Institution. It can neither stand the test of scrutiny, or abide the shock of popular indignation. A deep, searching and determined sentiment of hostility has gone abroad against the Fraternity. Its votaries have united to resist this sentiment, but neither overgrown wealth, heretofore controlling influence, or mystic modes of warfare, can oppose the current that is sweeping this relic of barbarism from our land.—Every freeman's voice raised against Masonry, adds a mournful note to the knell, which, with unerring footsteps, is marshalling their Institution to the tomb.

Horace Greeley on the Values of Reform*

*Cantankerous, opinionated, often unpredictable, Horace Gree-
ley had two qualities of mind and character that brought him
eminence and fame. One of these was a capacity for expressing
in crystal clear fashion the ideas that teemed in his brain; the
other was a passion for making the world a better place than he
found it. He was always at heart a moralist. This passage tells
why he and others in nineteenth century America prized the
role of reformer.*

And, indeed, though the life of the Reformer may seem
rugged and arduous, it were hard to say considerately that any
other were worth living at all. Who can thoughtfully affirm that
the career of the conquering, desolating, subjugating warrior,
—of the devotee of Gold, or Pomp, or Sensual Joys; the Monarch
in his purple, the Miser by his chest, the wassailer over his bowl,
—is not a libel on Humanity and an offence against God? But
the earnest, unselfish Reformer—born into a state of darkness,
evil, and suffering, and honestly striving to replace these by
light, and purity, and happiness,—he may fall and die, as so
many have done before him, but he cannot fail. His vindication
shall gleam from the walls of his hovel, his dungeon, his tomb;
it shall shine in the radiant eyes of uncorrupted Childhood, and
fall in blessings from the lips of high-hearted, generous Youth.
As the untimely death of the good is our strongest moral assurance of the Resurrection, so the life wearily worn out in doubtful
and perilous conflict with Wrong and Woe is our most conclusive evidence that Wrong and Woe shall yet vanish forever.
Luther, dying amid the agonizing tears and wild consternation
of all Protestant Germany,—Columbus, borne in regal pomp to
his grave by the satellites of the royal miscreant whose ingrati-

* Greeley, Horace, *Recollections of a Busy Life* (New York, 1868),
   526–527.

tude and perfidy had broken his mighty heart,—Lovejoy, pouring out his life-blood beside the Press whose freedom he had so gallantly defended,—yes, and not less majestic, certainly not less tragic, than either, the lowly and lonely couch of the dying 'Uncle Tom,' whose whole life had been a brave and Christian battle against monstrous injustice and crime,—these teach us, at least, that all true greatness is ripened, and tempered, and proved, in life-long struggle against vicious beliefs, traditions, practices, institutions; and that not to have been a Reformer is not to have truly lived. Life is a bubble which any breath may dissolve; Wealth or Power a snow-flake, melting momently into the treacherous deep across whose waves we are floated on to our unseen destiny; but to have lived so that one less orphan is called to choose between starvation and infamy,—one less slave feels the lash applied in mere wantonness or cruelty,—to have lived so that some eyes of those whom Fame shall never know are brightened and others suffused at the name of the beloved one,—so that the few who knew him truly shall recognize him as a bright, warm, cheering presence, which was here for a season and left the world no worse for his stay in it,—this surely is to have really *lived*,—and not wholly in vain.

Difficulties in Transportation*

The hardships of communication in early nineteenth century America are well illustrated by this lively account of travel between New York City and Philadelphia in the winter of 1834. The author was an Irish comedian who toured the United States and gave stage performances in the principal cities. Power visited the United States four times between 1833 and 1840. In 1841, en route from New York to Liverpool, the steamship on which he was traveling went down with all on board.

The smoothness of the sea enabled our boat to make rapid way; and by a little after ten o'clock we were landed at Amboy, where we found the train awaiting our arrival. As we left our first stage, Hights-town, an accident occurred similar to the one I had, on my last trip southward, seen attended by such fearful consequences. We were proceeding, luckily at a moderate rate, when the axle of the engine-tender broke in two: the car occupied by myself and three others led the van, yet the first intimation we got of the break-down of our tender was our running foul of it with a bump that fairly unshipped us all, pitching the occupiers of the hind-seats head-on into the laps of those *vis-à-vis* to them. Happily, this was the worst of the present mischance: the engine was speedily arrested, a sound axle drawn from the near car to replace the one fractured, myself and the others belonging to the carriage thus hauled out of the line were stowed in, as supernumeraries, elsewhere, and, after a delay, of some forty minutes, off we bowled again.

Halting for a few moments at Borden-town, where the Delaware steamer waits when the river is practicable, it now spread away below us in a solid mass; and we pursued our journey by the railroad provided for such seasons so far as it was at this

* Power, Tyrone, *Impressions of America; During the Years 1833, 1834 and 1835,* 2 Vols. (Philadelphia, 1836), I, 110–113.

time completed, that is, for some eight or nine miles farther on. This point achieved, we discovered a group of the clumsy-looking stage-coaches of the country, to the number of twelve, each having a team of four horses, ready harnessed, standing amongst the trees below.

The cold was by this time extreme; bustle was the word, therefore, amongst all parties,—drivers, porters, and passengers; and in a quarter of an hour the transfer was completed, the luggage packed, the people arranged, and the caravan in motion. The place had quite a wild, lone, forest air; and it was a curious scene to view the bustle, and hear the noise, so uncongenial to the spot, and no less so to observe the coaches wheeling about amongst the trees as each Jehu sought to make the best of his way into the lane at a little distance.

Miserably uncomfortable as the driver's seat is before these machines, I, as usual where the course was strange to me, requested leave to share it with him. I had cast about to select a team; and was soon seated, well rolled in broadcloth and bear-skin, behind four dark bays that might have done credit to a better judgment.

We soon got into a very narrow lane, through which lay the first few miles. In this the ruts, or track, as it is here called, was over a foot deep: on either side grew trees, thick and low-branched; therefore my companion and I had as much as we could do to avoid broken heads and keep the track. I looked impatiently, after practising this dodging exercise some time, for the great road which the driver told me was "a bit farther a-head;" and at last we broke from our leafy shelter into it, but with little advantage that I could discover; for, though our heads were in less peril, our necks, I considered, required more especial looking after than ever. We certainly had here wider space, and a free choice of ruts or tracks, for there were several; but not one of them less profound than those we had hitherto ploughed through. In one or two places, the road was deeply trenched in every direction, and the edges of these cuts so glazed with new-formed ice that I expected my friend who was pilot would pass the box and back out. But no such thing, faith! he steered round all impediments as coolly as the wind that whistled through the half-frozen reins he held.

Finding one place in the road quite impassable, he cast his eyes about him for a moment, and chose the best part of the right bank; when, gathering up his leaders, he first vexed them a little with the whip, and then, putting them fairly at it, gained its summit, drove along for a hundred yards, crashing through a thick cover of shrubs growing breast-high, when having thus turned the impracticable bit of highway, he coolly dropped down into it again. On looking back, I saw each team taking in succession the line we had thus led over.

This was all performed clumsily enough, as far as appearance went, I allow; but cleverly and confidently, though with leaders hardly within calling distance: and four snaffle-bits, and a pig-whip, being the only means of dictation and control possessed by the coachman. The more I see of these queer Whips the better I like them: it assuredly is impossible to conceive any thing more uncoachman-like than their outward man; but they grapple with the constantly occurring difficulties of their strange work hardily and with superior intelligence.

I have seen a pass on the high-road between Albany and New York, where a descending driver perceiving that collision with a coming carriage was from the slippery condition of the hill unavoidable, and also being aware that such an event would be fatal to both parties, on the instant turned his horses to the near bank, and dashed down into the bed of the Mohawk, a descent of more than a hundred feet, as nearly perpendicular as may well be. His presence of mind and courage saved both his own passengers and those in the other vehicle, with the loss of his coach and one of his horses only. The man was publickly thanked and rewarded, and, I believe, yet wagons the same road.

One might almost back one of these crack hands to hunt a picked team of their own, across country, with the Melton hounds, coach and all; and if it was not for the *pace,* it would not be such a very bad bet either.

At Camden we quitted our vehicular mode of progressing, and took once more to the water, or rather to the ice, since it certainly ruled over the broad Delaware. In many places this was strong enough to sustain the weight of our little steamer's bow, and only gave way beneath repeated heavy blows of the iron-sheathed paddles.

After a hard fight we forced a path through all obstacles, and as the clock struck four were alongside the Chestnut Street wharf; having, notwithstanding the delays occasioned by our mishap and various changes, accomplished the hundred miles in exactly ten hours. . . .

Inauguration Day at the White House, March 4, 1829*

The account here given is by the intelligent and charming Mrs. Margaret B. Smith, an authoress of considerable note who was a leader in Washington society in the early Nineteenth Century.

. . . . But what a scene did we witness! The *Majesty of the People* had disappeared, and a rabble, a mob, of boys, negros, women, children, scrambling fighting, romping. What a pity what a pity! No arrangements had been made no police officers placed on duty and the whole house had been inundated by the rabble mob. We came too late. The President, after having been *literally* nearly pressed to death and almost suffocated and torn to pieces by the people in their eagerness to shake hands with Old Hickory, had retreated through the back way or south front and had escaped to his lodgings at Gadsby's. Cut glass and china to the amount of several thousand dollars had been broken in the struggle to get the refreshments, punch and other articles had been carried out in tubs and buckets, but had it been in hogsheads it would have been insufficient, ice-creams, and cake and lemonade, for 20,000 people, for it is said that number were there, tho' I think the estimate exaggerated. Ladies fainted, men were seen with bloody noses and such a scene of confusion took place as is impossible to describe,—those who got in could not get out by the door again, but had to scramble out of windows. At one time, the President who had retreated and retreated until he was pressed against the wall, could only be secured by a number of gentlemen forming round him and making a kind of barrier of their own bodies, and the pressure was so great that

* Smith, Margaret B., *The First Forty Years of Washington Society,* Gaillard Hunt, ed. (New York, 1908), 295–296.

Col Bomford who was one said that at one time he was afraid they should have been pushed down, or on the President. It was then the windows were thrown open, and the torrent found an outlet, which otherwise might have proved fatal. . . .

Van Buren Describes His Doubts in 1829 Concerning President Jackson*

There can be no doubt that Jackson's career in the White House had a shaky start. Some of the good aspects that came later were owing to canny advisers, but a major part of the credit must go to the President's native intelligence, honesty and courage.

I had been from the beginning aware of the strong preference which Swartwout's apparently chivalrous character and engaging manners had excited in the breast of the President, but I had not anticipated nor was I at all prepared to witness its influence in so grave a form. The result came upon me at a moment when my health was feeble and my spirits depressed, and, tho' I had resisted all the reasonings that had been given to me, since my appointment, by men whose friendship I did not in the least doubt, my mind was not at ease in regard to my position. I took my hat and walked the streets of Washington until a late hour of the night deliberating whether I ought not to adopt the advice I had received and to resign a post surrounded by such embarrassments, but I returned to my lodgings and retired to my bed with my views in respect to the path of duty painfully unsettled. I need scarcely say that it was not by the possible consequences of a single appointment, important as that undoubtedly was, that I was induced to raise the question which I canvassed with so much earnestness. The evils I apprehended from a step of that character might, after all, not occur, or might be limited in extent, but the feeling which so deeply disturbed me arose from an apprehension, excited by what had just occurred that

* Van Buren, *Autobiography,* 266.

my dissatisfied friends might prove to have been right in their belief that persons who could never possess my confidence had acquired an influence over the President's mind which would force me to an ultimate resignation if they retained it.

Andrew Jackson on Rotation in Office, December 8, 1829 *

In his first annual message to Congress Jackson explained his philosophy of officeholding. Note the points on which he rested his case.

There are, perhaps, few men who can for any great length of time enjoy office and power without being more or less under the influence of feelings unfavorable to the faithful discharge of their public duties. Their integrity may be proof against improper considerations immediately addressed to themselves, but they are apt to acquire a habit of looking with indifference upon the public interests and of tolerating conduct from which an unpracticed man would revolt. Office is considered as a species of property, and government rather as a means of promoting individual interests than as an instrument created solely for the service of the people. Corruption in some and in others a perversion of correct feelings and principles divert government from its legitimate ends and make it an engine for the support of the few at the expense of the many. The duties of all public officers are, or at least admit of being made, so plain and simple that men of intelligence may readily qualify themselves for their performance; and I can not but believe that more is lost by the long continuance of men in office than is generally to be gained by their experience. I submit, therefore, to your consideration whether the efficiency of the Government would not be promoted and official industry and integrity better secured by a general extension of the law which limits appointments to four years.

In a country where offices are created solely for the benefit of the people no one man has any more intrinsic right to official station than another. Offices were not established to give support

* Richardson, *Messages and Papers,* II, 448–449.

to particular men at the public expense. No individual wrong is, therefore, done by removal, since neither appointment to nor continuance in office is matter of right. The incumbent became an officer with a view to public benefits, and when these require his removal they are not to be sacrificed to private interests. It is the people, and they alone, who have a right to complain when a bad officer is substituted for a good one. He who is removed has the same means of obtaining a living that are enjoyed by the millions who ever held office. The proposed limitation would destroy the idea of property now so generally connected with official station, and although individual distress may be sometimes produced, it would, by promoting that rotation which constitutes a leading principle in the republican creed, give healthful action to the system.

Calhoun's Theory of Interposition, December, 1828 *

John C. Calhoun (1782–1850), South Carolina statesman, was of Scotch-Irish descent. An ardent nationalist in his early career, he became the South's leading champion of states' rights. He developed his doctrine of interposition in his famous South Carolina Exposition and Protest, *written in response to the tariff bill of 1828 and adopted by the South Carolina legislature in December of that year. Interposition was the method he proposed for combating the growing power of the North in Congress. Humorless, logical and intense, Calhoun was a tragic figure torn between his love for the Union and his love for the South.*

The committee have thus arrived, by what they deem conclusive reasoning, and the highest authority, at the constitutional and appropriate remedy against the unconstitutional oppression under which this, in common with the other staple States, labors, —and the menacing danger which now hangs over the liberty and happiness of our country;—and this brings them to the inquiry,—How is the remedy to be applied by the States? In this inquiry a question may be made,—whether a State can interpose its sovereignty through the ordinary Legislature, but which the committee do not deem it necessary to investigate. It is sufficient that plausible reasons may be assigned against this mode of action, if there be one (and there is one) free from all objections. Whatever doubts may be raised as to the question,—whether the respective Legislatures fully represent the sovereignty of the States for this high purpose, there can be none as to the fact that a Convention fully represents them for all purposes whatever. Its authority, therefore, must remove every objection

* Calhoun, John C., *Works,* R. K. Cralle, ed., 6 Vols. (New York, 1853–1856), VI, 44–45.

as to form, and leave the question on the single point of the right of the States to interpose at all. When convened, it will belong to the Convention itself to determine, authoritatively, whether the acts of which we complain be unconstitutional; and, if so, whether they constitute a violation so deliberate, palpable, and dangerous, as to justify the interposition of the State to protect its rights. If this question be decided in the affirmative, the Convention will then determine in what manner they ought to be declared null and void within the limits of the State; which solemn declaration, based on her rights as a member of the Union, would be obligatory, not only on her own citizens, but on the General Government itself; and thus place the violated rights of the State under the shield of the Constitution.

Webster's Apostrophe to the Union, January 27, 1830*

Daniel Webster (1782–1852), statesman and lawyer, was one of the greatest orators that America has produced. His intellectual power, coupled with an imposing presence, a deep voice, and an overwhelming eloquence evoked an immense response from his auditors. He was also extravagant and a heavy drinker. While he relied upon the vested interests of his time for financial assistance, there is no real evidence that he ever supported a political cause in which he did not believe. This magnificent peroration of his second reply to Hayne was a favorite recitation piece for nineteenth century schoolboys.

I have not allowed myself, sir, to look beyond the Union, to see what might lie hidden in the dark recess behind. I have not coolly weighed the chances of preserving liberty, when the bonds that unite us together shall be broken asunder. I have not accustomed myself to hang over the precipice of disunion, to see whether, with my short sight, I can fathom the depth of the abyss below; nor could I regard him as a safe counsellor, in the affairs of this Government, whose thoughts should be mainly bent on considering, not how the Union should be best preserved, but how tolerable might be the condition of the people when it shall be broken up and destroyed. While the Union lasts, we have high, exciting, gratifying prospects spread out before us, for us and our children. Beyond that, I seek not to penetrate the veil. God grant that, in my day, at least, that curtain may not rise. God grant that, on my vision, never may be opened what lies behind. When my eyes shall be turned to behold, for the last time, the sun in heaven, may I not see him shining on

* *Register of Debates,* 21 Cong., 1 sess., 80.

the broken and dishonored fragments of a once glorious Union; on States dissevered, discordant, belligerent; on a land rent with civil feuds, or drenched, it may be, in fraternal blood! Let their last feeble and lingering glance, rather, behold the gorgeous ensign of the republic, now known and honored throughout the earth, still full high advanced, its arms and trophies streaming in their original lustre, not a stripe erased or polluted, nor a single star obscured, bearing for its motto no such miserable interrogatory as, What is all this worth? Nor those other words of delusion and folly, Liberty first, and Union afterwards: but every where, spread all over in characters of living light, blazing on all its ample folds, as they float over the sea and over the land, and in every wind under the whole heavens, that other sentiment, dear to every true American heart—Liberty *and* Union, now and forever, one and inseparable!

Jackson Frustrates Calhoun*

This is Van Buren's graphic account of the dramatic events connected with the Jefferson's Day dinner, April 13, 1830. Being short of stature, Van Buren stood on a chair in order to have a better view of the reception given by the assembled company to Jackson's toast.

If Mr. Calhoun had been blessed in a larger degree with that greatness of soul which finds gratification in the acknowledgment of error—if he had said, openly and frankly, to his Northern brethren, I contributed to the introduction of this principle of protection into our legislation, believing that it would work to the general advantage, but experience has shown that your section of the Country derives advantages from it to which ours can never attain, that it, on the contrary, enures to our injury, and that it bears within itself facilities for its abuse not at first foreseen but which the love of money will always induce those interested to seize upon to make bad worse,—if with such declarations, the truth of which could not have been controverted, he had appealed to the justice and fraternal feelings and obligations of the North, perseveringly, in season and out of season, as Cobden appealed to the landed interest of England, he must have established for himself an enviable renown and for his cause the full assurance if not the immediate enjoyment of triumph. But he seemed to attach as much importance to being consistent as to being right—perhaps more, and a large and an unprofitable share of his time, I say it with deference to his conceded and unquestionable abilities, was spent in defending his successive positions by showing their consistency with each other. For these and other reasons he was indisposed to trust himself in the beaten track but sought for a more enterprising

* Van Buren, *Autobiography*, 412–415.

as well as a more striking course, one which would overtop all past discussions and processes relating to this subject. In this frame of mind his attention was naturally attracted to the memorable proceedings of Jefferson, Madison, Taylor of Caroline, Nicholas and their compeers of Virginia and Kentucky in respect to the alien and sedition laws, and his ambition, [was] as naturally, fired by reflection upon the fame and influence which they contribute even to those illustrious names. There is indeed no doubt that in addition to a sincere desire to relieve his section from an offensive tariff Mr. Calhoun's action was strongly stimulated by an eager emulation, on behalf of himself, his political friends and the State of South Carolina, of the honors awarded for those proceedings to the Statesmen and to the States I have named, and if he and his associates had adhered to the model by which they claimed to be guided that laudable ambition might have been abundantly gratified.

The anniversary of the birth-day of Thomas Jefferson, a most appropriate day if such had been his design, was selected for the commencement of the movements he had in view. The circumstances under which that day was, for the first time, seized upon for special commemoration; the extent of the preparations that were set on foot to give to the proposed festival extraordinary celebrity and the names of the men most prominent in those preparations contrasted with the ominous suddenness of their reverence for the memory of Jefferson combined to attract the attention of well informed bystanders and especially of those whose province it was to see to the faithful execution of the laws. Neither the President nor myself were inattentive observers of these signs, but made them the subject of frequent conversations. Weighing them in connection with the ambiguous intimations to me and morbid speculations of Mr. Calhoun in 1828, my mind was strongly impressed with a belief that some irregular and unauthorized proceedings were contemplated which might menace the stability of the Union. We were slow to believe that gentlemen with whom the Virginia principles of Ninety Eight had, until quite recently, been in very bad odor would have become on the instant cordially disposed to carry them out in the pure and catholic spirit in which they were originally adopted by that noble old Commonwealth, and the suspicion was there-

fore irresistible that it was designed to use the Virginia model
and a mask or stalking horse, rather than as an armor of defence; and we doubted the ability, even conceding the desire, of
some of Mr. Calhoun's associates, who shared largely in his
councils and who would be likely to take the lead when acts
of violence became the order of the day, to preserve sufficient
self control to keep themselves within the pale of the Constitution.

The subject was one which in every aspect required the utmost prudence and circumspection on the part of the President,
and having both accepted invitations to the Dinner we agreed
to meet first at his office to consider the course proper for him
to pursue on the occasion. Major Donelson was the only other
person present at that meeting and became fully advised of
every thing that was said and determined. The safety and propriety of virtually assuming by the character of the toast to be
proposed by the President that the proceedings and ceremonies
of the day were portentous of danger to the Union, and the
question whether any advantage might be anticipated from his
abrupt and defiant presentation of himself as its ready guardian
and Champion, were deliberately considered and affirmatively
decided. The form of his toast was accordingly agreed upon and
my own, which was expected to be the third volunteer, was so
constructed as to follow suit with his in spirit and tenor. Thus
armed we repaired to the dinner with feelings on the part of the
old Chief akin to those which would have animated his breast
if the scene of this preliminary skirmish in defence of the Union
had been the field of battle instead of the festive board.

Less knowledge of the political characters of the men engaged
in getting up this drama and a very small degree of sagacity in
the interpretation of their movements would have been enough
to satisfy us of the justice of our suspicions that the convocation
had been designed for the advancement of a particular measure—
that of nullification, rather than for the object that had been
avowed, to wit, the promotion of the general interests of our
party. The prominent features in the plan, as disclosed to the
perception of any well informed observer were 1st to identify
the principles of the measure yet in embryo—but fore-shadowed
in the toasts and proceedings—with those of Virginia in her

resistance to the alien and sedition laws, and thus to arouse in their support the enthusiasm of her representatives and people and of the advocates of the same principles in other States, and 2dly to conciliate Georgia with which State South Carolina had long nourished hostile relations, by professing to adopt principles upon which she had recently acted and by panegyrizing her public men.

A Virginian was placed in the Chair. Of the twenty-four regular toasts all but six or seven spoke of Virginia and of Jefferson—referring to, describing and embracing political principles which he had at different times avowed and to others which were known to constitute parts of the political creed of the State. Gen. Hayne, of South Carolina, spoke long and eloquently of the glorious stand taken by Virginia in regard to the alien and sedition laws, based the resistance made by his State to the protective policy upon the ground that the old republicans had always sustained and pointed particularly to the course pursued by the State of Georgia in defence of the same principles. Alluding to her controversy about the Indians he said that she had "planted upon her borders, under the guidance of one of the noblest of her sons, the standard of State-rights, and had achieved a great and glorious victory."

The President and Vice President were seated near the Chair; my position being at the foot of the second table, under the care of my subsequently warm friend Grundy whose feelings were then evidently enlisted on the side of the nullifiers altho' he took great care to avoid identifying himself with their doctrines. When the President was called upon for his toast I was obliged to stand on my chair to get a distinct view of what passed in his vicinity. There was no misunderstanding the effect it produced upon the company neither could any sentiment from another have occasioned a tithe of the sensation that was witnessed throughout the large assemblage. The veil was rent—the incantations of the night were exposed to the light of day. Gen. Hayne left his seat and ran to the President to beg him to insert the word "federal," so that the toast should read "OUR FEDERAL UNION—IT MUST BE PRESERVED!" This was an ingenious suggestion as it seemed to make the rebuke less pungent, although it really had no such effect. The President cheerfully assented because in point of fact the addition only made the toast what he had originally designed it to be—he having rewritten it, in the bustle and excitement of the occasion, on the back of the list of regular toasts which had been laid before him, instead of using the copy in his pocket, and having omitted that word inadvertently.

The affair proceeded but the feeling of the guests was plainly manifested that the game was blocked.

Jackson and the Supreme Court in the Cherokee Case, 1832*

Greeley's account, based on the memory of George N. Briggs, a contemporary Massachusetts Congressman, is made the more trustworthy by a letter Jackson wrote to his friend, John Coffee, April 7, 1832. In this letter the President declared that the Court could not coerce Georgia and that the decision had "fell still born."

A Cherokee named Tassells was arrested on a Georgia warrant for killing another Indian within the Cherokee territory. His counsel obtained a writ of error from a United States court, requiring Georgia to show cause why he should not be discharged and his case remitted to the Cherokee authorities, according to existing treaties. Georgia defied the writ and hung the Indian. And this finished the case.

Some time thereafter, two missionaries of the American Board among the Cherokees were arrested on a Georgia process, tried for, and convicted of, inciting the Indians to resist the policy of the State of Georgia designed to effect the expulsion of the Indians from her soil. They were of course sentenced to the State Prison. They appealed by writ of error to the courts of the United States, and the final adjudication thereon was had before the Supreme Court at Washington, the decision being pronounced by Chief Justice Marshall. It was entirely in favor of the missionaries and against the pretensions of Georgia, holding that the treaties between the United States and the Cherokees were valid and binding on all the States, and paramount to all State laws, according to that provision of the Federal Constitution which prescribes:

* Greeley, Horace, *The American Conflict,* 2 Vols. (Hartford, 1864–1866), I, 106.

"Article VI., § 2. This Constitution, and the laws of the United States which shall be made in pursuance thereof; and all *treaties* made, or which shall be made, under the authority of the United States, shall be the *supreme law of the land;* and the judges in every State shall be bound thereby, anything in the constitution or laws of any State to the contrary notwithstanding."

The attorneys for the missionaries sought to have this judgment enforced, but could not. General Jackson was President, and would do nothing of the sort. "Well: John Marshall has made his decision: *now let him enforce it!*" was his commentary on the matter. So the missionaries languished years in prison, and the Cherokees were finally (1838) driven into exile, in defiance of the mandate of our highest judicial tribunal. Georgia was permitted to violate the faith of solemn treaties and defy the adjudications of our highest court. South Carolina was put down in a similar attempt: for the will of Andrew Jackson, not the Constitution, was in those years "the supreme law of the land."

Jackson on States' Rights in Internal Improvements*

This statement, made May 27, 1830, shows Jackson as a man regardful of states' rights. He was not an extreme states' rights man, but on this particular point his position was arbitrary.

The constitutional power of the Federal Government to construct or promote works of internal improvement presents itself in two points of view—the first as bearing upon the sovereignty of the States within whose limits their execution is contemplated, if jurisdiction of the territory which they may occupy be claimed as necessary to their preservation and use; the second as asserting the simple right to appropriate money from the National Treasury in aid of such works when undertaken by State authority, surrendering the claim of jurisdiction. In the first view the question of power is an open one, and can be decided without the embarrassments attending the other, arising from the practice of the Government. Although frequently and strenuously attempted, the power to this extent has never been exercised by the Government in a single instance. It does not, in my opinion, possess it; and no bill, therefore, which admits it can receive my official sanction.

* Richardson, *Messages and Papers*, II, 484–485.

Vetoing the Maysville Road Bill, May 27, 1830*

Here Jackson develops his arguments against the Maysville Road bill, and on the general subject of internal improvements at federal expense. Compare these opinions with the record of the Jackson administration as given in the text.

Independently of the sanction given to appropriations for the Cumberland and other roads and objects under this power, the Administration of Mr. Madison was characterized by an act which furnishes the strongest evidence of his opinion of its extent. A bill was passed through both Houses of Congress and presented for his approval, "setting apart and pledging certain funds for constructing roads and canals and improving the navigation of water courses, in order to facilitate, promote, and give security to internal commerce among the several States and to render more easy and less expensive the means and provisions for the common defense." Regarding the bill as asserting a power in the Federal Government to construct roads and canals within the limits of the States in which they were made, he objected to its passage on the ground of its unconstitutionality, declaring that the assent of the respective States in the mode provided by the bill could not confer the power in question; that the only cases in which the consent and cession of particular States can extend the power of Congress are those specified and provided for in the Constitution, and superadding to these avowals his opinion that "a restriction of the power 'to provide for the common defense and general welfare' to cases which are to be provided for by the expenditure of money would still leave within the legislative power of Congress all the great and most important measures of Government, money being the ordinary and necessary means of carrying them into execution." I

* Richardson, *Messages and Papers,* II, 486–491.

have not been able to consider these declarations in any other point of view than as a concession that the right of appropriation is not limited by the power to carry into effect the measure for which the money is asked, as was formerly contended.

The views of Mr. Monroe upon this subject were not left to inference. During his Administration a bill was passed through both Houses of Congress conferring the jurisdiction and prescribing the mode by which the Federal Government should exercise it in the case of the Cumberland road. He returned it with objections to its passage, and in assigning them took occasion to say that in the early stages of the Government he had inclined to the construction that it had no right to expend money except in the performance of acts authorized by the other specific grants of power, according to a strict construction of them, but that on further reflection and observation his mind had undergone a change; that his opinion then was "that Congress have an unlimited power to raise money, and that in its appropriation they have a discretionary power, restricted only by the duty to appropriate it to purposes of common defense, and of general, not local, national, not State, benefit;" and this was avowed to be the governing principle through the residue of his Administration. The views of the last Administration are of such recent date as to render a particular reference to them unnecessary. It is well known that the appropriating power, to the utmost extent which had been claimed for it, in relation to internal improvements was fully recognized and exercised by it.

This brief reference to known facts will be sufficient to show the difficulty, if not impracticability, of bringing back the operations of the Government to the construction of the Constitution set up in 1798, assuming that to be its true reading in relation to the power under consideration, thus giving an admonitory proof of the force of implication and the necessity of guarding the Constitution with sleepless vigilance against the authority of precedents which have not the sanction of its most plainly defined powers; for although it is the duty of all to look to that sacred instrument instead of the statute book, to repudiate at all times encroachments upon its spirit, which are too apt to be effected by the conjuncture of peculiar and facilitating circumstances, it is not less true that the public good and the nature of our political institutions require that individual differences should yield to a well-settled acquiescence of the people and confederated authorities in particular constructions of the Constitution on doubtful points. Not to concede this much to the spirit of our institutions would impair their stability and defeat the objects of the Constitution itself.

The bill before me does not call for a more definite opinion upon the particular circumstances which will warrant appropriations of money by Congress to aid works of internal improvement, for although the extension of the power to apply money beyond that of carrying into effect the object for which it is appropriated has, as we have seen, been long claimed and exercised by the Federal Government, yet such grants have always been professedly under the control of the general principle that the works which might be thus aided should be "of a general, not local, national, not State," character. A disregard of this distinction would of necessity lead to the subversion of the federal system. That even this is an unsafe one, arbitrary in its nature, and liable, consequently, to great abuses, is too obvious to require the confirmation of experience. It is, however, sufficiently definite and imperative to my mind to forbid my approbation of any bill having the character of the one under consideration. I have given to its provisions all the reflection demanded by a just regard for the interests of those of our fellow-citizens who have desired its passage, and by the respect which is due to a coordinate branch of the Government, but I am not able to view it in any other light than as a measure of purely local character; or, if it can be considered national, that no further distinction between the appropriate duties of the General and State Governments need be attempted, for there can be no local interest that may not with equal propriety be denominated national. It has no connection with any established system of improvements; is exclusively within the limits of a State, starting at a point on the Ohio River and running out 60 miles to an interior town, and even as far as the State is interested conferring partial instead of general advantages.

Considering the magnitude and importance of the power, and the embarrassments to which, from the very nature of the thing, its exercise must necessarily be subjected, the real friends of internal improvement ought not to be willing to confide it to accident and chance. What is properly *national* in its character or otherwise is an inquiry which is often extremely difficult of solution. The appropriations of one year for an object which is considered national may be rendered nugatory by the refusal of a succeeding Congress to continue the work on the ground that it is local. No aid can be derived from the intervention of corporations. The question regards the character of the work, not that of those by whom it is to be accomplished. Notwithstanding the union of the Government with the corporation by whose immediate agency any work of internal improvement is carried on, the inquiry will still remain, Is it national and conducive to the benefit of the whole, or local and operating only to the advantage of a portion of the Union?

But although I might not feel it to be my official duty to interpose the Executive veto to the passage of a bill appropriating money for the construction of such works as are authorized by the States and are national in their character, I do not wish to be understood as expressing an opinion that it is expedient at this time for the General Government to embark in a system of this kind; and anxious that my constituents should be possessed of my views on this as well as on all other subjects which they have committed to my discretion, I shall state them frankly and briefly. Besides many minor considerations, there are two prominent views of the subject which have made a deep impression upon my mind, which, I think, are well entitled to your serious attention, and will, I hope, be maturely weighed by the people.

From the official communication submitted to you it appears that if no adverse and unforeseen contingency happens in our foreign relations and no unusual diversion be made of the funds set apart for the payment of the national debt we may look with confidence to its entire extinguishment in the short period of four years. The exent to which this pleasing anticipation is dependent upon the policy which may be pursued in relation to measures of the character of the one now under consideration must be obvious to all, and equally so that the events of the present session are well calculated to awaken public solicitude upon the subject. By the statement from the Treasury Department and those from the clerks of the Senate and House of Representatives, herewith submitted, it appears that the bills which have passed into laws, and those which in all probability will pass before the adjournment of Congress, anticipate appropriations which, with the ordinary expenditures for the support of Government, will exceed considerably the amount in the Treasury for the year 1830. Thus, whilst we are diminishing the revenue by a reduction of the duties on tea, coffee, and cocoa the appropriations for internal improvement are increasing beyond the available means of the Treasury. And if to this calculation be added the amounts contained in bills which are pending before the two Houses, it may be safely affirmed that $10,000,000 would not make up the excess over the Treasury receipts, unless the payment of the national debt be postponed and the means now pledged to that object applied to those enumerated in these bills. Without a well-regulated system of internal improvement this exhausting mode of appropriation is not likely to be avoided, and the plain consequence must be either a continuance of the national debt or a resort to additional taxes.

Although many of the States, with a laudible zeal and under the influence of an enlightened policy, are successfully applying their separate efforts to works of this character, the desire to enlist the aid of the General Government in the construction of such as from their nature ought to devolve upon it, and to which the means of the individual States are inadequate, is both rational and patriotic, and if that desire is not gratified now it does not follow that it never will be. The general intelligence and public spirit of the American people furnish a sure guaranty that at the proper time this policy will be made to prevail under circumstances more auspicious to its successful prosecution than those which now exist. But great as this object undoubtedly is, it is not the only one which demands the fostering care of the Government. The preservation and success of the republican principle rest with us. To elevate its character and extend its influence rank among our most important duties, and the best means to accomplish this desirable end are those which will rivet the attachment of our citizens to the Government of their choice by the comparative lightness of their public burthens and by the attraction which the superior success of its operations will present to the admiration and respect of the world. Through the favor of an overruling and indulgent Providence our country is blessed with general prosperity and our citizens exempted from the pressure of taxation, which other less favored portions of the human family are obliged to bear; yet it is true that many of the taxes collected from our citizens through the medium of imposts have for a considerable period been onerous. In many particulars these taxes have borne severely upon the laboring and less prosperous classes of the community, being imposed on the necessaries of life, and this, too, in cases where the burthen was not relieved by the consciousness that it would ultimately contribute to make us independent of foreign nations for articles of prime necessity by the encouragement of their growth and manufacture at home. They have been cheerfully borne because they were thought to be necessary to the support of Government and the payment of the debts unavoidably incurred in the acquisition and maintenance of our national rights and liberties. But have we a right to calculate on the same cheerful acquiescence when it is known that the necessity for their continuance would cease were it not for irregular, improvident, and unequal appropriations of the public funds? Will not the people demand, as they have a right to do, such a prudent system of expenditure as will pay the debts of the Union and authorize the reduction of every tax to as low a point as the wise observance of the necessity to protect that portion of our manufactures and labor whose prosperity is essential to our national safety and independence will allow? When the national debt is paid, the duties upon those articles which we do not raise may be repealed with safety, and still leave, I trust, without oppression to any section of the country, an accumulating surplus fund, which may be beneficially applied to some well-digested system of improvement.

Under this view the question as to the manner in which the Federal Government can or ought to embark in the construction of roads and canals, and the extent to which it may impose burthens on the people for these purposes, may be presented on its own merits, free of all disguise and of every embarrassment, except such as may arise from the Constitution itself. Assuming these suggestions to be correct, will not our constituents require the observance of a course by which they can be effected? Ought they not require it? With the best disposition to aid, as far as I can conscientiously, in furtherance of works of internal improvement, my opinion is that the soundest views of national policy at this time point to such a course. Besides the avoidance of an evil influence upon the local concerns of the country, how solid is the advantage which the Government will reap from it in the elevation of its character! How gratifying the effect of presenting to the world the sublime spectacle of a Republic of more than 12,000,000 happy people, in the fifty-fourth year of her existence, after having passed through two protracted wars—the one for the acquisition and the other for the maintenance of liberty— free from debt and with all her immense resources unfettered! What a salutary influence would not such an exhibition exercise upon the cause of liberal principles and free government throughout the world! Would we not ourselves find in its effect an additional guaranty that our political institutions will be transmitted to the most remote posterity without decay? A course of policy destined to witness events like these can not be benefited by a legislation which tolerates a scramble for appropriations that have no relation to any general system of improvement, and whose good effects must of necessity be very limited. In the best view of these appropriations, the abuses to which they lead far exceed the good which they are capable of promoting. They may be resorted to as artful expedients to shift upon the Government the losses of unsuccessful private speculation, and thus, by ministering to personal ambition and self-aggrandizement, tend to sap the foundations of public virtue and taint the administration of the Government with a demoralizing influence.

In the other view of the subject, and the only remaining one which it is my intention to present at this time, is involved the expediency of embarking in a system of internal improvement without a previous amendment of the Constitution explaining and defining the precise powers of the Federal Government over it. Assuming the right to appropriate money to aid in the construction of national works to be warranted by the cotemporaneous and continued exposition of the Constitution, its insufficiency for the successful prosecution of them must be admitted by all candid minds. If we look to usage to define the extent of the right, that will be found so variant and embracing so much that has been overruled as to involve the whole subject in great uncertainty and to render the execution of our respective duties in relation to it replete with difficulty and embarrassment. It is in regard to such works and the acquisition of additional territory that the practice obtained its first footing. In most, if not all, other disputed questions of appropriation the construction of the Constitution may be regarded as unsettled if the right to apply money in the enumerated cases is placed on the ground of usage.

This subject has been one of much, and, I may add, painful, reflection to me. It has bearings that are well calculated to exert a powerful influence upon our hitherto prosperous system of government, and which, on some accounts, may even excite despondency in the breast of an American citizen. I will not detain you with professions of zeal in the cause of internal improvements. If to be their friend is a virtue which deserves commendation, our country is blessed with an abundance of it, for I do not suppose there is an intelligent citizen who does not wish to see them flourish. But though all are their friends, but few, I trust, are unmindful of the means by which they should be promoted; none certainly are so degenerate as to desire their success at the cost of that sacred instrument with the preservation of which is indissolubly bound our country's hopes. If different impressions are entertained in any quarter; if it is expected that the people of this country, reckless of their constitutional obligations, will prefer their local interest to the principles of the Union, such expectations will in the end be disappointed; or if it be not so, then indeed has the world but little to hope from the example of free government. When an honest observance of constitutional compacts can not be obtained from communities like ours, it need not be anticipated elsewhere, and the cause in which there has been so much martyrdom, and from which so much was expected by the friends of liberty, may be abandoned, and the degrading truth that man is unfit for self-government admitted. And this will be the case if *expediency* be made a rule of construction in interpreting the Constitution. Power in no government could desire a better shield for the insidious advances which it is ever ready to make upon the checks that are designed to restrain its action.

Benton's Attack on the Bank, February 2, 1831*

Thomas Hart Benton (1782–1858) had been an early friend of Andrew Jackson. Their relationship was broken in 1813 by what can only be described as an armed brawl. After 1824, however, Benton became a fervent Jacksonian. His devotion to hard money and his opposition to bank notes gave him the sobriquet of "Old Bullion." He had great vanity and very little humor, but he was a fervent nationalist and a firm believer in democratic principles. He expressed the sentiments of many citizens when he delivered this crashing attack upon what he called "a moneyed oligarchy."

. . . . This power to disparage the notes of all other banks, is a power to injure them; and, added to all the other privileges of the Bank of the United States, is a power to destroy them! If any one doubts this assertion, let him read the answers of the President of the bank to the questions put to him by the Chairman of the Finance Committee. These answers are appended to the committee's report of the last session in favor of the bank, and expressly declare the capacity of the federal bank to destroy the State banks. The worthy Chairman [Mr. SMITH, of Md.] puts this question: "Has the bank at any time oppressed any of the State banks?" The President, [Mr. Biddle,] answers, as the whole world would answer to a question of oppression, that it never had; and this response was as much as the interrogatory required. But it did not content the President of the bank; he chose to go further, and to do honor to the institution over which he presided, by showing that it was as just and generous as it was rich and powerful. He, therefore, adds the following words, for which, as a seeker after evidence, to show the alarming

* *Register of Debates,* 21 Cong., 2 sess., 60–61, 77–78.

and dangerous character of the bank, I return him my unfeigned and pardonable thanks: "There are very few banks which might not have been destroyed by an exertion of the power of the bank."

This is enough! proof enough! not for me alone, but for all who are unwilling to see a moneyed domination set up—a moneyed oligarchy established in this land, and the entire Union subjected to its sovereign will. The power to destroy all other banks is admitted and declared; the inclination to do so is known to all rational beings to reside with the power! Policy may restrain the destroying faculties for the present; but they exist; and will come forth when interest prompts and policy permits. They have been exercised; and the general prostration of the Southern and Western banks attests the fact. They will be exercised, (the charter being renewed,) and the remaining State banks will be swept with the besom of destruction. Not that all will have their signs knocked down, and their doors closed up. Far worse than that to many of them. Subjugation, in preference to destruction, will be the fate of many. Every planet must have its satellites; every tyranny must have its instruments; every knight is followed by his squire; even the king of beasts, the royal quadruped, whose roar subdues the forest, must have a small, subservient animal to spring his prey. Just so of this imperial bank, when installed anew in its formidable and lasting power. The State banks, spared by the sword, will be passed under the yoke. They will become subordinate parts in the great machine. Their place, in the scale of subordination will be one degree below the rank of the legitimate branches; their business, to perform the work which it would be too disreputable for the legitimate branches to perform. This will be the fate of the State banks which are allowed to keep up their signs, and to set open their doors; and thus the entire moneyed power of the Union would fall into the hands of one single institution, whose inexorable and invisible mandates, emanating from a centre, would pervade the Union, giving or withholding money according to its own sovereign will and absolute pleasure. To a favored State, to an individual, or a class of individuals, favored by the central power, the golden stream of Pactolus would flow direct. To all such the munificent mandates of the High Directory would come, as the fabled god made his terrestrial visit of love and desire, enveloped in a shower of gold. But to others—to those not favored—and to those hated—the mandates of this same directory would be as "the planetary plague which hangs its poison in the sick air:" death to them! death to all who minister to their wants! What a state of things! What a condition for a confederacy of States! What grounds for alarm and terrible apprehension, when, in a confederacy of such vast extent, so many independent States, so many rival commercial cities, so much sectional jealousy, such violent political parties, such fierce contests for power, there should be but one moneyed tribunal before which all the rival and contending elements must appear! but one single dispenser of money, to which every citizen, every trader, every merchant, every manufacturer, every planter, every corporation, every city, every State, and the Federal Government itself, must apply, in every emergency, for the most indispensable loan! and this, in the face of the fact, that, in every contest for human rights, the great moneyed institutions of the world have uniformly been found on the side of kings and nobles, against the lives and liberties of the people. . . .

The gains of such an institution defy calculation. There is no example on earth to which to compare it. The bank of England, in its proudest days, would afford but an inadequate and imperfect exemplar; for the power of that bank was counterpoised, and its exactions limited, by the wealth of the landed aristocracy, and the princely revenues of great merchants and private bankers. But with us, there would be no counterpoise, no limit, no boundary, to the extent of exactions. All would depend upon the will of the supreme central directory. The nearest approach to the value of this terrific stock, which my reading has suggested, would be found in the history of the famous South Sea Company of the last century, whose shares rose in leaps from 100 to 500, and from 500 to 1,000 per cent.; but, with this immeasurable and lamentable difference that that was a bubble! this, a reality! And who would be the owners of this imperial stock? Widows and orphans, think you? as ostentatiously set forth in the report of last session? No, sir! a few great capitalists; aliens, denizens, naturalized subjects, and some native citizens, already the richest of the land, and who would avail themselves of their intelligences, and their means, to buy out the small stockholders on the eve of the renewal. These would be the owners. And where would all this power and money centre? In the great cities to the northeast, which have been for forty years, and that by force of federal legislation, the lion's den of Southern and Western money—that den into which all the tracks point inwards; from which the returning track of a solitary dollar has never yet been seen. And, this is the institution for which a renewed existence is sought— for which the votes of the people's representatives are claimed! But, no! Impossible! It cannot be! The bank is done. The arguments of 1816 will no longer apply. Times have changed; and the policy of the Republic changes with the times. The war made the bank; peace will unmake it. The baleful planet of fire, and blood, and every human woe, did bring that pestilence upon us; the benignant star of peace shall chase it away.

Jackson on the Bank of the United States, 1829–1831 *

Jackson's dislike of the Second Bank of the United States is clearly indicated in these excerpts from three annual messages to Congress, December 8, 1829, December 6, 1830 and December 6, 1831. Note that, especially in the second selection, he suggests modification of the Bank's charter. This would have been a statesmanlike approach to the problem, as both friends and foes of the Bank partially recognized; unfortunately, however, the institution became a political football.

December 8, 1829. The charter of the Bank of the United States expires in 1836, and its stockholders will most probably apply for a renewal of their privileges. In order to avoid the evils resulting from precipitancy in a measure involving such important principles and such deep pecuniary interests, I feel that I can not, in justice to the parties interested, too soon present it to the deliberate consideration of the Legislature and the people. Both the constitutionality and the expediency of the law creating this bank are well questioned by a large portion of our fellow-citizens, and it must be admitted by all that it has failed in the great end of establishing a uniform and sound currency.

Under these circumstances, if such an institution is deemed essential to the fiscal operations of the Government, I submit to the wisdom of the Legislature whether a national one, founded upon the credit of the Government and its revenues, might not be devised which would avoid all constitutional difficulties and at the same time secure all the advantages to the Government and country that were expected to result from the present bank.

December 6, 1830. The importance of the principles involved in the inquiry whether it will be proper to recharter the

* Richardson, *Messages and Papers,* II, 462, 528–529, 558.

Bank of the United States requires that I should again call the attention of Congress to the subject. Nothing has occurred to lessen in any degree the dangers which many of our citizens apprehend from that institution as at present organized. In the spirit of improvement and compromise which distinguishes our country and its institutions it becomes us to inquire whether it be not possible to secure the advantages afforded by the present bank through the agency of a Bank of the United States so modified in its principles and structure as to obviate constitutional and other objections.

It is thought practicable to organize such a bank with the necessary officers as a branch of the Treasury Department, based on the public and individual deposits, without power to make loans or purchase property, which shall remit the funds of the Government, and the expense of which may be paid, if thought advisable, by allowing its officers to sell bills of exchange to private individuals at a moderate premium. Not being a corporate body, having no stockholders, debtors, or property, and but few officers, it would not be obnoxious to the constitutional objections which are urged against the present bank; and having no means to operate on the hopes, fears, or interests of large masses of the community, it would be shorn of the influence which makes that bank formidable. The States would be strengthened by having in their hands the means of furnishing the local paper currency through their own banks, while the Bank of the United States, though issuing no paper, would check the issues of the State banks by taking their notes in deposit and for exchange only so long as they continue to be redeemed with specie. In times of public emergency the capacities of such an institution might be enlarged by legislative provisions.

These suggestions are made not so much as a recommendation as with a view of calling the attention of Congress to the possible modifications of a system which can not continue to exist in its present form without occasional collisions with the local authorities and perpetual apprehensions and discontent on the part of the States and the people.

December 6, 1831. Entertaining the opinions heretofore expressed in relation to the Bank of the United States as at present organized, I felt it my duty in my former messages

frankly to disclose them, in order that the attention of the
Legislature and the people should be seasonably directed to that
important subject, and that it might be considered and finally
disposed of in a manner best calculated to promote the ends of
the Constitution and subserve the public interests. Having thus
conscientiously discharged a constitutional duty, I deem it proper
on this occasion, without a more particular reference to the
views of the subject then expressed, to leave it for the present
to the investigation of an enlightened people and their representatives.

Jackson on Banks and Bank Paper*

In this letter to Thomas Hart Benton, written probably in June, 1832, President Jackson states the reasons for his opposition to the Bank of the United States, and for his dislike of state banks that issue paper money.

The charge made of my being friendly to the Bank of the united states Bank until I found it could not be used for my political purposes, when I turned against it, is one of the foulest and basest calumnies ever uttered—all who know any thing about me know it to be such.

I have always been opposed to it upon constitutional grounds as well as expediency and policy—there was a time when the arristocratic few in Nashville made a movement to obtain a Branch there. judge White then being a member of the Legislature, to forestall this movement introduced a bill which passed into a law imposing a penalty of $50,000, on any bank, that would assume banking business within the state, not chartered by the legislature thereof. this put down that movement for years untill that law was repealed by a secrete and combined movement of the arristocracy. I was absent at the time, returned to [*mut.*] Washington [*mut.*] the night previous to its final passage by the senate, sent for the speaker, Robert C. Foster, Expostulated with him upon the danger of repealing that law, that the intention was to introduce a branch of the united states Bank, which would drain the state of its specie to the amount of its profits for the support and prosperity of other places, and the Lords, Dukes, and Ladies of foreign countries who held the greater part of its stock—no individual but one in our state owning any of its stock. my admonitions had no effect and the repealing law was passed, I think by one of a majority—this Mr Foster can vouch for. immediately thereafter a memorial was got up praying the

* Jackson, *Correspondence*, IV, 445–446.

President and directors to extend a branch to Nashville, this presented to me, which I preremptoraly refused to sign. soon afterwards Genl Cadwaleder came on as the agent of the Bank, he dinned with me, my oposition was open and known to every one, and major William B. Lewis who is now in the city, and judge Grundy can vouch for my hostility against the u.s. Bank on all and every occasion. Soon thereafter a Branch was established at Nashville, when a recommendation was presented for two Gentlemen for President and Cashier, with a request, as I was known in my public character to the President and directors of the mother Bank, and knew the Gentlemen to be capable and worthy of confidence, that I would recommend them for the office. The Branch being established at Nashville, and the people liable to be cursed with all its attendant evils and corruption, I with pleasure recommended them, believing that they were honest, and fit and would direct the institution well and as far as they had controle would not wield it to corrupt political principles. this recommendation, as I have been informed has been used to prove my approbation—nothing more false, or ridiculous. When organizing the Government of Florida, I was applied to by the mercantile interest in that place to aid them in procuring a branch there. my views were fully given to them of the impolicy of the measure, and my hostility to that institution, but upon their solicitation I forwarded, as Governor of the Territory, their memorial to the President of the Bank—this also has been aduced as evidence of my approval of the u.s. Bank—there can be nothing more unfounded and unjust. my duty as the Temporary Governor of Florida was to make known the wants and wishes of the people of the Territory—officially I did so by forwarding at their request their memorial. I have been opposed always to the Bank of the u.s. as well as all state Banks of paper issues, upon constitutional grounds believing as I do, that congress has no constitutional power to grant a charter and the states are prohibitted from granting charters of paper issues—their powers retained, are to charter Banks of deposit discount and exchange.

The Bank Veto Attacks Privilege, July 10, 1832*

This is the celebrated passage from the veto message in which Jackson presents his administration as the defender of "the farmers, mechanics and laborers" against the machinations of the wealthy and powerful. Note especially the President's concept of the proper function of the national government.

It is to be regretted that the rich and powerful too often bend the acts of government to their selfish purposes. Distinctions in society will always exist under every just government. Equality of talents, of education, or of wealth can not be produced by human institutions. In the full enjoyment of the gifts of Heaven and the fruits of superior industry, economy, and virtue, every man is equally entitled to protection by law; but when the laws undertake to add to these natural and just advantages artificial distinctions, to grant titles, gratuities, and exclusive privileges, to make the rich richer and the potent more powerful, the humble members of society—the farmers, mechanics, and laborers—who have neither the time nor the means of securing like favors to themselves, have a right to complain of the injustice of their Government. There are no necessary evils in government. Its evils exist only in its abuses. If it would confine itself to equal protection, and, as Heaven does its rains, shower its favors alike on the high and the low, the rich and the poor, it would be an unqualified blessing. In the act before me there seems to be a wide and unnecessary departure from these just principles.

Nor is our Government to be maintained or our Union preserved by invasions of the rights and powers of the several States. In thus attempting to make our General Government strong we make it weak. Its true strength consists in leaving individuals

* Richardson, *Messages and Papers*, II, 590–591.

and States as much as possible to themselves—in making itself
felt, not in its power, but in its beneficence; not in its control,
but in its protection; not in binding the States more closely to
the center, but leaving each to move unobstructed in its proper
orbit.

Experience should teach us wisdom. Most of the difficulties our
Government now encounters and most of the dangers which im-
pend over our Union have sprung from an abandonment of the
legitimate objects of Government by our national legislation,
and the adoption of such principles as are embodied in this act.
Many of our rich men have not been content with equal protection and equal benefits, but have besought us to make them
richer by act of Congress. By attempting to gratify their desires
we have in the results of our legislation arrayed section against
section, interest against interest, and man against man, in a
fearful commotion which threatens to shake the foundations of
our Union. It is time to pause in our career to review our
principles, and if possible revive that devoted patriotism and
spirit of compromise which distinguished the sages of the Revolution and the fathers of our Union. If we can not at once, in
justice to interests vested under improvident legislation, make
our Government what it ought to be, we can at least take a
stand against all new grants of monopolies and exclusive privileges, against any prostitution of our Government to the advancement of the few at the expense of the many, and in favor of compromise and gradual reform in our code of laws and system of
political economy.

South Carolina Ordinance of Nullification, November 24, 1832 *

The convention summoned by Governor Hamilton adopted this ordinance by a vote of 136 to 26. The first seven signatures were those of convention members who were Revolutionary War veterans. The rest of the delegates signed in alphabetical order.

AN ORDINANCE,

To Nullify certain Acts of the Congress of the United States, Purporting to be Laws, laying Duties and Imposts on the Importation of Foreign Commodities.

Whereas, the Congress of the United States, by various acts, purporting to be acts laying duties and imposts on foreign imports, but in reality intended for the protection of domestic manufactures, and the giving of bounties to classes and individuals engaged in particular employments, at the expense and to the injury and oppression of other classes and individuals, and by wholly exempting from taxation certain foreign commodities, such as are not produced or manufactured in the United States, to afford a pretext for imposing higher and excessive duties on articles similar to those intended to be protected, hath exceeded its just powers under the Constitution, which confers on it no authority to afford such protection, and hath violated the true meaning and intent of the Constitution, which provides for equality in imposing the burdens of taxation upon the several States and portions of the Confederacy. *And whereas,* the said Congress, exceeding its just power to impose taxes and collect revenue for the purpose of effecting and accomplishing the specific objects and purposes which the Constitution of the United

* *Statutes at Large of South Carolina,* I, 329–331.

States authorizes it to effect and accomplish, hath raised and collected unnecessary revenue, for objects unauthorized by the Constitution—

We, therefore, the People of the State of South Carolina, in Convention assembled, do Declare and Ordain, and it is hereby Declared and Ordained, That the several acts and parts of acts of the Congress of the United States, purporting to be laws for the imposing of duties and imposts on the importation of foreign commodities, and now having actual operation and effect within the United States, and more especially an act entitled "an act in alteration of the several acts imposing duties on imports," approved on the nineteenth day of May, one thousand eight hundred and twenty-eight, and also, an act entitled "an act to alter and amend the several acts imposing duties on imports," approved on the fourteenth day of July, one thousand eight hundred and thirty-two, are unauthorized by the Constitution of the United States, and violate the true meaning and intent thereof, and are null, void, and no law, nor binding upon this State, its officers, or citizens; and all promises, contracts and obligations, made or entered into, or to be made or entered into, with purpose to secure the duties imposed by said acts, and all judicial proceedings which shall be hereafter had in affirmance thereof, are, and shall be held, utterly null and void.

And it is further Ordained, That it shall not be lawful for any of the constituted authorities, whether of this State, or of the United States, to enforce the payment of duties imposed by the said acts, within the limits of this State; but it shall be the duty of the Legislature to adopt such measures and pass such acts as may be necessary to give full effect to this Ordinance, and to prevent the enforcement and arrest the operation of the said acts and parts of acts of the Congress of the United States, within the limits of this State, from and after the first day of February next; and the duty of all other constituted authorities, and of all persons residing or being within the limits of this State, and they are hereby required and enjoined, to obey and give effect to this Ordinance, and such acts and measures of the Legislature as may be passed or adopted in obedience thereto.

And it is further Ordained, That in no case of law or equity, decided in the Courts of this State, wherein shall be drawn in question the authority of this Ordinance, or the validity of such act or acts of the Legislature as may be passed for the purpose of giving effect thereto, or the validity of the aforesaid acts of Congress, imposing duties, shall any appeal be taken or allowed to the Supreme Court of the United States; nor shall any copy of the record be permitted or allowed for that purpose; and if any such appeal shall be attempted to be taken, the Courts of this State shall proceed to execute and enforce their judgments, according to the laws and usages of the State, without reference to such attempted appeal, and the person or persons attempting to take such appeal may be dealt with as for a contempt of the Court.

And it is further Ordained, That all persons now holding any office of honor, profit or trust, civil or military, under this State, (members of the Legislature excepted) shall, within such time, and in such manner as the Legislature shall prescribe, take an oath, well and truly to obey, execute and enforce this Ordinance, and such act or acts of the Legislature as may be passed in pursuance thereof, according to the true intent and meaning of the same; and on the neglect or omission of any such person or persons so to do, his or their office or offices shall be forthwith vacated, and shall be filled up as if such person or persons were dead or had resigned; and no person hereafter elected to any office of honor, profit or trust, civil or military, (members of the Legislature excepted) shall, until the Legislature shall otherwise provide and direct, enter on the execution of his office, or be in any respect competent to discharge the duties thereof, until he shall, in like manner, have taken a similar oath; and no juror shall be impannelled in any of the Courts of this State, in any cause in which shall be in question this Ordinance, or any act of the Legislature passed in pursuance thereof, unless he shall first, in addition to the usual oath, have taken an oath that he will well and truly obey, execute, and enforce this Ordinance, and such act or acts of the Legislature as may be passed to carry the same into operation and effect, according to the true intent and meaning thereof.

And we, the People of South Carolina, to the end that it may be fully understood by the Government of the United States, and the People of the co-States, that we are determined to maintain this, our Ordinance and Declaration, at every hazard, *Do further Declare,* that we will not submit to the application of force, on the part of the Federal Government, to reduce this State to obedience; but that we will consider the passage, by Congress, of any act authorizing the employment of a military or naval force against the State of South Carolina, her constituted authorities or citizens, or any act abolishing or closing the ports of this State, or any of them, or otherwise obstructing the free ingress and egress of vessels to and from the said ports, or any other act, on the part of the Federal Government, to coerce the State, shut up her ports, destroy or harrass her commerce, or to enforce the acts hereby declared to be null and void, otherwise than through the civil tribunals of the country, as inconsistent with the longer continuance of South Carolina in the Union: and that the People of this State will thenceforth hold themselves absolved from all further obligation to maintain or preserve their political connexion with the people of the other States, and will forthwith proceed to organize a separate Government, and to do all other acts and things which sovereign and independent States may of right do.

Done in Convention, at Columbia, the twenty-fourth day of November, in the year of our Lord one thousand eight hundred and thirty-two, and in the fifty-seventh year of the Declaration of the Independence of the United States of America.

Jackson on the Tariff, December 4, 1832*

Note here the skill with which the President develops his argument. He opposes high protection arbitrarily imposed but favors a "judicious" tariff. Within these broad guide lines he leaves the framing of the bill to Congress. This selection is from his fourth annual message to the national legislature.

Long and patient reflection has strengthened the opinions I have heretofore expressed to Congress on this subject, and I deem it my duty on the present occasion again to urge them upon the attention of the Legislature. The soundest maxims of public policy and the principles upon which our republican institutions are founded recommend a proper adaptation of the revenue to the expenditure, and they also require that the expenditure shall be limited to what, by an economical administration, shall be consistent with the simplicity of the Government and necessary to an efficient public service. In effecting this adjustment it is due, in justice to the interests of the different States, and even to the preservation of the Union itself, that the protection afforded by existing laws to any branches of the national industry should not exceed what may be necessary to counteract the regulations of foreign nations and to secure a supply of those articles of manufacture essential to the national independence and safety in time of war. If upon investigation it shall be found, as it is believed it will be, that the legislative protection granted to any particular interest is greater than is indispensably requisite for these objects, I recommend that it be gradually diminished, and that as far as may be consistent with these objects the whole scheme of duties be reduced to the revenue standard as soon as a just regard to the faith of the Government and to the preservation of the large capital invested in establishments of domestic industry will permit.

* Richardson, *Messages and Papers,* II, 597–598.

That manufactures adequate to the supply of our domestic consumption would in the abstract be beneficial to our country there is no reason to doubt, and to effect their establishment there is perhaps no American citizen who would not for awhile be willing to pay a higher price for them. But for this purpose it is presumed that a tariff of high duties, designed for perpetual protection, has entered into the minds of but few of our statesmen. The most they have anticipated is a temporary and, generally, incidental protection, which they maintain has the effect to reduce the price by domestic competition below that of the foreign article. Experience, however, our best guide on this as on other subjects, makes it doubtful whether the advantages of this system are not counterbalanced by many evils, and whether it does not tend to beget in the minds of a large portion of our countrymen a spirit of discontent and jealousy dangerous to the stability of the Union.

What, then, shall be done? Large interests have grown up under the implied pledge of our national legislation, which it would seem a violation of public faith suddenly to abandon. Nothing could justify it but the public safety, which is the supreme law. But those who have vested their capital in manufacturing establishments can not expect that the people will continue permanently to pay high taxes for their benefit, when the money is not required for any legitimate purpose in the administration of the Government. Is it not enough that the high duties have been paid as long as the money arising from them could be applied to the common benefit in the extinguishment of the public debt?

Those who take an enlarged view of the condition of our country must be satisfied that the policy of protection must be ultimately limited to those articles of domestic manufacture which are indispensable to our safety in time of war.

The "Proclamation to the People of South Carolina," December 10, 1832*

These excerpts are a superb illustration of Jackson's nationalism. Note the skill with which he portrays the risks South Carolina would run by separation from the Union. The reference to "civil discord" conjures up a picture of the slave rebellions that haunted the imaginations of many southerners, especially those to whom the Proclamation was addressed.

This, then, is the position in which we stand: A small majority of the citizens of one State in the Union have elected delegates to a State convention; that convention has ordained that all the revenue laws of the United States must be repealed, or that they are no longer a member of the Union. The governor of that State has recommended to the legislature the raising of an army to carry the secession into effect, and that he may be empowered to give clearances to vessels in the name of the State. No act of violent opposition to the laws has yet been committed, but such a state of things is hourly apprehended. And it is the intent of this instrument to *proclaim,* not only that the duty imposed on me by the Constitution "to take care that the laws be faithfully executed" shall be performed to the extent of the powers already vested in me by law, or of such others as the wisdom of Congress shall devise and intrust to me for that purpose, but to warn the citizens of South Carolina who have been deluded into an opposition to the laws of the danger they will incur by obedience to the illegal and disorganizing ordinance of the convention; to exhort those who have refused to support it to persevere in their determination to uphold the Constitution and laws of their country; and to point out to all the perilous situation into which the good people of that State

* Richardson, *Messages and Papers,* II, 652, 654–655.

have been led, and that the course they are urged to pursue is one of ruin and disgrace to the very State whose rights they affect to support. . . .

Contemplate the condition of that country of which you still form an important part. Consider its Government, uniting in one bond of common interest and general protection so many different States, giving to all their inhabitants the proud title of *American citizen,* protecting their commerce, securing their literature and their arts, facilitating their intercommunication, defending their frontiers, and making their name respected in the remotest parts of the earth. Consider the extent of its territory, its increasing and happy population, its advance in arts which render life agreeable, and the sciences which elevate the mind! See education spreading the lights of religion, morality, and general information into every cottage in this wide extent of our Territories and States. Behold it as the asylum where the wretched and the oppressed find a refuge and support. Look on this picture of happiness and honor and say, *We too are citizens of America.* Carolina is one of these proud States; her arms have defended, her best blood has cemented, this happy Union. And then add, if you can, without horror and remorse, This happy Union we will dissolve; this picture of peace and prosperity we will deface; this free intercourse we will interrupt; these fertile fields we will deluge with blood; the protection of that glorious flag we renounce; the very name of Americans we discard. And for what, mistaken men? For what do you throw away these inestimable blessings? For what would you exchange your share in the advantages and honor of the Union? For the dream of a separate independence—a dream interrupted by bloody conflicts with your neighbors and a vile dependence on a foreign power. If your leaders could succeed in establishing a separation, what would be your situation? Are you united at home? Are you free from the apprehension of civil discord, with all its fearful consequences? Do our neighboring republics, every day suffering some new revolution or contending with some new insurrection, do they excite your envy? But the dictates of a high duty oblige me solemnly to announce that you can not succeed. The laws of the United States must be executed. I have no discretionary power on the subject; my duty is emphatically pronounced in the Constitution. Those who told you that you might peaceably prevent their execution deceived you; they could not have been deceived themselves. They know that a forcible opposition could alone prevent the execution of the laws, and they know that such opposition must be repelled. Their object is disunion. But be not deceived by names. Disunion by armed force is *treason*. Are you really ready to incur its guilt? If you are, on the heads of the instigators of the act be the dreadful consequences; on their heads be the dishonor, but on yours may fall the punishment. On your unhappy State will inevitably fall all the evils of the conflict you force upon the Government of your country. It can not accede to the mad project of disunion, of which you would be the first victims. Its First Magistrate can not, if he would, avoid the performance of his duty.

READING NO. 38

The Force Bill, March 2, 1833 *

The provisions of this measure here cited show the national government's intent to compel obedience to federal law in the recalcitrant state. The Force Bill excited great wrath among the South Carolinians, who called it "The Bloody Bill."

President authorized to direct site of custom-house to be changed.

Be it enacted by the Senate and House of Representatives of the United States of America, in Congress assembled, That whenever, by reason of unlawful obstructions, combinations, or assemblages of persons, it shall become impracticable, in the judgment of the President, to execute the revenue laws, and collect the duties on imports in the ordinary way, in any collection district, it shall and may be lawful for the President to direct that the custom-house for such district be established and kept in any secure place within some port or harbour of such district, either upon land

Vessels to be detained, &c.

or on board any vessel; and, in that case, it shall be the duty of the collector to reside at such place, and there to detain all vessels and cargoes arriving within the said district until the duties imposed on said cargoes, by law, be paid in cash, deducting interest according to existing laws; and

Custody of detained vessels, &c.

in such cases it shall be unlawful to take the vessel or cargo from the custody of the proper officer of the customs, unless by process from some court of the United States; and in case of any attempt otherwise to take such vessel or cargo by any force, or combination, or assemblage of persons too great to be overcome by the officers of

* *The Public Statutes at Large of the United States,* IV, 632, 634–635.

the customs, it shall and may be lawful for the President of the United States, or such person or persons as he shall have empowered for that purpose, to employ such part of the land or naval forces, or militia of the United States, as may be deemed necessary for the purpose of preventing the removal of such vessel or cargo, and protecting the officers of the customs in retaining the custody thereof. . . .

President to issue proclamation and to suppress obstructions to the laws by military force or other means, within any state.

SEC. 5. *And be it further enacted,* That whenever the President of the United States shall be officially informed, by the authorities of any state, or by a judge of any circuit or district court of the United States, in the state, that, within the limits of such state, any law or laws of the United States, or the execution thereof, or of any process from the courts of the United States, is obstructed by the employment of military force, or by any other unlawful means, too great to be overcome by the ordinary course of judicial proceeding, or by the powers vested in the marshal by existing laws, it shall be lawful for him, the President of the United States, forthwith to issue his proclamation, declaring such fact or information, and requiring all such military and other force forthwith to disperse; and if at any time after issuing such proclamation, any such opposition or obstruction shall be made, in the manner or by the means aforesaid, the President shall be, and hereby is, authorized, promptly to employ such means to suppress the same, and to cause the said laws or process to be duly executed, as are authorized and provided in the cases therein mentioned by the act of the twenty-eighth of February, one thousand seven hundred and ninety-five, entitled "An act to provide for calling forth the militia to execute the laws of the Union, suppress insurrections, repel invasions, and to repeal the act now in force for that purpose;" and also, by the

Act of Feb. 28, 1795, ch. 36.

Act of
March 3,
1807, ch. 39.

act of the third of March, one thousand eight hundred and seven, entitled "An act authorizing the employment of the land and naval forces of the United States in cases of insurrection."

Places of
confinement.

SEC. 6. *And be it further enacted,* That in any state where the jails are not allowed to be used for the imprisonment of persons arrested or committed under the laws of the United States, or where houses are not allowed to be so used, it shall and may be lawful for any marshal, under the direction of the judge of the United States for the proper district, to use other convenient places, within the limits of said state, and to make such other provision as he may deem expedient and necessary for that purpose.

Judges to issue writs of habeas corpus.

SEC. 7. *And be it further enacted,* That either of the justices of the Supreme Court, or a judge of any district court of the United States, in addition to the authority already conferred by law, shall have power to grant writs of habeas corpus in all cases of a prisoner or prisoners, in jail or confinement, where he or they shall be committed or confined on, or by any authority or law, for any act done, or omitted to be done, in pursuance of a law of the United States, or any order, process, or decree, of any judge or court thereof, any thing in any act of Congress to the contrary not-

Penalty for
neglect or refusal to obey
the same.

withstanding. And if any person or persons to whom such writ of habeas corpus may be directed, shall refuse to obey the same, or shall neglect or refuse to make return, or shall make a false return thereto, in addition to the remedies already given by law, he or they shall be deemed and taken to be guilty of a misdemeanor, and shall, on conviction before any court of competent jurisdiction, be punished by fine, not exceeding one thousand dollars, and by imprisonment, not exceeding six months, or by either, according to the nature and aggravation of the case.

Provisions of the first and fifth sections limited.

SEC. 8. *And be it further enacted,* That the several provisions contained in the first and fifth sections of this act, shall be in force until the end of the next session of Congress, and no longer.

APPROVED, March 2, 1833.

South Carolina Nullifies the Force Bill, March 18, 1833*

This was the state's final gesture of defiance in the crisis of 1833. It was only a gesture, for the state accepted Clay's compromise tariff, but the whole affair had long range significance. South Carolinians continued to boast of the part they had played and to maintain the "rights" of nullification and secession. Many citizens of the state held from then on that the interests of North and South were directly opposed, and that this was especially true in regard to slavery.

AN ORDINANCE,

To Nullify an Act of the Congress of the United States, entitled "An Act further to provide for the Collection of Duties on Imports," commonly called the Force Bill.

We, the People of the State of South Carolina in Convention assembled, do *Declare and Ordain,* that the Act of the Congress of the United States, entitled "An Act further to provide for the collection of duties on imports," approved the 2d day of March, 1833, is unauthorized by the Constitution of the United States, subversive of that Constitution, and destructive of public liberty; and that the same is, and shall be deemed, null and void, within the limits of this State; and it shall be the duty of the Legislature, at such time as they may deem expedient, to adopt such measures and pass such acts as may be necessary to prevent the enforcement thereof, and to inflict proper penalties on any person who shall do any act in execution or enforcement of the same within the limits of this State.

We do further Ordain and Declare, That the allegiance of the

* *Statutes at Large of South Carolina,* I, 400–401.

citizens of this State, while they continue such, is due to the said State; and that obedience only, and not allegiance, is due by them to any other power or authority, to whom a controul over them has been, or may be delegated by the State; and the General Assembly of the said State is hereby empowered, from time to time, when they may deem it proper, to provide for the administration to the citizens and officers of the State, or such of the said officers as they may think fit, of suitable oaths or affirmations, binding them to the observance of such allegiance, and abjuring all other allegiance; and, also, to define what shall amount to a violation of their allegiance, and to provide the proper punishment for such violation.

Done in Convention, at Columbia, the eighteenth day of March, in the year of our Lord one thousand eight hundred and thirty-three, and in the fifty-seventh year of the Sovereignty and Independence of the United States of America.

ROBERT Y. HAYNE,
Delegate from the Parishes of St. Philip and St. Michael.

PRESIDENT OF THE CONVENTION.

ISAAC W. HAYNE, CLERK.

Jackson on Nullifiers, December 23, 1832 *

President Jackson regarded the nullifiers as dangerous men. Here his view of their doctrine is vigorously expressed. Note the threat in the last sentence of this letter to Martin Van Buren.

. . . . You see the course of the nullifyers in the virginia assembly. I was aware of the combination between them, and calhoun and Co, and the haste, the leaders in So. Carolina, had shewn was to get their Rebellious ordinance before the Virginia Legislature that their nullifying doctrines, and rights of secession, should be sustained by them. It was no time to temporise— the subject must be met, and to do it successfully, it must be boldly met at the threshold, or all was lost. This abominable doctrine that strikes at the root of our Government and the social compact, and reduces every thing to anarchy, must be met and put down or our union is gone, and our liberties with it forever. The true Republican doctrine is, that the people are the sovereign power, that they have the right to establish such form of Government they please, and we must look into the constitution which they have established, for the powers expressly granted, the ballance being retained to the people, and the States.

When we Look into the confederation of the thirteen *United* States of america, we find there a perpetual union and that it might last forever, we find the express power granted to Congress to settle all disputes that may arise between the States. What next—we find upon experience, that this perpetual union and confederation is not perfect. on this discovery, "We the people of these united states", "to form a more perfect union" etc. etc., do ordain and establish this constitution as the supreme law of the land. When we look into this instrument, we can find no reserved right to nullify or secede, but we find a positive provision, how it is to be altered or amended. These must be

* Jackson, *Correspondence,* IV, 504–505.

adopted or it must be changed by revolution—when this is attempted by a state a perfect right remains in the other states and the people, if they have the power, to coerce them to obay the laws and prese[r]ve their moral obligations to the other. Let us remark one absurdity out of thousands that could be named. Congress have power to admit new states into the union—under Territorial Govts. the[y] are bound by the laws of the Union, new states cannot force themselves into the Union; but the moment they are admitted, they have a right to secede and destroy the confederation and the Union with it. The virginia doctrine brings me in mind of a bag of sand with both ends opened, the moment the least pressure is upon it, the sand flows out at each end. The absurdity is too great to be dwelt on. The people of virginia are sound. The Union will be preserved, and Treators punished, by a due execution of the laws, by the *Possee* comitatus—

The Charles River Bridge Case, 1837 *

*In the passage reproduced here from Taney's opinion, which
was that of the Supreme Court, the Chief Justice depicts the consequences of upholding the contention of the Charles River
Bridge Company.*

Indeed, the practice and usage of almost every State in the
Union, old enough to have commenced the work of internal
improvement, is opposed to the doctrine contended for on the
part of the plaintiffs in error. Turnpike roads have been made in
succession, on the same line of travel; the latter ones interfering
materially with the profits of the first. These corporations have,
in some instances, been utterly ruined by the introduction of
newer and better modes of transportation and traveling. In some
cases railroads have rendered the turnpike roads on the same
line of travel so entirely useless, that the franchise of the turnpike corporation is not worth preserving. Yet in none of these
cases have the corporations supposed that their privileges were
invaded, or any contract violated on the part of the State.
Amid the multitude of cases which have occurred, and have
been daily occurring for the last forty or fifty years, this is
the first instance in which such an implied contract has been
contended for, and this court called upon to infer it from an
ordinary act of incorporation, containing nothing more than
the usual stipulations and provisions to be found in every such
law. The absence of any such controversy, when there must
have been so many occasions to give rise to it, proves that neither
States, individuals, nor corporations, ever imagined that such a
contract could be implied from such charters. It shows that the
men who voted for these laws never imagined that they were
forming such a contract; and if we maintain that they have
made it, we must create it by legal fiction, in opposition to the

* 11 Peters 420.

truth of the fact, and the obvious intention of the party. We cannot deal thus with the rights reserved to the States; and by legal intendments and mere technical reasoning take away from them any portion of that power over their own internal police and improvement, which is so necessary to their well being and prosperity.

And what would be the fruits of this doctrine of implied contracts on the part of the States, and of property in a line of travel by a corporation, if it should now be sanctioned by this court? To what results would it lead us? If it is to be found in the charter to this bridge, the same process of reasoning must discover it in the various acts which have been passed within the last forty years, for turnpike companies. And what is to be the extent of the privileges of exclusion on the different sides of the road? The counsel who have so ably argued this case, have not attempted to define it by any certain boundaries. How far must the new improvement be distant from the old one? How near may you approach without invading its rights in the privileged line? If this court should establish the principles now contended for, what is to become of the numerous railroads established on the same line of travel with turnpike companies; and which have rendered the franchises of the turnpike corporations of no value? Let it once be understood that such charters carry with them these implied contracts, and give this unknown and undefined property in a line of traveling, and you will soon find the old turnpike corporations awakening from their sleep, and calling upon this court to put down the improvements which have taken their place. The millions of property which have been invested in railroads and canals, up on lines of travel which had been before occupied by turnpike corporations, will be put in jeopardy. We shall be thrown back to the improvements of the last century, and obliged to stand still until the claims of the old turnpike corporations shall be satisfied, and they shall consent to permit these States to avail themselves of the lights of modern science, and to partake of the benefit of those improvements which are now adding to the wealth and prosperity, and the convenience and comfort, of every other part of the civilized world. Nor is this all. This court will find itself compelled to fix, by some arbitrary rule, the width of this new kind of property in a line of travel; for if such a right of property exists, we have no lights to guide us in marking out its extent, unless, indeed, we resort to the old feudal grants, and to the exclusive rights of ferries, by prescription, between towns; and are prepared to decide that when a turnpike road from one town to another had been made, no railroad or canal, between these two points, could afterwards be established. This court are not prepared to sanction principles which must lead to such results.

Jackson Protests Censure by the Senate, April 15, 1834*

Clay's declaration of censure passed the Senate by a vote of twenty-six to twenty, supported by Webster, Calhoun and Tyler. This excerpt is from Jackson's indignant protest, warning against the dangerous potential of a senatorial oligarchy. The Senate ordered that the President's protest not be entered on its Journal.

It appears by the published Journal of the Senate that on the 26th of December last a resolution was offered by a member of the Senate, which after a protracted debate was on the 28th day of March last modified by the mover and passed by the votes of twenty-six Senators out of forty-six who were present and voted, in the following words, viz:

Resolved, That the President, in the late Executive proceedings in relation to the public revenue, has assumed upon himself authority and power not conferred by the Constitution and laws, but in derogation of both.

Having had the honor, through the voluntary suffrages of the American people, to fill the office of President of the United States during the period which may be presumed to have been referred to in this resolution, it is sufficiently evident that the censure it inflicts was intended for myself. Without notice, unheard and untried, I thus find myself charged on the records of the Senate, and in a form hitherto unknown in our history, with the high crime of violating the laws and Constitution of my country.

It can seldom be necessary for any department of the Government, when assailed in conversation or debate or by the strictures of the press or of popular assemblies, to step out of its ordinary path for the purpose of vindicating its conduct

* Richardson, *Messages and Papers,* III, 69–70, 86.

or of pointing out any irregularity or injustice in the manner of the attack; but when the Chief Executive Magistrate is, by one of the most important branches of the Government in its official capacity, in a public manner, and by its recorded sentence, but without precedent, competent authority, or just cause, declared guilty of a breach of the laws and Constitution, it is due to his station, to public opinion, and to a proper self-respect that the officer thus denounced should promptly expose the wrong which has been done.

The resolution of the Senate as originally framed and as passed, if it refers to these acts, presupposes a right in that body to interfere with this exercise of Executive power. If the principle be once admitted, it is not difficult to perceive where it may end. If by a mere denunciation like this resolution the President should ever be induced to act in a matter of official duty contrary to the honest convictions of his own mind in compliance with the wishes of the Senate, the constitutional independence of the executive department would be as effectually destroyed and its power as effectually transferred to the Senate as if that end had been accomplished by an amendment of the Constitution. But if the Senate have a right to interfere with the Executive powers, they have also the right to make that interference effective, and if the assertion of the power implied in the resolution be silently acquiesced in we may reasonably apprehend that it will be followed at some future day by an attempt at actual enforcement. The Senate may refuse, except on the condition that he will surrender his opinions to theirs and obey their will, to perform their own constitutional functions, to pass the necessary laws, to sanction appropriations proposed by the House of Representatives, and to confirm proper nominations made by the President. It has already been maintained (and it is not conceivable that the resolution of the Senate can be based on any other principle) that the Secretary of the Treasury is the officer of Congress and independent of the President; that the President has no right to control him, and consequently none to remove him. With the same propriety and on similar grounds may the Secretary of State, the Secretaries of War and the Navy, and the Postmaster-General each in succession be declared independent of the President, the subordinates of Congress, and removable only with the concurrence of the Senate. Followed to its consequences, this principle will be found effectually to destroy one coordinate department of the Government, to concentrate in the hands of the Senate the whole executive power, and to leave the President as powerless as he would be useless—the shadow of authority after the substance had departed.

Jackson Rebukes and Then "Apologizes" to France*

In his message to Congress of December 1, 1834, Jackson tells the story of negotiations with France over the indemnity and proposes retaliation. In his message of December 7, 1835, he denies that he intended to "menace or insult" France, but as much as a generation later the American Minister to France, John Bigelow, found that Jackson's attitude still rankled in the minds of French statesmen.

December 1, 1834. If it shall be the pleasure of Congress to await the further action of the French Chambers, no further consideration of the subject will at this session probably be required at your hands. But if from the original delay in asking for an appropriation, from the refusal of the Chambers to grant it when asked, from the omission to bring the subject before the Chambers at their last session, from the fact that, including that session, there have been five different occasions when the appropriation might have been made, and from the delay in convoking the Chambers until some weeks after the meeting of Congress, when it was well known that a communication of the whole subject to Congress at the last session was prevented by assurances that it should be disposed of before its present meeting, you should feel yourselves constrained to doubt whether it be the intention of the French Government, in all its branches, to carry the treaty into effect, and think that such measures as the occasion may be deemed to call for should be now adopted, the important question arises what those measures shall be. . . .

It is my conviction that the United States ought to insist on a prompt execution of the treaty, and in case it be refused or longer delayed take redress into their own hands. After the de-

* Richardson, *Messages and Papers,* III, 105, 106–107, 157–158.

lay on the part of France of a quarter of a century in acknowl-
edging these claims by treaty, it is not to be tolerated that another quarter of a century is to be wasted in negotiating about
the payment. The laws of nations provide a remedy for such
occasions. It is a well-settled principle of the international code
that where one nation owes another a liquidated debt which it
refuses or neglects to pay the aggrieved party may seize on the
property belonging to the other, its citizens or subjects, sufficient
to pay the debt without giving just cause of war. This remedy
has been repeatedly resorted to, and recently by France herself
toward Portugal, under circumstances less unquestionable.

The time at which resort should be had to this or any other
mode of redress is a point to be decided by Congress. If an
appropriation shall not be made by the French Chambers at
their next session, it may justly be concluded that the Government of France has finally determined to disregard its own
solemn undertaking and refuse to pay an acknowledged debt.
In that event every day's delay on our part will be a stain
upon our national honor, as well as a denial of justice to our
injured citizens. Prompt measures, when the refusal of France
shall be complete, will not only be most honorable and just, but
will have the best effect upon our national character.

Since France, in violation of the pledges given through her
minister here, has delayed her final action so long that her decision will not probably be known in time to be communicated
to this Congress, I recommend that a law be passed authorizing
reprisals upon French property in case provision shall not be
made for the payment of the debt at the approaching session
of the French Chambers. Such a measure ought not to be considered by France as a menace. Her pride and power are too
well known to expect anything from her fears and preclude the
necessity of a declaration that nothing partaking of the character
of intimidation is intended by us. She ought to look upon it as the
evidence only of an inflexible determination on the part of the
United States to insist on their rights. That Government, by
doing only what it has itself acknowledged to be just, will be
able to spare the United States the necessity of taking redress into
their own hands and save the property of French citizens from
that seizure and sequestration which American citizens so long

endured without retaliation or redress. If she should continue to refuse that act of acknowledged justice and, in violation of the law of nations, make reprisals on our part the occasion of hostilities against the United States, she would but add violence to injustice, and could not fail to expose herself to the just censure of civilized nations and to the retributive judgments of Heaven.

Collision with France is the more to be regretted on account of the position she occupies in Europe in relation to liberal institutions, but in maintaining our national rights and honor all governments are alike to us. If by a collision with France in a case where she is clearly in the wrong the march of liberal principles shall be impeded, the responsibility for that result as well as every other will rest on her own head.

December 7, 1835. The conception that it was my intention to menace or insult the Government of France is as unfounded as the attempt to extort from the fears of that nation what her sense of justice may deny would be vain and ridiculous. But the Constitution of the United States imposes on the President the duty of laying before Congress the condition of the country in its foreign and domestic relations, and of recommending such measures as may in his opinion be required by its interests. From the performance of this duty he can not be deterred by the fear of wounding the sensibilities of the people or government of whom it may become necessary to speak; and the American people are incapable of submitting to an interference by any government on earth, however powerful, with the free performance of the domestic duties which the Constitution has imposed on their public functionaries. The discussions which intervene between the several departments of our Government belong to ourselves, and for anything said in them our public servants are only responsible to their own constituents and to each other. If in the course of their consultations facts are erroneously stated or unjust deductions are made, they require no other inducement to correct them, however informed of their error, than their love of justice and what is due to their own character; but they can never submit to be interrogated upon the subject as a matter of right by a foreign power. When our discussions terminate in acts, our responsibility to foreign powers commences, not as individuals, but as a nation. The principle which calls in question the President for the language of his message would equally justify a foreign power in demanding explanation of the language used in the report of a committee or by a member in debate.

How Two of His Contemporaries Viewed Jackson*

The first of these excerpts is by Miss Harriet Martineau, a distinguished English writer who traveled in the United States in 1834. Her comments on American society were both astute and comprehensive. Nathan Sargent, author of the second excerpt, was a newspaper reporter and, for a time in the 1840s, Sergeant-at-arms in the House of Representatives. His estimate of President Jackson is all the more interesting because Sargent was a self-confessed "old line Whig."

1. General Jackson was brought into office by an overpowering majority, and after a series of strong party excitements. If ever there was a possibility of a President marking his age, for good or for evil, it would have been done during Jackson's administration. He is a man made to impress a very distinct idea of himself on all minds. He has great personal courage, much sagacity, though frequently impaired by the strength of his prejudices, violent passions, an indomitable will, and that devotion to public affairs in which no President has ever failed. He had done deeds of war which flattered the pride of the people; and in doing them, he had acquired a knowledge of the people, which has served him instead of much other knowledge in which he is deficient. He has known, however, how to obtain the use, though not the reputation, of the knowledge which he does not possess. Notwithstanding the strength of his passions, and the awkward positions in which he has placed himself by the indulgence of his private resentments, his sagacity has served him well in keeping him a little way

* Martineau, H., *Society in America,* 3 Vols. (London, 1837), I, 81–83; Sargent, N., *Public Men and Events,* 2 Vols. (Philadelphia, 1875), I, 345–347.

a-head of the popular convictions. No physician in the world ever understood feeling the pulse, and ordering his practice accordingly, better than President Jackson. Here are all the requisites for success in a tyrannical administration. Even in England, we heard rumours in 1828, and again in 1832, about the perils of the United States, under the rule of a despotic soldier. The cry revived with every one of his high-handed deeds; with every exercise of the veto,—which he has used oftener than all the other Presidents put together,—with every appointment made in defiance of the Senate; with the removal of the deposites; with his messages of menace to the French government. Yet to what amounts the power now, at the close of his administration, of this idol of the people, this man strong in war, and subtle in council, this soldier and statesman of indomitable will, of insatiable ambition, with the resources of a huge majority at his disposal? The deeds of his administration remain to be justified in as far as they are sound, and undone if they are faulty. Meantime, he has been able to obtain only the barest majority in the Senate, the great object of his wrath: he has been unable to keep the slavery question out of Congress,—the introduction of which is by far the most remarkable event of his administration. One of the most desponding complaints I heard of his administration was, not that he had strengthened the general government—not that his government had tended to centralisation—not that he had settled any matters to his own satisfaction, and left the people to reconcile themselves to his pleasure as they best might,—but that every great question is left unsettled; that it is difficult now to tell any party by its principles; that the principles of such affairs as the currency, land, slavery, internal improvements, &c. remain to be all argued over again.

2. General Jackson was a remarkable man: remarkable, first, for an indomitable *will;* remarkable, second, for his sagacity in judging men, his clear insight into human character and the motives which actuate men; remarkable, in the third place, for his great moral and physical courage; remarkable, in the fourth place, that he never took a backward step. Whatever he fully determined to do, he persevered in until it was accomplished, stand who would in his way. It was flatteringly said by his ad-

miring friends that he was "an old Roman," and that he was "born to command." Much as there was of obsequiousness in these expressions, which did not fail to reach his ears, there was still more of truth. It cannot be denied that "he was bountifully endowed by Providence with those high gifts which qualified him to lead, both as a soldier and a statesman;" and he had many of the noble qualities which we usually attribute to the "old Roman." He was restive of restraint, contradiction, opposition, or censure, and looked upon all who indulged in either as personal enemies; and, having a large share of combativeness, he was pretty sure to throw down the gage of battle to all such. But to his trusted friends his kindness and gentleness, his affability and frankness, were unbounded.

That he was patriotic, no one can doubt. That all the measures he adopted he believed to be for the best interests of the country, I do not doubt; though his strong feelings of hostility to Mr. Clay, and his antagonism to the opposition, often blinded his judgment and induced him to adopt and persevere in measures which were highly injurious to the country; his enmities being as powerful in moving him as his desire to promote the public interests, sometimes perhaps even more so,—as, for instance, in the war he waged against the United States Bank, and in uttering, perseveringly, charges of bargain and corruption against Messrs. Adams and Clay, but especially the latter, after he had failed to prove anything of the kind.

That some, perhaps many, of his measures which were strongly opposed by the Whigs were wise and beneficial to the country the test of time has proven,—one of these being what was called the "Sub-Treasury," or "Independent Treasury," still in existence.

General Jackson's popularity was most extraordinary; especially with the less informed,—"the unsophisticated classes" of people,—with whom he was, indeed, an idol. It was a common remark, and sometimes the boast of his supporters, that "his popularity could stand anything;" and there was in it more truth than boasting. No matter what he did, with the classes I have mentioned, he "could do no wrong." They believed him honest and patriotic; that he was the friend of the *people,* battling for them against corruption and extravagance, and opposed only by dishonest politicians. They loved him as their friend, and admired him as all admire heroic characters,—men of "iron will" and courage, who grapple with and overcome all opposing obstacles. He seemed to have an intuitive knowledge of the people,—how to move them and to win their confidence, as was evinced in his Dauphin County letter, and in his communication to the Legislature of Tennessee resigning his seat in the Senate. His power over his party was absolute, and enabled him to crush any one who manifested a disposition to act independently, or who failed to support any one of his measures; and this was done so promptly, remorselessly, and effectually as to strike terror into others. The discipline of his party was the discipline of his army,—the head only must command, all below implicitly obey, and every deserter be shot. No doubt the effect of this discipline was to give strength and unity to the party. It was no uncommon thing for members of the party, in conversation with gentlemen opposed to them, to condemn earnestly a government measure and yet to vote faithfully for it. And the explanation was that though they deemed it wrong and injurious to the country, yet to vote against their party or an Executive measure would be committing political suicide.

The Democratic Party as a
Passive Policeman*

The following excerpt is from a magazine established in 1837 by John L. O'Sullivan, a prominent Jacksonian Democrat. His aim, he averred, was to "strike the hitherto silent strings of the democratic genius of the country." The Review *was the outstanding expositor of Democratic thought in this period.*

The best government is that which governs least. No human depositories can, with safety, be trusted with the power of legislation upon the general interests of society so as to operate directly or indirectly on the industry and property of the community. Such power must be perpetually liable to the most pernicious abuse, from the natural imperfection, both in wisdom of judgment and purity of purpose, of all human legislation, exposed constantly to the pressure of partial interests; interests which, at the same time that they are essentially selfish and tyrannical, are ever vigilant, persevering, and subtle in all the arts of deception and corruption. In fact, the whole history of human society and government may be safely appealed to, in evidence that the abuse of such power a thousand fold more than overbalances its beneficial use. Legislation has been the fruitful parent of nine-tenths of all the evil, moral and physical, by which mankind has been afflicted since the creation of the world, and by which human nature has been self-degraded, fettered, and oppressed. Government should have as little as possible to do with the general business and interests of the people. If it once undertake these functions as its rightful province of action, it is impossible to say to it 'thus far shalt thou go, and no farther.' It will be impossible to confine it to the public interests of the *com-*

* *The United States Magazine and Democratic Review,* I (October, 1837), 6–7.

monwealth. It will be perpetually tampering with private interests, and sending forth seeds of corruption which will result in the demoralization of the society. Its domestic action should be confined to the administration of justice, for the protection of the natural equal rights of the citizen, and the preservation of social order. In all other respects, the VOLUNTARY PRINCIPLE, the principle of FREEDOM, suggested to us by the analogy of the divine government of the Creator, and already recognized by us with perfect success in the great social interest of Religion, affords the true 'golden rule' which is alone abundantly competent to work out the best possible general result of order and happiness from that chaos of characters, ideas, motives, and interests—human society. Afford but the single nucleus of a system of administration of justice between man and man, and, under the sure operation of this principle, the floating atoms will distribute and combine themselves, as we see in the beautiful natural process of crystallization, into a far more perfect and harmonious result than if government, with its 'fostering hand,' undertake to disturb, under the plea of directing, the process. The natural laws which will establish themselves and find their own level are the best laws. The same hand was the Author of the moral, as of the physical world; and we feel clear and strong in the assurance that we cannot err in trusting, in the former, to the same fundamental principles of spontaneous action and self-regulation which produce the beautiful order of the latter.

Jacksonian Democracy's
Agrarian Foundation*

This frank statement by a magazine devoted to promoting the interests of the Democratic party is valuable testimony as to the chief source of the party's strength. Note especially Jackson's own comment, as reported by editor O'Sullivan.

As a general rule, we are free to confess that we prefer the suffrages of the country to those of the city. It is on the former that the main reliance of our party has always rested. The farmer is naturally a Democrat—the citizen may be so, but it is in spite of many obstacles. In the country a more healthy moral atmosphere may be said to exist, untainted by the corruptions and contagions of the crowded city, analogous to its purer breezes which the diseased and exhausted denizen of the latter is from time to time compelled to seek for the renovation of his jaded faculties of mind and body. In the city men move in masses. They catch the current opinion of the hour from their class, and from those public organs of the press on which they are accustomed to depend for their daily supply of superficial thought—for their morning dose of mental stimulus, in those flaming appeals to their passions, their interests, or their vanity, which it is the vocation of the latter daily to administer. They have little leisure to reflect calmly and independently for themselves. They are like men in a troubled crowd, swept hither and thither by the current of the huge mass, with a force which the individual can rarely nerve himself to stem. Individuality in fact loses itself, almost of necessity, in the constant pressure of surrounding example, of the general habit and tone of society, and in the contagious excitements which rapidly chase each other in

* *The United States Magazine and Democratic Review, VI (December, 1839), 500–502.*

their successive sway over the multitudinous aggregate of minds.

In the city, too, men live more for artificial, deceptive "appearances"—for a petty pride of silly fashion—for a mean ostentation of wealth and luxury, in all its relative degrees—in a constant state of jealous sensitiveness to their position in those classifications which naturally arise out of the dense, heterogeneous mass of men that compose the population of a city—in a perpetual, even though unconscious, habit of self-comparison, of an upward looking envy, and a downward looking contempt. And how injurious must be the influence of the all-pervading social atmosphere thus generated, to all true independence and elevation of character—to all mental freedom and fearlessness—to that proud democratic dignity of manhood, to that noble love and respect for the equal human nature and human rights of the humblest of our fellow men, alone worthy of the American Citizen—it cannot be necessary for us to expatiate upon. Well, indeed, notwithstanding their unquestionable industrial utility, as vast labor-saving machines, did Jefferson term all great cities, in view of their deleterious moral character and influence, "festering sores on the surface of the body politic."

In the country, on the other hand, man enjoys an existence of a healthier and truer happiness, a nobler mental freedom, a higher native dignity—for which a poor equivalent is found in that superficial polish produced by the incessant mutual attrition, and that more intense life, if we may so speak, excited by the perpetual surrounding stimulus that belong to cities. He is thrown more on himself. Most of his labors are comparatively solitary, and of such kind as to leave his mind meanwhile free for reflection. Every thing around him is large, open, free, unartificial, and his mind insensibly, to a greater or less extent, takes a corresponding tone from the general character of the objects and associations in the midst of which he lives and moves and has his being. He is less dependent on the hourly aid of others, in the regular routine of his life, as likewise on their opinions, their example, their influence. The inequalities of social distinctions, the operation of which is attended with equal moral injury to the higher and the lower, affect less his more simple and independent course of life. He is forced more constantly to think and act for himself, with reference to those broad principles of natural right, of which all men alike, when unperverted by artificial circumstances, carry with them a common general understanding. And to live he must labor—all the various modes by which, in great congregations of men, certain classes are ingeniously able to appropriate to themselves the fruits of the general toil of the rest, being to him alike unknown and impracticable. Hence does he better appreciate the true worth and dignity of labor, and knows how to respect, with a more manly and christian sympathy of universal brotherhood, those oppressed masses of the laboring poor, whose vast bulk constitutes the basis on which alone rests the proud apex of the social pyramid. In a word, he is a more natural, a more healthy, a more independent, a more genuine *man*,—and hence, as we have said above, the farmer is naturally a democrat; the citizen may be so, but it is in spite of many obstacles.

We have here briefly, in passing, alluded to the reasons for our preference of the political support of the country over that of the city; and to the causes of the fact that, as a general rule, the former has always been found to be the true home of American democracy; while in the latter, and in their circumradiated influence, has usually been found the main strength of that party by which, under one form and name or another, the progress of the democratic principle has, from the outset, been so bitterly and unremittingly opposed. And hence the frequent saying of General Jackson, that in the cities and towns his opponents were all powerful, but that at the first country cross-road, there his land began. How generally true this is still at the present day, our readers do not need to be here told.

Throughout all the late contest between our two parties, commencing with that of General Jackson's first election, this natural bias of the cities and towns against the Democratic party— the general truth of which is not invalidated by particular exceptions—was promoted by the fact that it was the Paper-Money Credit System which constituted the chief force in the field against it. This fact necessarily involved in the struggle the whole commercial system of the country which was almost wholly administered and controlled through the former. In the cities this being the paramount influence, and comprising not the mercantile community alone, but extensive other classes, professional and laboring, more or less directly connected with it, it embraced of course a large proportion of those classes whose natural instincts and sympathies, as well as their substantial interests, ought more properly to have attached them to the Democratic party, and would have done so, but for this peculiar conjunction of causes, and the overpowering pressure of influence upon them from above, by the great mercantile community, on whose patronage depended their daily bread.

Van Buren's Concept of the National Government as a Relief Agency*

This selection is from Van Buren's Special Session of Congress message, September 4, 1837. He called this session not to provide a general relief program, but to assist the national government in keeping its financial house in order. A large part of the message was an argument in favor of severing the connection of the national government with the banks of the country.

. . . . Those who look to the action of this Government for specific aid to the citizen to relieve embarrassments arising from losses by revulsions in commerce and credit lose sight of the ends for which it was created and the powers with which it is clothed. It was established to give security to us all in our lawful and honorable pursuits, under the lasting safeguard of republican institutions. It was not intended to confer special favors on individuals or on any classes of them, to create systems of agriculture, manufactures, or trade, or to engage in them either separately or in connection with individual citizens or organized associations. If its operations were to be directed for the benefit of any one class, equivalent favors must in justice be extended to the rest, and the attempt to bestow such favors with an equal hand, or even to select those who should most deserve them, would never be successful.

All communities are apt to look to government for too much. Even in our own country, where its powers and duties are so strictly limited, we are prone to do so, especially at periods of sudden embarrassment and distress. But this ought not to be. The framers of our excellent Constitution and the people who approved it with calm and sagacious deliberation acted at the time on a sounder principle. They wisely judged that the less

* Richardson, *Messages and Papers*, III, 344–345.

government interferes with private pursuits the better for the general prosperity. It is not its legitimate object to make men rich or to repair by direct grants of money or legislation in favor of particular pursuits losses not incurred in the public service. This would be substantially to use the property of some for the benefit of others. But its real duty—that duty the performance of which makes a good government the most precious of human blessings—is to enact and enforce a system of general laws commensurate with, but not exceeding, the objects of its establishment, and to leave every citizen and every interest to reap under its benign protection the rewards of virtue, industry, and prudence.

I can not doubt that on this as on all similar occasions the Federal Government will find its agency most conducive to the security and happiness of the people when limited to the exercise of its conceded powers. In never assuming, even for a well-meant object, such powers as were not designed to be conferred upon it, we shall in reality do most for the general welfare. To avoid every unnecessary interference with the pursuits of the citizen will result in more benefit than to adopt measures which could only assist limited interests, and are eagerly, but perhaps naturally, sought for under the pressure of temporary circumstances. If, therefore, I refrain from suggesting to Congress any specific plan for regulating the exchanges of the country, relieving mercantile embarrassments, or interfering with the ordinary operations of foreign or domestic commerce, it is from a conviction that such measures are not within the constitutional province of the General Government, and that their adoption would not promote the real and permanent welfare of those they might be designed to aid.

One Whig Rebukes Another*

On April 16, 1840, Whig Congressman Levi Lincoln of Massachusetts, replied to the remarks of Congressman Charles Ogle of Pennsylvania, also a Whig, on "The Royal Splendor of the President's Palace," which depicted the President as wasting the people's money in luxurious living. Ogle was widely quoted by the Whig orators and in the Whig press. Needless to say, Lincoln's remarks received little Whig publicity.

. . . . Mr. Chairman, it can only be necessary to review the remarks of the member to show the absurdity of their intended application. While he condemns the extravagance of the furniture, he is silent in respect to the appropriations through which it was procured. *These appropriations are the grants of legislation by the Representatives of the people.* Whose was the work of constructing the costly mansion, and to what end was it reared? More than forty years have now elapsed since the building was erected, at the charge of more than half a million of dollars to the nation, and from that time to the present it has been occupied in the manner in which it is now used. Congress, through all this intervening period, have voted the sums for furnishing the house, as they had previously done for its construction. If it were intended that the occupant should himself provide the furniture, wherefore these grants? They commenced before the house was first taken possession of by the elder Adams, and the occasions for further supplies have since been voluntarily anticipated upon every succession to the Presidency. Besides, the spacious halls and lofty ceilings of such a mansion require much which would be suited to no other residence. The reasonableness of compelling a President elect to an outlay exceeding his annual salary in the purchase of furniture for a

* *Cong. Globe,* 26 Cong., 1 sess., App. 701.

house, the occupancy of which he has not the election to refuse, and the tenancy of which, at the expiration of every four years, is at the disposal of the popular voice, with the certainty of the sacrifice upon the cost of the property in the attempt to dispose of it for any other place or use, cannot gravely be contended for. The credit of the country itself would suffer by such an arrangement; for either the officer, by the absorption of his salary in the purchase of suitable and sufficient furniture for the house, would be deprived of the appointed means for his proper support in the office, or, by the neglect of such provision, would exhibit to the world, in his public station, the discreditable contrast of magnificent apartments meanly destitute or scantily furnished with whatever was appropriate to their occupation. It is a great mistake to suppose that these accommodations are for the personal relief, or to the private advantage of the President. He is made by them, and by the amplitude of his salary, emphatically the *host* of the nation. His guests are the guests of the people. The Executive mansion is the place for their reception. This house of the people is the fitting position in which, in the person of their Chief Magistrate, they receive from the representatives of other people the homage due to the sovereignty of this great Republic. Here ambassadors and ministers, the accredited messengers from the proudest and most powerful, the enlightened and most refined of the kingdoms of the earth, are received and entertained in the name of the hospitality of the nation! And here, too, the courtesies of official station are exchanged between the high functionaries of the Government, and extended to all classes of the citizens. The House, it is well known, is open to all, and is daily visited by many. Is it too much, then, that the place and its appendages are beyond the requirements of private station? I venture the assertion, that so far as the personal interest of the President is concerned, (I speak not of the present incumbent, but of whoever has been or may be in the office,) it would be preferable, far preferable, to him to occupy, at his own cost, a smaller and more humble humble dwelling, than to submit to the inconveniences and heavy exactions which his required residence in the Executive mansion necessarily imposes. Sure I am that, in a pecuniary point of view, it would be much better for any incumbent in the office to receive ten thousand dollars, and furnish his own habitation, than with twenty-five thousand to maintain the style of living and public hospitality which every President in succession has deemed but in conformity with the design, as well as the liberality of present provisions.

But the member complains of it as a monstrous abuse, that the President of the United States, in addition to his salary, and the use of a furnished house, should have the grounds about the latter kept in order at the public expense. He says the President ought to furnish his own house and employ his own gardener, as his salary is amply sufficient. I have only to add to what I have before said on this subject, that such has not been the judgment or the pleasure of the people. For forty years, their Representatives sitting in these halls, without division in sentiment or vote, have provided the house, supplied the furniture, directed the enclosure and improvement of the grounds, and required their occupation by the Chief Magistrate. The salary may be sufficient for the officer. On this point I take no issue with the member. So may the per diem of eight dollars be ample compensation for a Representative in Congress. But does the scrupulous member himself receive nothing more? I demand of him to say if eight dollars a day is not abundant recompense for the value of his labors here; and yet, does he keep his hands clean from all the perquisites of place? Has he no Government stationery in his room? no Congressional penknife of costly extravagance at this very moment in his pocket? Has he never ordered to his lodgings the beautiful "embossed and lace-edged note paper" and "fancy sealing wax," for the use of any of his family, or received to his own use a distributive share of the "spoils," in costly editions of books printed at the expense of the Treasury? Sir, let me not be misunderstood. I do not condemn him in this, for the legislation of the House allows it. But I say he receives these things by a more questionable authority than does the President of the United States the accommodations which are made the burden of his complaint. When, therefore, the member goes to his constituents and to mine with the objections that the Chief Magistrate of the nation is (in his most courteous language) robbing and cheating the people in receiving, under an appropriation of Congress, the use of a furnished house and the care of a garden, in addition to his salary, let him, at the same time, honestly admit, that to his own pay he adds, at the public charge, perquisites of considerable value, and which a colleague of his, [Mr. PETRIKIN,] on another occasion, pronounced, although I think by gross exaggeration, equal in amount to the per diem. Sir, the President is much rather to be justified in the use of his furnished lodgings than the member in the enjoyment of his perquisites; for the latter may be refused, while the former, consistently with the existing arrangements of the Government, cannot be declined.

John L. O'Sullivan's View of the American Destiny*

O'Sullivan is usually credited with being the first to use the concept of "Manifest Destiny" in relation to the expansion of United States territory. The concept is clearly outlined in these passages taken from the issue of the Democratic Review *for July and August, 1845.*

No—Mr. Clay was right when he declared that Annexation was a question with which slavery had nothing to do. The country which was the subject of Annexation in this case, from its geographical position and relations, happens to be—or rather the portion of it now actually settled, happens to be—a slave country. But a similar process might have taken place in proximity to a different section of our Union; and indeed there is a great deal of Annexation yet to take place, within the life of the present generation, along the whole line of our northern border. Texas has been absorbed into the Union in the inevitable fulfilment of the general law which is rolling our population westward; the connexion of which with that ratio of growth in population which is destined within a hundred years to swell our numbers to the enormous population of *two hundred and fifty millions* (if not more), is too evident to leave us in doubt of the manifest design of Providence in regard to the occupation of this continent. It was disintegrated from Mexico in the natural course of events, by a process perfectly legitimate on its own part, blameless on ours; and in which all the censures due to wrong, perfidy and folly, rest on Mexico alone. And possessed as it was by a population which was in truth but a colonial detachment from our own, and which was still bound by myriad

* *The United States Magazine and Democratic Review*, XVII (July and August, 1845), 7–10.

ties of the very heart-strings to its old relations, domestic and political, their incorporation into the Union was not only inevitable, but the most natural, right and proper thing in the world—and it is only astonishing that there should be any among ourselves to say it nay. . . .

California will, probably, next fall away from the loose adhesion which, in such a country as Mexico, holds a remote province in a slight equivocal kind of dependence on the metropolis. Imbecile and distracted, Mexico never can exert any real governmental authority over such a country. The impotence of the one and the distance of the other, must make the relation one of virtual independence; unless, by stunting the province of all natural growth, and forbidding that immigration which can alone develope its capabilities and fulfil the purposes of its creation, tyranny may retain a military dominion which is no government in the legitimate sense of the term. In the case of California this is now impossible. The Anglo-Saxon foot is already on its borders. Already the advance guard of the irresistible army of Anglo-Saxon emigration has begun to pour down upon it, armed with the plough and the rifle, and marking its trail with schools and colleges, courts and representative halls, mills and meeting-houses. A population will soon be in actual occupation of California, over which it will be idle for Mexico to dream of dominion. They will necessarily become independent. All this without agency of our government, without responsibility of our people —in the natural flow of events, the spontaneous working of principles, and the adaptation of the tendencies and wants of the human race to the elemental circumstances in the midst of which they find themselves placed. And they will have a right to independence—to self-government—to the possession of the homes conquered from the wilderness by their own labors and dangers, sufferings and sacrifices—a better and a truer right than the artificial title of sovereignty in Mexico a thousand miles distant, inheriting from Spain a title good only against those who have none better. Their right to independence will be the natural right of self-government belonging to any community strong enough to maintain it—distinct in position, origin and character, and free from any mutual obligations of membership of a common political body, binding it to others by the duty of loyalty

and compact of public faith. This will be their title to independence; and by this title, there can be no doubt that the population now fast streaming down upon California will both assert
and maintain that independence. Whether they will then attach
themselves to our Union or not, is not to be predicted with any
certainty. Unless the projected rail-road across the continent to
the Pacific be carried into effect, perhaps they may not; though
even in that case, the day is not distant when the Empires of the
Atlantic and Pacific would again flow together into one, as soon
as their inland border should approach each other. But that
great work, colossal as appears the plan on its first suggestion,
cannot remain long unbuilt. Its necessity for this very purpose
of binding and holding together in its iron clasp our fast settling
Pacific region with that of the Mississippi valley—the natural
facility of the route—the ease with which any amount of labor
for the construction can be drawn in from the overcrowded
populations of Europe, to be paid in the lands made valuable by
the progress of the work itself—and its immense utility to the
commerce of the world with the whole eastern coast of Asia,
alone almost sufficient for the support of such a road—these
considerations give assurance that the day cannot be distant which
shall witness the conveyance of the representatives from Oregon
and California to Washington within less time than a few years
ago was devoted to a similar journey by those from Ohio; while
the magnetic telegraph will enable the editors of the "San Fran-
cisco Union," the "Astoria Evening Post," or the "Nootka Morning News" to set up in type the first half of the President's Inaugural, before the echoes of the latter half shall have died away
beneath the lofty porch of the Capitol, as spoken from his lips.

Away, then, with all idle French talk of *balances of power* on
the American Continent. There is no growth in Spanish America!
Whatever progress of population there may be in the British
Canadas, is only for their own early severance of their present
colonial relation to the little island three thousand miles across
the Atlantic; soon to be followed by Annexation, and destined
to swell the still accumulating momentum of our progress. And
whosoever may hold the balance, though they should cast into
the opposite scale all the bayonets and cannon, not only of
France and England, but of Europe entire, how would it kick

the beam against the simple solid weight of the two hundred and fifty, or three hundred millions—and American millions—destined to gather beneath the flutter of the stripes and stars, in the fast hastening year of the Lord 1945!

READING NO. 50

Calhoun on Slavery, April 18, 1844 *

Why Calhoun wrote the letter to Pakenham from which this excerpt comes is still something of a mystery. Some think it was meant to unite southerners on the issues of Texas and slavery; some believe it was designed to prevent Van Buren's nomination in 1844. C. M. Wiltse, an outstanding authority on Calhoun, says that it was never meant to be published, and was intended "to force the British government to stop dealing with the abolitionists." The census of 1840, on which Calhoun relied in comparing the condition of the blacks in the slave and free states, was grossly inaccurate.

. . . . It is with still deeper concern the President regards the avowal of Lord Aberdeen of the desire of Great Britain to see slavery abolished in Texas, and, as he infers, is endeavoring, through her diplomacy, to accomplish it, by making the abolition of slavery one of the conditions on which Mexico should acknowledge her independence. It has confirmed his previous impressions as to the policy of Great Britain in reference to Texas, and made it his duty to examine with much care and solicitude what would be its effects on the prosperity and safety of the United States, should she succeed in her endeavors. The investigation has resulted in the settled conviction that it would be difficult for Texas, in her actual condition, to resist what she desires, without supposing the influence and exertions of Great Britain would be extended beyond the limits assigned by Lord Aberdeen; and this, if Texas could not resist the consummation of the object of her desire, would endanger both the safety and prosperity of the Union. Under this conviction, it is felt to be the imperious duty of the Federal Government, the common representative and protector of the States of the Union, to adopt, in self-defence, the most effectual measures to defeat it.

* Calhoun, *Works,* V, 334–335, 336–338.

This is not the proper occasion to state at large the grounds of this conviction. It is sufficient to say, that the consummation of the avowed object of her wishes in reference to Texas would be followed by hostile feelings and relations between that country and the United States, which could not fail to place her under the influence and control of Great Britain. This, from the geographical position of Texas, would expose the weakest and most vulnerable portion of our frontier to inroads, and place in the power of Great Britain the most efficient means of effecting in the neighboring States of this Union what she avows to be her desire to do in all countries where slavery exists. To hazard consequences which would be so dangerous to the prosperity and safety of this Union, without resorting to the most effective measures to prevent them, would be, on the part of the Federal Government, an abandonment of the most solemn obligation imposed by the guarantee which the States, in adopting the Constitution, entered into to protect each other against whatever might endanger their safety, whether from without or within. Acting in obedience to this obligation, on which our federal system of Government rests, the President directs me to inform you that a treaty has been concluded between the United States and Texas, for the annexation of the latter to the former as a part of its territory, which will be submitted without delay to the Senate, for its approval. This step has been taken as the most effectual, if not the only means of guarding against the threatened danger, and securing their permanent peace and welfare. . . .

A large number of the States has decided, that it is neither wise nor humane to change the relation which has existed, from their first settlement, between the two races; while others, where the African is less numerous, have adopted the opposite policy.

It belongs not to the Government to question whether the former have decided wisely or not; and if it did, the undersigned would not regard this as the proper occasion to discuss the subject. He does not, however, deem it irrelevant to state that, if the experience of more than half a century is to decide, it would be neither humane nor wise in them to change their policy. The census and other authentic documents show that, in all instances in which the States have changed the former relation between the two races, the condition of the African, instead of being improved, has become worse. They have been invariably sunk into vice and pauperism, accompanied by the bodily and mental inflictions incident thereto—deafness, blindness, insanity, and idiocy—to a degree without example; while, in all other States which have retained the ancient relation between them, they have improved greatly in every respect—in number, comfort, intelligence, and morals—as the following facts, taken from such sources, will serve to illustrate:

The number of deaf and dumb, blind, idiots, and insane, of the negroes in the States that have changed the ancient relation between the races, is one out of every ninety-six; while in the States adhering to it, it is one out of every six hundred and seventy-two—that is, seven to one in favor of the latter, as compared with the former.

The number of whites, deaf and dumb, blind, idiots, and insane, in the States that have changed the relation, is one in every five hundred and sixty-one; being nearly six to one against the free blacks in the same States.

The number of negroes who are deaf and dumb, blind, idiots, and insane, paupers, and in prison in the States that have changed, is one out of every six; and in the States that have not, one out of every one hundred and fifty-four; or twenty-two to one against the former, as compared with the latter.

Taking the two extremes of North and South—in the State of Maine, the number of negroes returned as deaf and dumb, blind, insane, and idiots, by the census of 1840, is one out of every twelve; and in Florida, by the same returns, is one out of every eleven hundred and five; or ninety-two to one in favor of the slaves of Florida, as compared with the free blacks of Maine.

In addition, it deserves to be remarked, that in Massachusetts, where the change in the ancient relation of the two races was first made (now more than sixty years since), where the greatest zeal has been exhibited in their behalf, and where their number is comparatively few (but little more than 8,000 in a population of upwards of 730,000), the condition of the African is amongst the most wretched. By the latest authentic accounts, there was one out of every twenty-one of the black population in jails or houses of correction; and one out of every thirteen was either deaf and dumb, blind, idiot, insane, or in prison. On the other hand, the census and other authentic sources of information establish the fact that the condition of the African race throughout all the States, where the ancient relation between the two has been retained, enjoys a degree of health and comfort which may well compare with that of the laboring population of any country in Christendom; and it may be added, that in no other condition, or in any other age or country, has the negro race ever attained so high an elevation in morals, intelligence, or civilization. . . .

Benton on the Annexation of Texas*

Benton supported the Polk administration during the Mexican War, but he believed the war never should have been fought. The first selection here, from a long speech, May 16–20, 1844, makes it clear that he regarded precipitate annexation as bound to result in conflict. The second selection, from a speech on February 24, 1847, is a slashing attack on Calhoun, charging him with the responsibility for the war. In both speeches Benton makes Texas the issue.

1. Mr. B. resumed. He said: I draw a broad line of distinction between the Province of Texas and the Republic of Texas. The Province laid between the Sabine and the lower Rio del Norte, and between the Gulf of Mexico and the Red river. It was wholly a southern Province—the land of verdure and of flowers—forever warm with balmy sunshine, and fresh with perpetual spring. The Republic of Texas stretches to the whole extent of the left bank of the Rio del Norte—penetrates the region of eternal snow—has a northern limit in the hyperborean latitude of Marblehead and Cape Cod—and embraces the territory between the Red river and the Arkansas, so wantonly and impiously thrown away by the treaty of 1819. Of these two Texases, I go for the recovery of the old one, and all the dismembered part of the valley of the Mississippi between the Red river and the Arkansas. I go for this recovery whenever it can be made without the crime and infamy of unjust war. I—the first denouncer of the treaty of 1819—the first advocate for the recovery of Texas—the consistent, uniform, and disinterested advocate for this recovery: I go for it when it can be accomplished without crime and infamy, as declared in the third resolution which I have submitted; and I wash my hands of all attempts to dis-

* *Cong. Globe*, 28 Cong., 1 sess., Appendix, 475–476; 29 Cong., 2 sess., p. 496.

member the Mexican republic by seizing her dominions in New Mexico, Chihuahua, Coahuila, and Tamaulipas.

2. . . . . Here are the avowals of the fact, and the reasons for it—that honor required us to fight for Texas, if we intrigued her into a war. I admit that would be a good reason between individuals, and in a case where a big bully should involve a little fellow in the fight again after he had got himself parted; but not so between nations, and under our Constitution. The engagement to fight Mexico for Texas, while we were at peace with Mexico, was to make war with Mexico!—a piece of business which belonged to the Congress, and which should have been referred to them! and which, on the contrary, was concealed from them, though in session, and present! and the fact only found out after the troops had marched, and then by dint of calls from the Senate.

The proof is complete that the loan of the land and naval forces was to fight Mexico while we were at peace with her! and this becomes a great turning point in the history of this war. Without this pledge given by our Secretary of State—without his reversal of Mr. Tyler's first decision—there could have been no war! Texas and Mexico would have made peace, and then annexation would have followed of itself. The victor of San Jacinto, who had gone forth and recovered by the sword, and erected into a new republic the beautiful domain given away by our Secretary in 1819, was at the head of the Texas Government, and was successfully and honorably conducting his country to peace and acknowledged independence. If let alone, he would have accomplished his object; for he had already surmounted the great difficulty of the first step—the armistice and the commencement of peace negotiations; and under the powerful mediation of Great Britain and France, the establishment of peace was certain. A heavenly benediction rests upon the labors of the peace-maker; and what is blessed of God must succeed. At all events, it does not lie in the mouth of any man—and least of all, in the mouth of the mischief-maker—to say that the peaceful mediation would not have succeeded. It was the part of all men to have aided, and wished, and hoped for success; and had it not been for our Secretary's letter of April 11th, authentic facts warrant the assertion that Texas and Mexico would have

made peace in the spring of 1844. Then Texas would have come
into this Union as naturally, and as easily, and with as little
offence to anybody, as Eve went into Adam's bosom in the garden
of Eden. There would have been no more need for intriguing
politicians to get her in, by plots and tricks, than there was for
some old hag of a match-making beldame, with her arts and
allurements, her philters and her potions, to get Eve into Adam's
bosom. And thus, the breaking up of the peace negotiations becomes the great turning point in the problem of the Mexican
war. . . .

The Mexican War in Retrospect*

Here Benton, in his Thirty Years' View, *recounts the steps that, after the annexation of Texas, brought on hostilities between the United States and Mexico. Most American historians today are in substantial agreement with Benton's explanation. The best defense of American policy in regard to Mexico is to be found in Justin H. Smith,* The War with Mexico, *2 Vols.* (New York, 1919).

The state of war had been produced between the United States and Mexico by the incorporation of Texas: hostilities between the two countries were brought on by the advance of the American troops to the left bank of the Lower Rio Grande—the Mexican troops being on the opposite side. The left bank of the river being disputed territory, and always in her possession, the Mexican government had a right to consider this advance an aggression—and the more so as field-works were thrown up, and cannon pointed at the Mexican town of Matamoros on the opposite side of the river. The armies being thus in presence, with anger in their bosoms and arms in their hands, that took place which every body foresaw must take place: collisions and hostilities. They did so; and early in May the President sent in a message to the two Houses of Congress, informing them that American blood had been spilt upon American soil; and requesting Congress to recognize the existence of war, as a fact, and to provide for its prosecution. It was, however, an event determined upon before the spilling of that blood, and the advance of the troops was a way of bringing it on. The President in his message at the commencement of the session, after an enumeration of Mexican wrongs, had distinctly intimated that he should have recommended measures of redress if a minister had not been

* Benton, T., *Thirty Years' View,* II, 679.

sent to effect a peaceable settlement; but the minister having gone, and not yet been heard from, "he should forbear recommending to Congress such ulterior measures of redress for the wrongs and injuries we have so long borne, as it would have been proper to make had no such negotiation been instituted." This was a declared postponement of war measures for a contingency which might quickly happen; and did. Mr. Slidell, the minister, returned without having been received, and denouncing war in his retiring despatch. The contingency had therefore occurred on which the forbearance of the President was to cease, and the ulterior measures to be recommended which he had intimated. All this was independent of the spilt blood; but that event producing a state of hostilities in fact, fired the American blood, both in and out of Congress, and inflamed the country for immediate war. Without that event it would have been difficult—perhaps impossible—to have got Congress to vote it: with it, the vote was almost unanimous. Duresse was plead by many members—duresse in the necessity of aiding our own troops. In the Senate only two senators voted against the measure, Mr. Thomas Clayton of Delaware, and Mr. John Davis of Massachusetts. In the House there were 14 negative votes: Messrs. John Quincy Adams, George Ashmun, Henry Y. Cranston, Erastus D. Culver, Columbus Delano, Joshua R. Giddings, Joseph Grinnell, Charles Hudson, Daniel P. King, Joseph M. Root, Luther Severance, John Strohm, Daniel R. Tilden and Joseph Vance. Mr. Calhoun spoke against the bill, but did not vote upon it. He was sincerely opposed to the war, although his conduct had produced it—always deluding himself, even while creating the *status belli,* with the belief that money, and her own weakness, would induce Mexico to submit, and yield to the incorporation of Texas without forcible resistance: which would certainly have been the case if the United States had proceeded gently by negotiation. . . .

The Nomination of Van Buren in 1848 *

This anecdote of the Free Soil convention of 1848 is recounted by a man who was journalist, author and, eventually, a Sweden-borgian minister. In 1848–1849 he was a reporter in the United States Senate, close to the political events of the period.

And now, when everything seemed to be at cross-purposes, the friends of Van Buren played their winning card. It was proposed, in order to simplify matters, and maintain that harmony which should characterize the deliberations of freemen met to carry out a great and holy cause, that a committee on nominations should be appointed, who could consult calmly and quietly upon the situation, come to definite conclusions, and report the same to the Convention, for its approval or rejection, as the case might be. This proposition was adopted, and the committee on nominations was appointed. What the views of a majority of that committee were, it is easy to imagine, when it is remembered that Butler and his helpers knew just exactly what they were about, and that the friends of Hale were taken unawares by the proposition. The committee went into secret session. Butler was a member of it, and so was Salmon P. Chase, the President of the Convention, who up to that time had been a Van Buren Democrat, and who didn't like Hale nearly as well as he liked Chase.

Butler soon took the lead in the committee. He had made elaborate and profound preparation for this very crisis, and his management was so consummately able that it would have excited the admiration of Van Buren himself, could he have witnessed it. He first convinced the committee that Van Buren would accept the nomination, if it were unanimously tendered to him. Then he set at work to persuade them that Van Buren

* Dyer, Oliver, *Great Senators of the United States Forty Years Ago* (New York, 1889), 98–103.

was nothing less than a providential candidate. Here was a man who for more than a generation had enjoyed the confidence of his countrymen; who had filled every official position, from a State legislator to President of the United States, with conspicuous ability and integrity; whose name was known and honored throughout the civilized world—this great, good and renowned man they could now have for their standard bearer in the desperate contest in which they were about to engage for the cause which was so dear to their hearts. His appeal was successful. The committee began to be satisfied that it would give them national *prestige* to have Van Buren for their candidate. Butler then discoursed upon Van Buren's admirable personal character, and in winning words set forth the purity and virtues of his private life. He gave an animated and picturesque description of a visit he had recently made him, at his home in Kinderhook. As he was describing the almost boyish activity with which Van Buren went over his farm, and the pride he took in his fields of grain and cabbages and turnips, a tall, gaunt delegate from Ohio, named Brinkerhoff, slowly and spirally elevating himself like a jackscrew, shrieked out, in shrill, piercing tones:

"Damn his cabbages and turnips! What does he say about the abolition of slavery in the Deestrick of Columby!"

This was a thunderclap. Silence reigned, but not long. The committee spontaneously burst into a roar of mingled laughter and cheers.

To understand the terrific impact of that question, it should be remembered that only eleven years before (March 4, 1837), in his inaugural address, Van Buren, quoting from his letter accepting the nomination to the Presidency, had said:

"I must go into the Presidential chair the inflexible and uncompromising opponent of every attempt on the part of Congress to abolish slavery in the District of Columbia against the wishes of the slaveholding States."

The explosion of such an interrogative bombshell as Brinkerhoff hurled at Van Buren's eulogist would have utterly disconcerted an ordinary speaker. But the veteran Butler was equal to the occasion, and turned what might have been a disaster into a means of triumph. Thanking his "friend from Ohio" for thus bringing forward the important subject of the abolition of slavery in the District of Columbia, he would answer, from personal knowledge of the views and convictions of Mr. Van Buren on that subject, that if he should be elected President of the United States, and if a bill abolishing slavery in the District of Columbia should be passed by Congress, it would receive the President's signature. This assurance occasioned great enthusiasm and was received with prolonged applause and cheers. The feeling thus excited decided the contest in the committee. It was unanimously resolved to recommend Martin Van Buren to the Convention as the Free-soil candidate for the Presidency, and Charles Francis Adams for Vice-President. A platform of principles was also prepared, which was so extreme in its expression of Free-soil and anti-slavery views that it could not fail to satisfy the most uncompromising members of the party. The Convention adopted the report of the committee entire, both as to candidates and platform, and Van Buren and Adams were nominated with enthusiasm.

A Judgment on the Compromise of 1850 *

Economic prosperity in both the North and the South was largely responsible for the widespread approval of the Compromise of 1850. But the South's acquiescence was conditional on the North's acceptance of the fugitive slave law, and on that point many Northerners had strong reservations. Here is a distinguished historian's judgment on the Compromise. Note his reference to the subsequent repeal of the Missouri Compromise, as well as to the rendition of fugitive slaves.

James Schouler (1839–1920), a Civil War veteran, had a successful career in law until increasing deafness limited his legal practice. His historical work is primarily political and constitutional, although it also considers social and economic forces. He displays a pro-Northern bias, but gives a spirited defense of Andrew Johnson.

For the present, at least, secession's guns were spiked. Texas, by her legislative action on the price which Congress now offered for quiet possession of the New Mexican territory, completed the dismay of that disunion spirit, which Clayton, of the late cabinet, pledged himself in a public speech at home, could never have gained headway had President Taylor's wise and sagacious policy been carried out. The legislature of the Lone Star State met at Austin, November 18th, and within a single week a bill for accepting the new settlement of boundary passed both branches with scarcely a dissentient vote and received the governor's approval.

The North had humiliations and struggles of her own with reference to this new immutable compact. Nor took it long to discern that the new fugitive slave act, which Southern Unionists seemed to think the golden link of loyalty, was, from the oppo-

* Schouler, James, *History of the United States of America*, 6 Vols. (New York, 1899), V, 201–202.

site standpoint the most damnable in the chain. It was not, perhaps, the weakest; for that, in more remote consequences, was the
new principle now grafted upon the territories, whereby Congress, not content to omit quietly the Wilmot Proviso, expressly
abnegated its rights of guardianship and left freedom and slavery
to antagonize to the end. The mischief of that new principle was
not apparent for years, but that of the fugitive slave act was
palpable at once. Clay warned his Kentucky friends, and sensibly
enough, that under this new act the South would not get back all
its fugitives, but that with disunion it would recover not one.
Drafted by a haughty Virginian, this new act was made revolting
in the last degree to free-State pride and then pronounced un-
changeable. It put the whole slave-catching machinery under
the active charge of Federal marshals and Federal commissioners,
clothing the latter with absolute judicial functions over the
liberty of human beings. The process to be invoked was secret
and summary; there could be no jury trial upon the question of
identity; the defendant's own testimony was not admissible
against the claimant of ownership; and any person hindering the
arrest, attempting to rescue, aiding to escape, or even harboring
the supposed fugitive, was liable to fine and imprisonment. Good
citizens were "commanded" to lend their aid, and the marshal
was liable for the full value of a slave who escaped from his
custody. If the older act of 1793 shrunk under the meridian
light of the nineteenth century, this new one, which replaced
it, was, to minds not habituated to slave institutions, like stepping
backwards to Draconism. The whole process, the whole offensive invasion of free States by the slave hunters, in brutal defiance
of local authorities and local jurisdiction, and to the imminent
risk of kidnapping free colored citizens under one pretext or
another and enslaving them, touched Northern sentiment on
that most sensitive point in both sections—State pride; perhaps
no more confiding process could have compassed the ends which
slaveholders had in view, but it was inhuman for all that, and
scarcely within the full shelter of the Federal constitution.

Horace Greeley on the Kansas-Nebraska Bill, February 15, 1854 *

In the New York Tribune *of February 15, 1854, Horace Greeley denounced the Kansas-Nebraska bill and its repudiation of the Missouri Compromise of 1820 in one of the most powerful editorials ever written. These excerpts show Greeley's mastery of logical analysis and the power of his moral judgments.*

We regard this Nebraska movement of Douglas and his backers as one of measureless treachery and infamy. Founded on a gigantic and impudent falsehood—the assumption that the Adjustment of 1850 in spirit if not in letter repealed so much of the Compromise of 1820 as was favorable to Freedom—it seeks to discomfit and humiliate the North by a surprise—a snap-judgment—an ambuscade surmounted by a flag of truce. . . .

We are charged by some of the open and active promoters of as well as by the more timid and cowardly connivers at Douglas's meditated repudiation of the Missouri Compromise, with using harsh and uncharitable language in reference to that scheme and its abettors. Our answer to the charge is, that no other language than that we use would faithfully express our sentiments or do justice to our convictions. Were it simply a bad measure, we might speak of it calmly and measuredly; but as an act of deliberate bad faith, impelled by the most sordid motives and threatening the most calamitous results ,we must treat it as we do other gigantic perfidies and crimes. The conflagration it threatens is not to be extinguished by jets of rose-water. . . .

Consider how sternly this Compromise was resisted by Calhoun, Butler, and every Representative from South Carolina—by the two Senators and most of Democratic [sic] Representatives

* New York *Tribune,* February 15, 1854.

from Virginia—by the delegations from Arkansas and Mississippi (Gen. Foote only, we believe, excepted)—by Venable and Yulee, and nearly every extreme pro-Slavery man in Congress. What did they all mean, what *could* they mean, if the Adjustment they fought so savagely was to have the effect which Mr. Douglas now ascribes to it? . . . .

It is our earnest conviction that the bill of Douglas, in so far as it proposes to disturb the Missouri Compromise, involves great perfidy, and is bolstered up by the most audacious false pretenses and frauds. If we are wrong in this conviction, let it be shown, and we stand condemned; but if we are right in our view of it, who can truly say that we speak of the plot and its contrivers more harshly than they deserve?

The Breach Between Douglas and Buchanan, December 3, 1857 *

Here is the story of the fateful clash between Douglas and the President as recounted by one of America's great historians.

James Ford Rhodes (1848–1927) made a fortune in coal and iron before he retired from business in 1885 to devote himself to the study and writing of American history. By 1891 he had completed the first two volumes of his History of the United States from the Compromise of 1850. *Historians and other lovers of history acclaimed it for its thoroughness in research and its objectivity of approach, and in 1898 the American Historical Association elected Rhodes its president.*

Many Northern Democrats, however, were excited when they learned of the Lecompton scheme. Forney opposed it in his Philadelphia newspaper, and the Democratic press of Illinois immediately denounced the action of the convention. The sentiment among the Democrats of Ohio and the Northwest was in general the same, but the opposition would have protested vainly against the scheme had not the ablest leader of the Democratic party, Douglas, put himself at its head. On receipt of the news at Chicago, he immediately made it known that he should strenuously oppose the pro-slavery plan. On arriving at Washington to attend the session of Congress, he called on the President to discuss the matter. The radical difference between the two became apparent. When Buchanan said he must recommend the policy of the slave power, Douglas said he should denounce it in open Senate. The President became excited, rose and said: "Mr.

* Rhodes, James Ford, *History of the United States from the Compromise of 1850,* 7 Vols. (New York, 1893–1906), II, 282, 283–285.

Douglas, I desire you to remember that no Democrat ever yet differed from an administration of his own choice without being crushed. Beware of the fate of Tallmadge and Rives." Douglas also rose, and in an emphatic manner replied: "Mr. President, I wish you to remember that General Jackson is dead." . . .

On December 9th, Douglas spoke boldly and resolutely against the Lecompton scheme. At the time the delegates to the constitutional convention were chosen, he said, it was understood by the national government, by the territorial government, and by the people of the territory that they were to be elected only to frame a constitution and to submit it to the people for their ratification or rejection. "Men high in authority, and in the confidence of the territorial and national government, canvassed every part of Kansas during the election of delegates, and each one pledged himself to the people that no snap judgment was to be taken . . . Up to the time of meeting of the convention, in October last, the pretence was kept up, the profession was openly made, and believed by me, and I thought believed by them, that the convention intended to submit a constitution to the people, and not to attempt to put a government in operation without such a submission." But instead of that, "All men must vote for the constitution, whether they like it or not, in order to be permitted to vote for or against slavery. . . . That would be as fair an election as some of the enemies of Napoleon attributed to him when he was elected First Consul. He is said to have called out his troops and had them reviewed by his officers with a speech, patriotic and fair in its professions, in which he said to them: 'Now, my soldiers, you are to go to the election and vote freely just as you please. If you vote for Napoleon, all is well; vote against him, and you are to be instantly shot.' *That was a fair election*. This election is to be *equally fair*," exclaimed the senator, in a tone of exquisite irony. "All men in favor of the constitution may vote for it—all men against it shall not vote at all. Why not let them vote against it? . . . I have asked a very large number of the gentlemen who framed the constitution, quite a number of delegates, and a still larger number of persons who are their friends, and I have received the same answer from every one of them. . . . They say if they allowed a negative vote, the constitution would have been voted down by an over-whelming majority, and hence the fellows shall not be allowed to vote at all."

It was a manly speech. His language was courteous, but his manner was bold, haughty, and defiant. "Henceforth," wrote Seward to his wife, "Douglas is to tread the thorny path I have pursued. The administration and slave power are broken. The triumph of freedom is not only assured, but near." "He never seemed to have so much heart in any of his public discussions as now," wrote Simonton to the New York *Times*; "never was he more resolute and scornfully defiant of all assaults or opposition." "He met the issue fairly and manfully," wrote the correspondent of the *Independent*, "and acquitted himself triumphantly. It was the forensic effort of his lifetime, and will live long after himself and his opponents in his party have passed from the stage of political action." This speech will "mark an important era in our political history." "The struggle of Douglas with the slave power will be a magnificent spectacle to witness," wrote the correspondent of the *Tribune*. It seemed curious to read his praises in the *Tribune* and *Independent*, yet he was far from coming on to Republican ground. For he declared: "If Kansas wants a slave-State constitution, she has a right to it; if she wants a free-State constitution, she has a right to it. It is none of my business which way the slavery clause is decided. I care not whether it is voted down or voted up."

The Rock on Which the Democratic Party Split in 1860 *

There were numerous points of difference between Northern and Southern Democrats in 1860, such as tariff, land policy and internal improvements at federal expense, but the chief cause of division was the status of slavery in the territories of the Union. Both groups affirmed their allegiance to the Democratic platform of 1856, which pledged "non-interference by Congress with slavery in state and territory, or in the District of Columbia." Note, however, the difference in the two 1860 platforms regarding what the people of a territory could do about slavery. Compare the Democratic pronouncements with that of the Republican convention.

1. *The Northern Democratic platform:* Inasmuch as difference of opinion exists in the Democratic party as to the nature and extent of the powers of a Territorial Legislature, and as to the powers and duties of Congress, under the Constitution of the United States, over the institution of slavery within the Territories,

Resolved, That the Democratic party will abide by the decision of the Supreme Court of the United States upon these questions of Constitutional law.

2. *The Southern Democratic platform: Resolved,*—That the Government of a Territory organized by an act of Congress is provisional and temporary, and during its existence all citizens of the United States have an equal right to settle with their property in the Territory, without their rights, either of person or

* *Democratic Party. National Convention Proceedings, 1832–1852* (Washington, D.C. 1958), pp. 48, 58.
* *Proceedings of the Republican National Convention Held at Chicago, May 16, 17 and 18, 1860* (Albany, 1860), p. 81.

property, being destroyed or impaired by Congressional or Territorial legislation.

3.   *The Republican platform:*—We deny the authority of Congress, of a territorial legislature, or of any individuals, to give legal existence to slavery in any territory of the United States.

Bibliography

PRIMARY MATERIALS

Adams, John Quincy, *Memoirs,* C. F. Adams, ed., 12 Vols., Philadelphia, 1874–1877.
Benton, Thomas Hart, *Twenty Years' View,* 2 Vols., New York, 1863.
Hammond, Jabez D., *The History of Political Parties in the State of New York,* 3 Vols., 4th ed., Cooperstown, 1846–1848.
Hone, Philip, *Diary,* Allan Nevins, ed., 2 Vols., New York, 1927.
Jackson, Andrew, *Correspondence,* J. S. Bassett, ed., 7 Vols., Washington, D. C., 1926–1935.
Welles, Gideon, "Diary," Huntington Library, San Marino, California.

BOOKS

Abernethy, Thomas P., *From Frontier to Plantation in Tennessee,* Chapel Hill, 1932.
Bassett, John Spencer, *The Life of Andrew Jackson,* 2 Vols. in one, New York, 1928.
Bemis, Samuel Flagg, *John Quincy Adams and the Union,* New York, 1956.
Benson, Lee, *The Concept of Jacksonian Democracy. New York as a Test Case,* New York, 1964.
Blau, Joseph L., ed., *Social Theories of Jacksonian Democracy,* New York, 1947.
Bruchey, Stuart, *The Roots of American Economic Growth,* New York, 1965.
Buley, R. Carlyle, *The Old Northwest,* 2 Vols., Indianapolis, 1950.
Cave, Alfred A., *Jacksonian Democracy and the Historians,* Gainesville, Florida, 1964.
Craven, Avery, *The Coming of the Civil War,* 2d. ed., Chicago, 1957.
Dangerfield, George, *The Era of Good Feelings,* New York, 1952.
Darling, Arthur B., *Political Changes in Massachusetts, 1824–1848,* New Haven, 1925.
Doherty, Herbert J., *The Whigs of Florida,* Gainesville, 1959.
Freehling, William W., *Prelude to Civil War. The Nullification Controversy in South Carolina, 1816–1836,* New York, 1966.
Hamilton, Holman, *Prologue to Conflict,* University of Kentucky Press, 1964.
Hamilton, James A., *Reminiscences,* New York, 1869.

Handlin, Oscar and Mary F., *Commonwealth. A Study of the Role of Government in the American Economy: Massachusetts, 1774–1861*, New York, 1947.

Hartz, Louis, *Economic Policy and Democratic Thought: Pennsylvania, 1776–1860*, Cambridge, 1948.
The Liberal Tradition in America, New York, 1955.

Hoffman, William S., *Andrew Jackson and North Carolina Politics*, Chapel Hill, 1958.

Hofstadter, Richard, *The American Political Tradition*, New York, 1954.

Howard, Perry H., *Political Tendencies in Louisiana, 1812–1952*, Baton Rouge, 1957.

Hubbart, Henry C., *The Older Middle West, 1840–1880*, New York, 1936.

Hugins, Walter, *Jacksonian Democracy and the Working Class*, Stanford, 1960.

Klein, Philip S., *Pennsylvania Politics, 1817–1832; A Game Without Rules*, Philadelphia, 1940.

McCormick, Richard P., *The Second American Party System*, Chapel Hill, 1966.

Miles, Edwin A., *Jacksonian Democracy in Mississippi*, Chapel Hill, 1960.

Nevins, Allan, *Ordeal of the Union*, 2 Vols., New York, 1947.
The Emergence of Lincoln, 2 Vols., New York, 1950.

Nichols, Roy F., *The Invention of the American Political Parties*, New York, 1967.
The Stakes of Power, 1845–1877, New York, 1961.
The Disruption of American Democracy, New York, 1948.

North, Douglas C., *Economic Growth in the United States, 1790–1860*, Englewood Cliffs, New Jersey, 1961.
Growth and Welfare in the American Past, Englewood Cliffs, New Jersey, 1966.

Remini, Robert H., *Andrew Jackson and the Bank War*, New York, 1967.
Andrew Jackson, New York, 1969.
Martin Van Buren and the Making of the Democratic Party, New York, 1959.

Rothbard, Murray N., *The Panic of 1819: Reactions and Policies*, New York, 1962.

Schlesinger, Arthur M., Jr., *Orestes A. Brownson*, Boston, 1939.
The Age of Jackson, Boston, 1945.

Shugg, Roger W., *Origins of Class Struggle in Louisiana*, University, Louisiana, 1939.

Silbey, Joel H., *The Shrine of Party: Congressional Voting Behavior, 1841–1852*, Pittsburgh, 1967.

Snyder, Charles McCool, *The Jacksonian Heritage. Pennsylvania Politics, 1833–1848*, Harrisburg, 1958.

Stevens, Harry R., *The Early Jackson Party in Ohio*, Durham, 1957.

Sullivan, William A., *The Industrial Worker in Pennsylvania, 1800–1840*, Harrisburg, 1955.

Taylor, George R., *The Transportation Revolution, 1815–1860*, New York, 1951.

Thompson, Arthur W., *Jacksonian Democracy on the Florida Frontier*, Gainesville, 1961.

Van Buren, Martin, *Autobiography*, John C. Fitzpatrick, ed., Washington, D. C., 1920.

Ward, John W., *Andrew Jackson: Symbol for an Age*, New York, 1955.

Weed, Thurlow, *Autobiography*, Harriet A. Weed, ed., Boston, 1883.

White, Leonard D., *The Jacksonians. A Study in Administrative History, 1829–1861*, New York, 1954.

Wilburn, Jean A., *Biddle's Bank: The Crucial Years*, New York, 1967.

Williamson, Chilton, *American Suffrage. From Property to Democracy, 1760–1860*, Princeton, 1960.

Wiltse, Charles, *The New Nation, 1800–1845*, New York, 1961.

ARTICLES

Anderson, Hattie M., "The Jackson Men in Missouri in 1828," *Missouri Historical Review*, XXXIV (April, 1940), 301–334.

Dorfman, Joseph, "The Jackson Wage-Earner Thesis," *American Historical Review*, LIV (January, 1949), 296–306.

Franklin, John H., "The Southern Expansionists of 1846," *Journal of Southern History*, XXV (August, 1959), 323–338.

Gatell, Frank O., "Money and Party in Jacksonian America: A Quantitative Look at New York's Men of Quality," *Political Science Quarterly*, LXXXII (June, 1967), 235–252.

"Secretary Taney and the Baltimore Pets: A Study in Banking and Politics," *Business History Review*, XXXIX (Summer, 1965), 205–227.

"Sober Second Thoughts on Van Buren, The Albany Regency, and the Wall Street Conspiracy," *The Journal of American History*, LIII (June, 1966), 19–40.

"Spoils of the Bank War: Political Bias in the Selection of State Banks," *American Historical Review*, LXX (October, 1964), 35–58.

Haller, Mark H., "The Rise of the Jackson Party in Maryland, 1820–1829," *Journal of Southern History*, XXVIII (August, 1962), 307–326.

Harrison, Joseph H., Jr., "Martin Van Buren and His Southern Supporters," *Journal of Southern History*, XXII (November, 1956), 438–458.

McWhiney, Grady, "Were the Whigs a Class Party in Alabama?", *Journal of Southern History*, XXIII (November, 1957), 510–522.

Marshall, Lynn L., "The Genesis of Grass-Roots Democracy in Kentucky," *Mid-America*, XLVII (October, 1965), 269–287.

Morris, Richard B., "Andrew Jackson, Strikebreaker," *American Historical Review,* LV (October, 1949), 54–68.

Nagel, Paul C., "The Election of 1824: A Reconsideration Based on Newspaper Opinion," *Journal of Southern History,* XXVI (August, 1960), 314–329.

Pessen, Edward, "The Workingmen's Movement of the Jacksonian Era," *The Mississippi Valley Historical Review,* XLIII (December, 1956), 428–443.

Remini, Robert V., "Martin Van Buren and the Tariff of Abominations," *American Historical Review,* LXIII (July, 1958), 903–917.

Schaar, John H., "Equality of Opportunity and Beyond," in J. R. Pennock and J. W. Chapman, *Equality* (New York, 1967).

Scheiber, Harry N., "The Pet Banks in Jacksonian Politics and Finance, 1833–1841," *Journal of Economic History,* XXIII (June, 1963), 196–214.

Sellers, Charles G., Jr., "Andrew Jackson Versus the Historians," *The Mississippi Valley Historical Review,* XLIV (March, 1958), 615–634.

"Banks and Politics in Jackson's Tennessee, 1817–1827," *Mississippi Valley Historical Review,* XLI (June, 1954), 61–84.

"Jackson Men With Feet of Clay," *American Historical Review,* LXII (April, 1957), 537–551.

"Who Were the Southern Whigs?", *American Historical Review,* LIX (January, 1954), 335–346.

Sullivan, William A., "Did Labor Support Andrew Jackson?", *Political Science Quarterly,* LXII (December, 1947), 569–580.

Van Deusen, Glyndon G., "Some Aspects of Whig Thought and Theory in the Jacksonian Period," *American Historical Review,* LXIII (January, 1958), 305–322.

Ward, John W., "The Age of the Common Man," in John Higham, ed., *The Reconstruction of American History* (London, 1963).

Index

VAN NOSTRAND REINHOLD ANVIL BOOKS